About the author

Stefan Andreasson is lecturer in comparative politics in the School of Politics, International Studies and Philosophy at Queen's University Belfast. He received his PhD in political science from Arizona State University and was a research associate with the Institute for Global Dialogue in Johannesburg. His primary interests are in post-colonial politics, the political economy of development, the philosophical origins of development as a concept and southern African politics. His research has appeared in peer-reviewed journals such as *Journal of Contemporary African Studies*, *Third World Quarterly*, *Capitalism Nature Socialism*, *Political Studies*, *Democratization* and *Business and Society*. He is currently writing a book on conservatism and post-colonial politics and is a consultant editor of the *British Journal of Politics and International Relations*.

AFRICA'S DEVELOPMENT IMPASSE

Rethinking the political economy of transformation

Stefan Andreasson

Zed Books

LONDON | NEW YORK

Africa's Development Impasse: Rethinking the political economy of transformation was first published in 2010 by Zed Books Ltd, 7 Cynthia Street, London N1 9JF, UK and Room 400, 175 Fifth Avenue, New York, NY 10010, USA

www.zedbooks.co.uk

Set in OurType Arnhem and Futura Bold by Ewan Smith, London
Cover designed by Rogue Four Design
Cover image © iStockphoto/Geoffrey Holman
Printed and bound in Great Britain by CPI Antony Rowe, Chippenham and Eastbourne

Distributed in the USA exclusively by Palgrave Macmillan, a division of St Martin's Press, LLC, 175 Fifth Avenue, New York, NY 10010, USA

A catalogue record for this book is available from the British Library
Library of Congress Cataloging in Publication Data available

ISBN 978 1 84277 971 2 hb
ISBN 978 1 84277 972 9 pb
ISBN 978 1 84813 544 4 eb

Contents

Acknowledgements

Given what I deem to be a reasonable division of intellectual labour, there are essentially two kinds of scholars who write on Africa. There are those who either live in or know Africa intimately and those who study the continent from outside. My contribution here is that of the outsider who, equipped with the visitor's eye for the broader, and in this case comparative, perspective and the occasionally enlightening first-hand experience, reflects on developments in Africa with the aim of understanding not only what is happening there, but also in the hope of gaining a better understanding of what our impressions of Africa tell us about the greater context of the modern age in which we all exist. Working on any subject with some significant degree of abstraction from that subject entails both advantages and disadvantages. It is my hope that the outsider's perspective presented in this book will be of interest to anyone fascinated by Africa and the politics of development, irrespective of their location or particular knowledge of the subject matter.

Some of the ideas underpinning this book came into being during my time as a PhD student at Arizona State University under the supervision of Patrick McGowan, Hendrik Spruyt and Peter McDonough. While this book would not have been written without the research undertaken at that time, it is only very loosely based on the theories and empirical research with which I then engaged. This book concerns itself instead with some of the questions regarding development and socio-economic transformation in post-colonial societies that conventional frameworks leave aside. It asks a fundamentally different set of questions, and it therefore identifies other problems and arrives at new conclusions. In the end, writing this book did not come easy. It required me to confront ideas that I initially resisted considering but which I have eventually come to accept as being of great importance. At the very least these ideas pose disturbing questions that we should attempt finding answers to, and which we ignore at our peril.

In writing this book I am indebted to my former PhD supervisors, in particular to Patrick McGowan, on account of the scholarly foundation they provided, and also to the Institute for Global Dialogue in Johannesburg, where I was provided with a 'home away from home' and conducted research on corporatism, which constituted a valuable background context for this book. A subsequent research project on corporate governance funded by the Economic and Social Research Council (ESRC) allowed me to undertake further research in Johannesburg and Pretoria, some of which has also been valuable in refining ideas presented herein. At Queen's University Belfast I have benefited greatly from a most supportive Head of School, Shane O'Neill, and Director of Research, Adrian Guelke, as well as having kind and helpful colleagues with whom I have exchanged ideas and thereby cultivated my thoughts on many issues I thought I knew about all too well. I have been fortunate to have colleagues working in areas outside my own, such as Robert Harmsen and Keith Breen, to bounce ideas off and thereby come away much the wiser. Andrew Baker has been not only a colleague with a shared interest in the intersection of politics and economics in a historical context, but also an exemplar from whom I have been able to draw generous support and an appreciation for the sort of professionalism to which any successful scholar ought to aspire. I am also indebted to my editors at Zed Books, Ellen Hallsworth and Ken Barlow, for their support and patience in seeing this book completed.

In South Africa, generous help and valuable insights have been offered by friends and fellow scholars alike. Patrick Bond, Garth le Pere, David Moore, Ian Taylor and many others have provided thoughtful perspectives on the politics of southern Africa, as has Sabelo Ndabazandile from his vantage point outside the academy. Without friends like Johann Abrahams and Kagiso Molefhe my interest in southern Africa would not have emerged in the first place. I owe a deep debt of gratitude in particular to my dear friend Kagiso, who passed away much too soon and whose friendship and many lengthy discussions about life in southern Africa I still recall and consider when I write.

Lastly, it is of course to my own family that I owe the greatest debt for all their love and support, and in particular to my grandfather Gösta Wallberg, who encouraged me from an early age to further my studies. My wife Tracie has lent me more support over the years than I could ever account for, and our sons, Karl and Victor, are a constant source of inspiration as well as a reminder to get things done when there is a quiet moment in the house. For the writing that follows I am myself solely responsible.

Stefan Andreasson
Bangor, County Down,
August 2009

Key abbreviations

ANC	African National Congress
ANCYL	African National Congress Youth League
ASGISA	Accelerated and Shared Growth Initiative for South Africa
BC	Black Consciousness
BCM	Black Consciousness Movement
BDP	Botswana Democratic Party (Bechuanaland Democratic Party)
BEE	Black Economic Empowerment
COPE	Congress of the People
COSATU	Congress of South African Trade Unions
CSR	corporate social responsibility
DA	Democratic Alliance
ESAP	Economic Structural Adjustment Programme
GEAR	Growth, Employment and Redistribution programme
HDI	Human Development Index
IFIs	international financial institutions
IFP	Inkatha Freedom Party
IMF	International Monetary Fund
MDC	Movement for Democratic Change
NDR	National Democratic Revolution
NEDLAC	National Economic Development and Labour Council
NP	National Party
PAC	Pan-Africanist Congress
RDP	Reconstruction and Development Programme
SACP	South African Communist Party
UDI	Unilateral Declaration of Independence
ZANU	Zimbabwe African National Union
ZANU-PF	Zimbabwe African National Union – Patriotic Front
ZAPU	Zimbabwe African People's Union
ZCTU	Zimbabwe Congress of Trade Unions

Introduction

The basic question with which this book is concerned is whether genuine alternatives to orthodox development policies can be envisioned and implemented in southern Africa. And if so, on what social and political basis these alternatives can be founded, and by what means they can best be pursued. In particular, this book investigates the degree to which southern African countries in the wake of transitions from settler colonialism contain the sort of cultural, social and political impulses that can support a new thinking about development and the means thereto. This rethinking of the political economy of development is about the *possibility* of pursuing alternatives to orthodox development strategies, but not about providing a new blueprint for what that future should look like. Given the deep sense of despair at Africa's post-independence developmental impasse, and given southern Africa's volatile post-transition environment, the question of possibilities for alternatives is a critical one indeed.

The primary point of departure for this study is the transition from a settler colonial to a post-colonial southern Africa in which states and politics are now dominated by the African majorities previously relegated to the sidelines of society in the period of colonization and industrialization that fundamentally reshaped southern Africa over the last few centuries. The official end of apartheid and the election of Nelson Mandela in 1994 as South Africa's first president with a genuine democratic mandate became the crowning achievement of southern Africa's many liberation struggles during the latter half of the twentieth century. Indeed, Mandela's inauguration on 10 May 'stands out as one of the epic moments of the second half of the twentieth century, on a par with the breaching of the Berlin Wall ... But unlike the fall of communism in eastern Europe, which took place suddenly, the triumph of democracy in South Africa was a culmination of a longer process' (Guelke 1999: vii).

With the exception of the North African struggle against French colonialism, eternalized in the incisive accounts and analyses by Fanon (1963) and Memmi (2003), no other anti-colonial struggle in Africa captured the imagination of peoples and politicians outside the continent, not least academics and intellectuals, as did the struggles against South African apartheid, Rhodesian intransigence and Portuguese reaction. Leaders emerging from nationalist and liberation movements, foremost among them Nelson Mandela and Robert Mugabe, became global icons of the struggle against what was often portrayed and perceived as the last remnants of Western imperialism and neocolonial exploitation in Africa.

The hopes for southern Africa on the cusp of independence were high. By the 1980s disappointing post-independence political and economic trajectories were well established elsewhere across sub-Saharan Africa, as illustrated by Sandbrook's (1985) influential statement on Africa's economic stagnation. At the very outset of what became described as Africa's 'lost decade', the World Bank's (1981) *Accelerated Development in Sub-Saharan Africa: An Agenda for Action* set the stage for a host of market-oriented analyses of Africa's shortcomings and prescriptions for their potential remedies. But in southern Africa there was a palpable sense that things were different, and that countries like Zimbabwe and eventually also South Africa could offer hope for a continent where 'Afro-pessimism' had become conventional wisdom in political and economic analysis and where the hopefulness of independence had been deferred and betrayed time and again. 'Colonialism of a special type' in southern Africa had not only thrown up formidable tasks for independence movements coming to power (ANC 1977; Saul 1986: 10–12), but also provided the region with a generation of liberation fighters well versed in engaging with colonial power, most importantly the economic and social structures erected to dominate and exploit Africans in their very midst.[1] In that sense, the struggle with this special type of colonialism produced a more particularly sophisticated civil society and leadership cadre among the oppressed than existed elsewhere on the continent, as well as arguably more skilful means of domination and exploitation on the part of the region's white regimes.

Southern Africa was, and continues to be, the most Westernized and modernized region in sub-Saharan Africa. Economic infrastructure and sophistication of political organizations were superior to what had developed during the colonial era elsewhere on the continent. A vibrant civil society emerged in South Africa with the African National Congress's (ANC) and its affiliates' near-century-long struggle against oppression, and structures of opposition proliferated and gained in sophistication and experience following the 1970s wave of strikes and the emerging global anti-apartheid movement during the 1980s. In Zimbabwe, independence ushered in an era of expanded education and health provision, as well as a renewed civil society activism. Such developments coexisted increasingly uneasily with a government veering from its revolutionary commitments to the people towards desperate attempts at reconciling demands of local and global capital with a burgeoning neo-patrimonial system of governance, leading eventually to the complete breakdown of democracy that fuels the current crisis. In Botswana, largely bypassed by the modernization transforming its larger neighbours, albeit integrated into the regional apartheid system as a labour reserve for South African farms and mines (Harvey and Lewis 1990: 36), a quasi-traditional yet in some aspects highly modernist post-independence dispensation managed to achieve impressive levels of economic growth and infrastructural development in the 1970s and 1980s, earning it the label Africa's 'miracle' (Samatar 1999).

The initial hopefulness about a post-colonial southern Africa produced a wealth of literature analysing the region's historical legacy, most notably that of European settler colonialism, industrialization and the creation of segregated and deeply divided societies. Liberal and socialist accounts alike offered insights into the dynamics of southern African societies, identified their particular problems and offered solutions that new governments with a democratic mandate would be able to pursue and implement. It is this literature, in particular that which broadly may be labelled the political economy of development, and the broad regional trajectories in southern Africa since the transitions from colonial rule, which are examined and assessed here with the aim of better understanding whether alternatives to the modern development paradigm could genuinely be pursued given contemporary social, political and economic imperatives circumscribing the room for manoeuvre of both states and civil societies.

The argument in brief

The key argument of this book is that a rethinking of the political economy of development, which crucially includes a renewed examination of post-development perspectives on southern Africa's future, offers the best opportunity to transcend the current developmental impasse where orthodox strategies for socio-economic development have failed spectacularly, both those strategies relying on the pursuit of a developmental state, *à la étatisme*, and those relying on neoliberal reforms to achieve development via the market-oriented route.

A comparative case study of post-transition reforms and trajectories in Botswana, Zimbabwe and South Africa provides three variations on the theme of failure, i.e. the denouement of attempts to overcome a debilitating colonial legacy. Shared regional experiences of settler-dominated colonialism culminating in a regional apartheid system make these

3

former British territories and colonies ideal for comparison (see du Toit 1995: 4–14). High hopes for the future were to a greater degree than elsewhere in Africa readily apparent in all three countries in the time period immediately preceding and following independence: in Botswana owing to a peaceful transition and plentiful natural resource wealth wisely managed; in Zimbabwe owing to a relatively modern economy and expanding health and educational programmes in the early independence years; and in South Africa owing to a modern economy and infrastructure, along with a history (albeit racially circumscribed) of parliamentary democracy and an active civil society. Initial promise did not, however, lead to envisioned socio-economic transformations. In all three countries, transitions to democracy and a range of development programmes have failed to break the stranglehold imposed on poor people by structural inequalities inherited from previous regimes. Nor have development strategies been able to address key problems of societal and cultural disruption that follow from conventional development thinking and policies. Given these three cases of fundamentally disappointing and untenable outcomes, the modernist development paradigm, which has dominated political and economic thinking since the Industrial Revolution, has effectively been exhausted. Hence the urgent need for alternatives.

The arguments put forth herein pose a fundamental challenge to influential scholarship on the political economy of development which remains wedded to a narrower vision of what development entails and what kind of political and economic institutional configurations are likely to promote such development (e.g. Englebert 2000; van de Walle 2001; Moss 2007). Dominant visions of development remain dependent on accommodation of global and local market forces, often within the confines of a 'thin' liberal and procedural democracy in order to pursue growth and accumulation more efficiently, with the assumption that greater generation of wealth will result in alleviation of poverty and increased well-being (Easterly 2001; Mistry 2004). While the importance of critical analysis and interventionist strategies in producing societies that are socially inclusive and sustainable is acknowledged with increasing frequency (e.g. Rapley 2002; J. D. Sachs 2005), there are no examples of systematic attempts to combine research on the political economy of developing countries with the genuinely critical development studies literature, most obviously that of post-development theory. Thus, the comparative analysis in this study of southern Africa's political economy in a heterodox development studies context brings attention to a neglected interface between politics and economy, as well as culture and ideology.

Three core theses inform the analysis of southern Africa's developmental dilemma to be developed in ensuing chapters. They are as follows:

1 A *communal* effort at reinventing, or reimagining, societal goals and aspirations – distinguishing novel considerations of development, and beyond, from previous scholarly work based on narrow assumptions of growth and accumulation (see Andreasson 2005b) – is necessary for any fundamental socio-economic transformation to occur. A political economy approach alone does not allow for this reinventing; hence the need for a conscious engagement with core tenets of post-development theorizing.

2 Two types of *alienation* central to human existence in late modernity must be resolved in order to move beyond development as conventionally understood. The first type is alienation of mankind from nature, which is introduced in the Western tradition with the Book of Genesis as it is commonly if not necessarily correctly interpreted and later, following what Parfitt (2002: 14–15) describes as the 'desacralisation' of nature, in the works of Bacon and Descartes. The second type is the alienation of human beings from each other, which is symptomatic of liberalism and social Darwinism and which runs counter to a communitarian understanding of human nature, including that embodied in the traditional African philosophy of *ubuntu* – an African humanism emphasizing empathy, understanding, reciprocity, harmony and cooperation (E. D. Prinsloo 1998: 42). An underlying assumption here is that a genuinely holistic perspective on development depends on an essentially communitarian view of human nature and relations. It is primarily with the second, societal, form of alienation that this study is concerned, as overcoming such alienation is a necessary precondition for anchoring any move beyond development in societal structures reflecting an African post-colonial order.

3 The theses put forth in (1) and (2) are grounded in the hypothesis that modern civilization, as it has developed and exists today, is not compatible with genuinely broad-based and sustainable development for humanity as a whole as it has been envisioned by orthodox approaches to the subject (Rist 2002). This is the core assumption on which relies the argument to be developed herein.

It is essential to note at the outset that the approach pursued in developing the central theses and arguments in this book does not sever itself from the historical context of a critical political economy. Nor does the present approach amount to merely yet another post-development critique of modernity and orthodox political economy. Rather, the central criticism put forth echoes Parfitt's (2002: 6) argument, *pace* Derrida, that any attempt at a 'complete definition' of development – i.e. what it *is* and how it can be achieved, and, therefore, how it ought to be pursued – 'is bound to fail since it will inevitably omit and repress projects that may legitimately be identified as falling within the ambit of development'. Any new approach attempting to overcome the developmental impasse is necessarily open-ended, with no teleological assumptions being made about an end stage towards which development must move and against which 'success' must be measured. This approach, then, does not constitute a rejection of all conceivable forms of development, but is rather a caution against hubris of both the intellectual kind displayed in a variety of modernization accounts, such as Rostow's (1960) stages of development and the many subsequent accounts of development that they inspired, and of the managerial kind commonplace to policies of governments and international organizations such as the World Bank. Most importantly, this caution regarding the orthodox pursuit of development, at both theoretical and practical levels, does not preclude an active engagement between the insights of mainstream political economy and post-development thinking that combine to form the context in which a search for emancipatory politics oscillates between the strictures of modernity and the potentialities of post-development.

How, then, can this proposed analysis be most effectively pursued, given the theoretical material and empirical evidence already available? First, the post-development theorizing of the 1980s and 1990s constitutes a useful tool for a new approach to development by acting as an ideational springboard for moving 'beyond development' in a way that is novel yet reconnects with traditional insights of critical, and per definition inherently historicist, approaches to political economy. An idealist element is integral to the approach developed here, as it is necessary to avoid simply producing yet another blueprint for development (considering the great volume of contributions already to that aspect of development studies), but to instead engage in some detail with why a move beyond development is necessary in the first place and on what ideational grounds such a move could be contemplated and justified. To accomplish this, the goals and aspirations of those who have traditionally taken an interest in development are redefined, and indeed reimagined, to approximate the more general aspirations of key thinkers associated with the post-development tradition. These aspirations revolve around the concepts of emancipation, the restoration of individual dignity in the context of indigenous cultural values and the casting of development as a genuinely holistic process including material as well as ideal/spiritual aspects. Identifying these aspirations makes it possible to apply a political economy analysis to concrete empirical situations (in this case southern Africa), thus better understanding the possibility of moving from the 'here' (the current developmental impasse) to 'there' (transformation of society and a move beyond development) while at the same time being conscious of not reproducing problematic linear assumptions of progress that underpin orthodox development thinking.

Outline of the book

The crucial problem that remains following decades of theorizing, strategizing and prescribing development is that 'new' thinking on development is based on mere tinkering with existing models (whether state-led or market-driven) rather than an exploration of genuinely novel alternatives that recognize paradoxes inherent in the concept of development, as well as the formidable constraints on pursuing alternatives posed by the region's capitalist economies and their linkages to vested interests in the global arena. It is therefore necessary to resuscitate and re-examine radical alternatives to conventional development. Research on such alternatives, falling under the post-development rubric (e.g. Rahnema and Bawtree 1997; Munck and O'Hearn 1999), provides a useful source for finding workable substitutes to development as well as a basis for a new South–South dialogue about what kind of societies peoples across the global South may wish to create.

To that end, the first section of this book examines changes in the nature of a 'developmental nexus' of state–market–society relations in post-colonial southern Africa and how regional political and economic dynamics affect prospects for socio-economic transformation. It is argued that the political economy of development must be reconceptualized so that key tenets of post-development thinking can be accommodated. These tenets are: first, the importance of including marginalized peoples, and *their own* particular ways of thinking and living, in decisions affecting their future; second, a holistic conceptualization of social harmony and well-being that does not separate cultural, spiritual and ecological facets of development from economic and political ones; and, third, a rejection of the modernist notion that 'becoming developed' must be based on material values manifested in ever-increasing exploitation of natural and human resources, economic growth, material accumulation and mass consumption. Translating these post-development ideas into

7

actual politics, producing a clear break with the modern development project, would constitute one conceivable path towards transformation and a sustainable future – the potential for such a future being the main issue under consideration and investigation here. Without such a transformation, which has not so far been achieved in the post-colonial world, there can no longer be genuine and lasting improvement to human and natural well-being.

Chapter 1 introduces the central developmental dilemma in southern Africa: how generations of uneven development, symptomatic of the region's historical evolution and its evolving political economy, combined with the increasingly competitive global economy and its attendant strictures of neoliberal economic reform, produce converging pressures on states and peoples. These pressures make it very difficult for the 'targets of development' to formulate and advocate independent strategies that are suited to their own particular needs. This environment does not encourage serious consideration of issues such as social harmony and the importance of belonging, nor of other aspects of acceptable living conditions not easily incorporated in traditional accounts of development. It is argued that the continued social, political and economic marginalization of peoples in southern Africa and their indigenous sources of knowledge and legitimacy explain why political transitions to independence and nominal democracy have not produced radical socio-economic transformations.

Chapter 2 introduces the concept of a 'developmental nexus', a site of political action where state, market and societal actors converge and interact to produce policies aimed at socio-economic development and where, in the end, a conceptual transformation of these actors' understanding of what development actually consists of – what development *is* – must occur. Traditionally this nexus has been understood as the institutional location – e.g. a corporatist forum such as South Africa's National Economic Development and Labour Council (NEDLAC) – where states, businesses and organized labour make decisions on economic policies and development strategies. Underhill and Zhang's (2005) conceptual innovation, the 'state–market condominium', is elaborated on and engaged with in the post-colonial context of southern Africa's developing countries. Understanding why the traditional pursuit of development within this nexus has not produced broad-based and sustainable development in Africa becomes the starting point for thinking 'beyond development'. Analysing this nexus suggests that all actors involved must rethink relations with each other and the ends pursued in shaping policy. The failure of

8

development strategies in southern Africa offers these actors an excellent reason and opportunity for doing so. Only when the developmental nexus becomes securely anchored in a deeper indigenous epistemology, manifested in the communal concept of *ubuntu*, can it exercise a legitimate, broadly democratic and therefore sustainable influence beyond that of the narrow 'utility' of existing corporatist arrangements. This anchoring is ultimately how the elusive developmental nexus can be transformed and thereby able to incorporate a post-development critique of the foundering mainstream development project. This constitutes the conceptual and theoretical framework within which the case studies are evaluated, emphasizing the origins and nature of capitalist relations in southern Africa, the defining characteristics of these relations and how both these relations and the actors involved have changed over time following the granting of independence in Botswana, the war of liberation in Zimbabwe and a negotiated transition from apartheid to democracy in South Africa.

To combat the pervasive 'Afro-pessimism' resulting from disappointing conclusions regarding prospects for development in Africa, and from Africa's perceived difficulties negotiating what is conventionally understood as the complexities and inherent stresses of modernity, Chapter 3 articulates a new vision by which developing countries can transcend current predicaments. This vision builds on path-breaking work by post-development theorists (e.g. W. Sachs 1992; Escobar 1995; Esteva and Prakash 1998), as well as work on post-development theorizing in the African context (Matthews 2004). By engaging with criticisms of the radical stipulations of post-development theory (e.g. Hettne 1995; Corbridge 1998; Pieterse 1998, 2000), and analysis of the post-colonial approach more generally (Abrahamsen 2003), it is argued that a post-development vision offers the global South genuinely new means to reclaim indigenous knowledge, ways of thinking and being, for purposes of pursuing an emancipatory politics radically different from past attempts at development – thereby also taking seriously the many exhortations to inclusiveness, respect for tradition and sustainability that are increasingly prominent in development blueprints emanating from Western governments and international organizations. The chapter concludes with a consideration of how post-development thinking can form the basis for a new dialogue among countries in the global South on how to pursue a worthy way of living, free from imposition of a (Western) modernization paradigm that, in both its traditional liberal and socialist variants, has for too long constrained thinking on development and progress. This new dialogue will leave old debates on how to best import Western 'success'

9

into Africa aside and instead consider how unique characteristics of southern African societies can be turned into strengths on which alternatives to development can be built.

Three case studies constitute a second, empirical section of the book and highlight different aspects of the region's developmental trajectories. These case studies examine what sociocultural and political foundations exist in the region, upon which a post-development vision of well-being can be based, by examining relations between states, markets and civil societies in the historical context of a regional apartheid system and in the theoretical context of the flawed ideological prescriptions of the post-Second World War 'Era of Development' (see Rist 2002). The end result, in terms of theoretical contribution, is a synthesis of the political economy and development literatures as they relate to southern Africa (and the global South more generally). This synthesis moves beyond orthodox accounts of how to find optimal arrangements of productive forces geared towards growth-led development by also accounting for non-economic aspects of development. Informed by post-development theory, this perspective does not abandon all traditional concerns of mainstream political economy but recognizes that existing actors and institutions must be transformed to work for different purposes: i.e. if states and markets are to remain relevant, they must support rather than direct societal needs. On this theoretical and empirical basis, possibilities for thinking 'beyond development' are identified.

Chapter 4 examines competing claims about Botswana being either Africa's premier developmental state (Samatar 1999) or an initially successful democracy where serious shortcomings in terms of democratic governance, the persistence of socio-economic inequalities and lack of economic and social diversification have mounted to dangerous proportions (Good 2002; I. Taylor 2003). The ultimate 'verdict' on Botswana is important, because it is the one African country that has been held up as evidence of an ability to pursue development in Africa via traditional means of export-led growth and orthodox development policies. Botswana's impressive record of economic growth and political stability is scrutinized in light of its continued reliance on a paternalistic form of democratic governance that encourages deference and passivity among its citizens and a developmental policy-making that remains too dependent on exploitation of natural resources. It is argued that Botswana's government finds it increasingly difficult to resist authoritarian ways of dealing with dissent, and that persistent attempts at co-optation of policy-makers by business are eroding state autonomy and the ability to consistently implement developmental policies. At the same time, a higher degree of traditional state legitimacy than in most African countries and a less traumatic experience with modernization and volatile social change than in Zimbabwe or South Africa offers Botswana a more readily apparent foundation on which to consider indigenous alternatives to development.

Zimbabwe has popularly become identified as yet another one of post-colonial Africa's 'failed states'. While this kind of assessment is preoccupied with the origins of Zimbabwe's disastrous trajectory in the violent and counterproductive land redistribution of the last decade, Chapter 5 provides a broader historical context of the crisis that builds on but also critically re-evaluates previous analyses (e.g. Bond 1998; Bond and Manyanya 2002; Darnolf and Laakso 2003) by highlighting the volatile legacy of the 'Second *Chimurenga*' (the war of liberation) and subsequent relations between established white economic power and African political ascendancy. This chapter argues that war-related volatility and the limitations on independence and development imposed by entrenched economic interests have prevented any fundamental considerations of how to promote broad-based development. State, market and societal actors have instead remained preoccupied with a reconfiguration of power relations that has been ongoing since independence and has culminated in the present crisis. This catastrophe, where there is little left of the post-independence development project to salvage, is forcing Zimbabweans to look for radical alternatives to the restoration of development on offer from either 'moderates' within the ruling Zimbabwe African National Union – Patriotic Front (ZANU-PF) or from the official opposition, the Movement for Democratic Change (MDC), suggesting some potential for a post-development alternative rising out of the contemporary ruins of Zimbabwe.

By virtue of the country's pivotal economic and political role in Africa, as well as the worldwide interest in the South African people's struggle for liberation, the South African transition from apartheid to democracy and its post-apartheid trajectory continues to attract high levels of attention by scholars who either laud or lament its outcome. By one measure, South Africa is characterized as a country that has become a model of responsible economic policy-making and commitment to democracy, managing to overcome an oppressive past, a difficult political transition and inherited structural inequalities (e.g. Hirsch 2005). Alternatively, post-apartheid South Africa is defined by a lack of genuine socio-economic transformation and by the social and political normalization of a society that is grossly unequal, very violent and offering a majority of its inhabit-

11

ants scant access to the benefits of economic growth and relative political stability (e.g. Marais 2001; Bond 2004b). On balance, Chapter 6 argues that the goals of transformation and development are not being achieved. This is particularly problematic given South Africa's status as Africa's most powerful and modern state. While South Africa's greater degree of socio-economic sophistication has in some ways anchored the country more solidly in the Western vision of modernity, a resurgent civil society and new challenges to the government's market-driven approach suggest a fertile ground for new thinking. The key challenge in South Africa is how to transcend well-entrenched liberal and socialist discourses on development, thereby producing a societal transformation that could serve as an inspiration for the region and beyond.

The book concludes with an overview of findings and a discussion of comparative lessons from the region's experiences with economic and political reforms, most importantly concerning the need to move 'beyond development' as traditionally understood and pursued. Several related conclusions are expounded: post-independence trajectories in southern Africa demonstrate that conventional development strategies based on accumulation and growth are insufficient and cannot provide a better future for all its inhabitants. Countries in southern Africa can learn important lessons from their divergent political and economic trajectories, as well as the general and deeply problematic trend towards consolidation of structural inequalities across the region. The pursuit of development by governments in the region provides important lessons for other developing countries characterized by high income inequalities, concentrated land ownership and deep societal divisions. Hopes for a sustainable future in southern Africa, and the global South more generally, will be extinguished if the insights of post-development are not heeded and the ways of transcending traditional development strategies not embraced. It is not possible to pursue socio-politically, economically or ecologically sustainable development in southern Africa, or elsewhere in the global South, today in the same way as such goals were pursued in cases of successful industrialization and modernization such as that represented by the 'Asian tigers'.[2] The East Asian 'developmental state' model is unlikely to solve southern Africa's present problems with poverty and marginalization. In the end, these conclusions provide a theoretical and empirical foundation from which to pursue better accounts of how sociocultural, political and economic factors shape prospects for a way out of the current quagmire of development.

ONE | **From development to post-development**

1 | Foundations for development in southern Africa

Capitalism is not a success. It is not intelligent, it is not beautiful, it is not just, it is not virtuous – and it doesn't deliver the goods. In short, we dislike it, and we are beginning to despise it. But when we wonder what to put in its place, we are extremely perplexed. – John Maynard Keynes

Capitalism and development

As anticipated by Keynes, writing in the *Yale Review* in 1933 on the eve of Europe's descent into a second phase of the collective madness initiated by the First World War (during which time Lenin wrote his influential pamphlet *Imperialism: The Highest Stage of Capitalism*), capitalism remains the central organizing principle of economic and often also social activity worldwide. Having weathered the storm of fascist and Stalinist challenges, global capitalism seemed to be shrugging off the persistence of poverty and inequality affecting a large majority of the world's population ever since. But the question raised by Keynes about capitalism not delivering the goods remains central to the most marginalized people of the global South, who see few benefits of global wealth creation accruing to them. Moreover, the currently unfolding global economic crisis that might become a new Great Depression has not produced a rejection of the market as a core element of contemporary societies, but merely a populist backlash against the neoliberal vision dominant in recent decades. Attempting to understand how poor people's aspirations for a better life clash with capitalist imperatives of accumulation and profit, this chapter examines how capitalism in southern Africa has shaped and in turn been shaped by the region's political transitions over the last several decades. It does so by considering general post-liberation trajectories in Botswana, Zimbabwe and South Africa in a historical context. The aim is to understand how capitalism in southern Africa impacts struggles to transform the region's social and economic relations in the pursuit of broad-based and sustained improvements in well-being.[1]

The core assumption here is that an unreconstructed or blandly reformed kind of capitalism will merely entrench southern Africa's inequalities and unacceptable levels of underdevelopment, and that this is essentially the only kind of vision on offer by the region's political leaders

– although what, precisely, is 'on offer' in Zimbabwe is presently not very clear at all. Despite heady liberation rhetoric, the region's post-liberation governments have, with the notable exception of Zimbabwe in recent years, remained largely accommodating to the demands by international and local capital for continuity in relations and the protection of business interests from excessively redistributive politics. Consequently, the renewed integration of a southern African region characterized by uneven development into the global world economy as currently constituted along neoliberal lines is likely to exacerbate its severe social and economic problems (Andreasson 2003). This is not simply a process of 'betrayal' on the part of post-liberation governments, since long-established and well-entrenched (economic) forces work against the many social and economic changes that those leading these liberation struggles thought, perhaps in earnest, that they would be able to bring about. Southern Africa therefore constitutes a particularly good case study for understanding both the destructive aspects, economically as well as socially and culturally, of global capitalism and the difficulties in organizing alternatives to the current system in which these problems originate.

Consequently, this chapter addresses the fundamental 'developmental dilemma' in southern Africa: how generations of uneven development, symptomatic of the region's historical evolution and political economy (the regional apartheid system in which the logic of a race-based and exploitative settler colonialism shaped regional developments far beyond the national borders of South Africa within which the actual policy of apartheid emerged), combined with the increasingly competitive global economy and its attendant strictures of neoliberal economic reform to produce converging pressures on states and peoples to accept the market (and *haute finance*) and its harsh demands as the *sine qua non* of any feasible socio-economic system. These pressures make it very difficult for the so-called 'targets' of development to formulate and implement independent strategies suited to their own particular needs. Such an environment does not encourage serious consideration of issues ranging from social harmony and belonging, what is in the African context usually encompassed by the concept of *ubuntu*, to sustainability and other aspects of acceptable living conditions not easily incorporated into orthodox economistic accounts of development. Continued social, political and economic marginalization of peoples, and of indigenous sources of knowledge and legitimacy, explains why political transitions to independence and procedural democracy have not produced socio-economic transformation.

Reform or revolution? For genuine socio-economic transformation to be possible, capitalism must itself be transformed and, in terms of it being a core organizing principle and signifier of life, eventually transcended. Any such development should be considered entirely open-ended in terms of how it may unfold and cannot be dependent on the Marxist understanding of how capitalism will (inevitably) collapse under the weight of its own inherent contradictions. Although a project seriously derailed by the late twentieth century, not least by the gross transgressions of those states and rulers claiming to lead the building of 'really existing socialism', struggles against exploitation remain on the agenda with the efforts of its proponents renewed in the twenty-first century and now given increasing impetus by the unfolding economic crisis originating in the central banks, financial centres and housing markets of the world's core economies. Such efforts against exploitation are imagined, retold and examined in a rich vein of recent scholarly work, ranging from Saul's (2005) writings on the 'next liberation struggle' in southern Africa and Moyo and Yeros's (2005) chronicling of resurgent movements to reclaim land across the global South, to de Angelis's (2007) anthropological-economic account of contemporary social struggles against global capital and Budgen et al.'s (2007) re-examination of the 'idea' of Lenin and the potential for revolutionary thought and action in the twenty-first century.

Despite continued marvelling at economic growth rates in countries like India and China (from whence Western leaders return with tales of uncompromising competition and danger that can be met only by a ratcheting up of the pressures to conform to market forces at home) that seldom translate into sustained improvements for the poor (R. H. Wade 2004), the continued immiseration of peoples across the global South makes the hubris and arrogant triumphalism on the part of the global markets' most avid supporters seem foolhardy indeed. While Friedman (2006) comes to the startling conclusion that the world 'is flat', i.e. globalization inevitably lowers transaction costs, thereby providing new and increasing opportunities for enrichment, while playing golf in India's high-tech oasis Bangalore, tens of thousands of the nation's peasants are committing suicide owing to the stress and hopelessness of their marginal existence that is further exacerbated by pressures of globalization (Shiva 2004). From the imperialist, indeed quasi-fascist,[2] fantasies of a future United States hegemony (including military 'full-spectrum dominance') in the neoconservative Project for a New American Century to nuclear brinkmanship in Iran, a powerful state-led and populist challenge to American dominance and entrenched capitalist power structures in Venezuela,

17

and a re-emergence of nationalistic and militaristic authoritarianism in Russia, Fukuyama's 'end of history' (1992) never seemed more distant.[3] These are all struggles related to an intensifying global competition for the control over natural resources and the ability to define the future of power relations in an increasingly volatile post-cold-war era (see Harvey 2003).

Yet the difficulty of challenging the received wisdom of our age should not be underestimated:

> At a time when global capitalism appears as the only game in town and the liberal-democratic system as the optimal political organization of society, it has indeed become easier to imagine the end of the world than a far more modest change in the mode of production. This liberal-democratic hegemony is sustained by a kind of unwritten *Denkverbot* ... The 'return to ethics' in today's political philosophy shamefully exploits the horrors of the Gulag or the Holocaust as the ultimate scare tactic for blackmailing us into renouncing all serious radical commitment. In this way, the conformist liberal scoundrel can find hypocritical satisfaction in their defense of existing order: they know there is corruption, exploitation, and so forth, but they denounce every attempt to change things as ethically dangerous and unacceptable, resuscitating the ghost of totalitarianism. (Budgen et al. 2007: 1–2)

Pace Luxemburg's (1970 [1909]) argument for revolution and against reform on the question of whether capitalism can overcome its internal contradictions, the arguments put forth herein align with contemporary critiques of capitalism and the global economy by suggesting that reform is in itself not a sufficient force for transformation. Indeed, the evidence of persistent underdevelopment worldwide, most obviously manifested in mass poverty and attendant suffering and death, is not an indication of the 'failure' of global capitalism:

> On the contrary, poverty is proof of the 'good health' of the capitalist system; it is the spur that stimulates new efforts and new forms of accumulation. To put it differently, economic growth – widely hailed as a prerequisite to prosperity – takes place only at the expense of either the environment or human beings. (Rist 2007: 489; cf. Seabrook 1998)[4]

While the need for revolution rather than reform is obviously not a new idea, the question of how to think constructively about transcending the developmental dilemma posed by capitalism in southern Africa today must allow for, and facilitate, novel ways of conceptualizing and criticizing the problem of development and reconnecting with its historical origins. In doing so, it is necessary to bring the post-development critique of the concept of development itself into the analysis. On its own, the traditional Marxist critique of liberalism, where a transition to socialism results in radical redistribution of goods and the eventual dissolution of class and state, is not sufficient for bringing about a real transformation towards a sustainable future, as is now recognized by a range of contemporary neo-Marxist analyses that adopt 'red-green' perspectives on development (Andreasson 2005b: 63–5). After all,

> while Marx proposed a remarkable *internal critique* of the Western system, he did not succeed in making a critique *of* the Western system. 'Development of the productive forces' was the common objective of capitalism and socialism, even if, as [Enrique Fernando] Cardoso stressed, the benefits were not distributed to the same classes ... [Hence the failure to] consider the cultural aspects of 'development,' or the possibility of models resting upon different foundations, or the ecological consequences of treating industrialization as necessary to collective well-being. (Rist 2002: 121)

One way of articulating a new way of thinking about improvements in well-being that move beyond orthodox strategies of the industrial era is by clarifying the challenges posed by southern Africa's particular capitalist formations and then by asking whether capital, when officially democratized and deracialized, becomes a potential agent of transformation, or whether deeply entrenched historical processes of accumulation prevail so that capital remains a key guarantor of perpetual elitist privilege and inequality. The latter course is by no means exceptional, as suggested by N. Alexander's (2003) analysis of post-liberation South Africa as an 'ordinary country' and by Habib and Kotzé's (2004: 266) argument that 'the post-apartheid era has witnessed the "normalisation" of South African society in a neo-liberal global environment'. Similar trajectories of increasing inequality can be observed in racially divided Brazil, post-Soviet Russia and market-reforming China. These trajectories constitute the empirical manifestation of what Seers (1963) termed the 'general case' of persistent underdevelopment in the Third World which ran counter to the expectations of modernization theory. This general case stands in sharp contrast to the unique experience of broad-based development in the post-Second World War European social democracies and East Asian 'tigers' (a window of opportunity now likely closed to the poorest and most unevenly developed countries), constituting Seers's 'special case'

19

from which neoclassical economists have been all too prone to draw conclusions about how economies work in general.

Two critiques of capitalism Two strands of contemporary critiques are relevant for assessing the nature of capitalism and prospects for development in southern Africa. The first is a critique that is Marxist in origin and which emphasizes the continuation of both primitive and capitalist forms of accumulation in southern Africa today – capital's continued capacity to 'loot' (Bond 2006).[5] From the international looting of natural resources in the Congo to the violent reshuffling of ownership and exploitation that is a central feature of Zimbabwe's 'Third *Chimurenga*', the interaction between coercion, violence and accumulation remains similar to that process which Luxemburg (1951 [1913]) described at the height of an earlier era of economic globalization as a (colonial) policy of 'force, fraud, oppression, looting ... openly displayed without any attempt at concealment', therefore requiring a considerable effort 'to discover within this tangle of political violence and contests of power the stern laws of the economic process'. The key issue here is continuity into the post-liberation era of old forms of economic and social exploitation that originate in the African context with imperialism and colonial conquest, later exacerbated by grafting the harsh processes of the early Industrial Revolution in Europe on to African societies (Andreasson 2006a).[6]

The second critique originates in post-development theory and thus poses a fundamental challenge to growth and accumulation-based orthodox theories of development, liberal and Marxist alike (Andreasson 2005b). From this point of view, the entire post-Second World War development project, the 'Era of Development', has been a failure and could not be otherwise given the unrealistic assumptions and promises of 'development for all' upon which it was based (Rist 2002; cf. Escobar 1995). According to Rist's analysis of 'development as a buzzword':

> The height of absurdity was reached when the Brundtland Commission (WCED 1987) tried to reconcile the contradictory requirements to be met in order to protect the environment from pollution, deforestation, the greenhouse effect, and climatic change, and, at the same time, to ensure the pursuit of economic growth that was still considered a condition for the general happiness. (Rist 2007: 487)

The challenge, theoretically speaking, is to show how a critique of capitalism that accepts the Marxist argument regarding capitalist accumulation and exploitation can engage and combine with the post-development notion of failure of development and fundamentally unworkable assumptions about growth-led development. It is in the context of these broadly defined theoretical contexts that the reassessment of southern Africa's developmental trajectories will unfold – a rich historical process providing fertile ground for investigating Africa's developmental dilemma.

The political economy of southern Africa

Southern Africa constitutes a distinct political and economic subsystem in Africa,[7] sharing some points of reference with colonial experiences elsewhere in Africa but also with other regions characterized by uneven development, very high levels of socio-economic inequality and racial/communal divisions (e.g. parts of Central and South America). It is, according to Bond (2001b: 31), 'probably the world's most extreme site of uneven capitalist development', and according to Lee (2003: 62) its 'most pronounced economic realities' are 'South Africa's economic hegemony and the unequal level of development among and within [its] states'. The region has been profoundly shaped by European settler colonialism from the seventeenth century onwards, and most obviously by the period of large-scale industrialization beginning with the discovery of diamonds and gold in nineteenth-century South Africa and the subsequent development of a regional apartheid system of race-based oppression and exploitation (Stadler 1987).[8] While recognizing that historical, economic and political developments across the region include significant national variation, it is nevertheless appropriate to speak of important developments that transcend national boundaries. Commercial farming and the 'minerals-energy complex', to use Fine and Rustomjee's (1996) description of the post-war South African political economy, constitute distinct and important influences on the region and its peoples as a whole.

Setting the southern African experience apart from that of other industrializing regions (in particular western Europe), and indeed the experiences of other African regions less affected by forces of modern industry and farming (i.e. settler colonialism), the process of industrialization in southern Africa is inextricably intertwined with continued degrading of the rights of Africans – Stadler's (1987: 34) 'special circumstances of industrialisation'.

During the last quarter of the nineteenth century and the first few decades of the twentieth, a pattern of coerced labour was established which precluded the extension of political rights on the pattern followed in England, France and the United States ... indeed, the most significant

21

effect of the labour system on politics was that political rights acquired by Africans and other racial groups during colonial times [hardly a great success story to begin with] were dismantled during the period of industrial growth and development in the twentieth century. (ibid.: 34; cf. Trapido 1971)

For Africans more generally, European imperialism was a driving force of the continent's modern transformation. As noted by Tanzania's Julius Nyerere: 'for Lenin imperialism was the last stage of capitalism, but for us in Africa it was the first' (quoted in Bernstein 2005: 68).

Nowhere was the link between imperial capital, local settler populations and their African neighbours-cum-helots more obvious than in southern Africa following the discovery of rich mineral deposits and the emergence of a global economic interest in the region's potential wealth, even though Hyam and Henshaw (2003: 10–12) caution strongly against exaggerating the link between British imperial interests and South African politics. According to Beinart, on discussing the problem of reading the history of South Africa through the lens of European presence and agency:

> Markets, empire, industry, capital, railways, and political union in 1910 were the new motors of change. None of these forces had to do simply with white or black, but in dealing with them the agency of the settler and metropolitan worlds must be emphasized. (Beinart 2001: 9)

The industrialization and urbanization that followed in the wake of discoveries of diamonds in Kimberley and of gold in the Witwatersrand would necessitate new, more innovative and devious ways of dispossessing Africans of their livelihoods, so as to produce a dependent and easily exploitable pool of labour for European farms, the mines and an emerging menial urban service industry. These were policies culminating in the administrative arrangement called apartheid following the National Party's (NP) victory at the white-only polls in South Africa in 1948. Apartheid constituted the codification, expansion and intensifying of existing racially discriminatory legislation known by Africans region-wide, a policy built in South Africa on 'the foundations of the segregationist legacy laid by Rhodes and Milner, Kruger and Shepstone, Hertzog and Smuts' (ibid.: 143).[9] Similarly in Zimbabwe, the increasing exploitation of Africans was driven by commercial transformation of agriculture and industry, most obviously linked to the South African experience via Cecil Rhodes's British South Africa Company (see Bond 1998: 39–42). The link to socio-economic transformation and increasing exploitation in Botswana is perhaps less obvious. But in this case, too, the peoples of the Bechuanaland Protectorate, ruled by Europeans from the Imperial Reserve in Mafeking, South Africa, were increasingly incorporated into the migrant labour system designed to supply South African farms, mines and factories (Parson 1985: 40).[10]

Economic and political/legal means alike were employed in this process of dispossessing Africans and consolidating the fundamental structures of modern inequality and uneven development. Revisiting Sol Plaatje's classic political account, *Native Life in South Africa*,[11] on the modern-day (but by no means earliest) origins of systematic dispossession of African lands, the novelist Bessie Head rightly suggests that

> [i]t is possible that no other legislation has so deeply affected the lives of black people in South Africa as the Natives' Land Act of 1913. It created overnight a floating landless proletariat whose labour could be used and manipulated at will, and ensured that ownership of the land had finally and securely passed into the hands of the ruling white race. On it rest the pass laws, the migratory labour system, influx control and a thousand other evils which affect the lives of black people in South Africa today. (Plaatje 1982 [1916]: ix)[12]

This lament on pondering the ominous 1913 legislation haunts politics and people in South Africa, and across the former southern African settler colonies, to this day. Systematic dispossession of African peoples by European settlers produced extreme inequalities and resulted in serious impediments to socio-economic development in the region (Bundy 1982: 228–30; C. H. Feinstein 2005: 43–6). Thus Plaatje (1982 [1916]: 21): 'Awakening on Friday morning, June 20, 1913, the South African native found himself, not actually a slave, but a pariah in the land of his birth.'

And no historical account of the indignities visited upon the native population by this act renders the despair more vividly than does Plaatje's:

> It was cold that afternoon as we cycled into the 'Free' State from Transvaal, and towards the evening the southern winds rose. A cutting blizzard raged during the night, and native mothers evicted from their homes shivered with their babies by their sides. When we saw on that night the teeth of the little children clattering through the cold ... we wondered what these little mites had done that a home should suddenly become to them a thing of the past ... Mrs Kgobadi carried a sick baby when the

23

eviction took place, and she had to transfer her darling from the cottage to the jolting ox-wagon in which they left the farm. Two days out the little one began to sink as the result of privation and exposure on the road, and the night before we met them its little soul was released from its earthly bonds. The death of the child added a fresh perplexity to the stricken parents. They had no right or title to the farmlands through which they trekked: they must keep to the public roads – the only places in the country open to the outcasts if they are possessed of travelling permit. The deceased child had to be buried, but where, when, and how? This young family decided to dig a grave under cover of the darkness of that night, when no one was looking, and in that crude manner the dead child was interred – and interred amid fear and trembling, as well as the throbs of a torturing anguish, in a stolen grave, lest the proprietor of the spot, or any of his servants, should surprise them in the act. Even criminals dropping straight from the gallows have an undisputed claim to six feet of ground on which to rest their criminal remains, but under the cruel operation of the Natives' Land Act little children, whose only crime is that God did not make them white, are sometimes denied that right in their ancestral home. (ibid.: 89–90)

These, then, are the foundations of imperialism and settler colonialism from which the region's various liberation movements and post-liberation governments have attempted to wrest control of their own destinies. Echoing the biblical dictum in the Gospel of Matthew, which Ghana's Kwame Nkrumah paraphrased as 'Seek ye first the political kingdom, and all else shall be added onto you', the political victory over white minority rule became understood as the rupture from which opportunity to promote socio-economic transformation would emanate. While the so-called legacy of apartheid is well recognized by governments and policy-makers throughout the region, and while historical factors generally feature prominently in accounts of why genuine improvements in the lives of the region's inhabitants have been so difficult to achieve (e.g. Hirsch 2005: 9–28), there is an important sense in which the relationship between political developments following liberation and historical processes of exploitation and underdevelopment is misconstrued.

This misconstruction can be illustrated in the following way. Rather than taking every opportunity to rectify and mitigate the consequences of pre-liberation-era policies of exploitation, governments and their lobbyists find themselves, for a variety of reasons, pursuing and promoting policies that exacerbate the very problems that liberation was supposed to overcome. From Zimbabwe's structural adjustment policies to South Africa's quasi-liberal Black Economic Empowerment (BEE) scheme and the paternalistic and increasingly non-transparent politics in Botswana, a disturbing trend is discernible: post-liberation policies have contributed to increased social fragmentation rather than healing of communities; marginalization of the poor continues despite the granting of political rights, such as the advent of universal suffrage, which is rightly celebrated as a triumph of liberation; economic policies ensure increased exposure to the volatility of global markets for the workers and poor who are least able to cope with such forces; there is a deepening of inequalities between mainly urban elites with political connections and the predominantly rural poor, whose voice can too often be taken for granted or simply ignored.

On this reading, the advent of liberation, for all its important political gains and the potential for further improvements across a wide range of issues that such a transition entails, was not so much a break with the region's political economy of underdevelopment as it was a reorganization of administration and management that political economy left largely intact, with disastrous consequences, both intended and unintended, for its inhabitants.[13] According to this account, both external and domestic elites, established and emerging state officials and captains of industry alike share a responsibility for what Saul (2001) terms South Africa's 'post-apartheid denouement' and what Bond (2001b: xi) describes as 'shining, rather than breaking' the chains of global apartheid – a failure to deliver on the promises of liberation, the implications of which are reflected in people's persistent experiences with relentless hardships across the region.

The nature of capitalism in present-day southern Africa If the twentieth century in southern Africa was an era in which European settler control over land, labour, production and finance was consolidated at the expense of Africans, the beginning of the twenty-first century represents a time in which post-liberation governments grapple with how to pursue socio-economic development by increasingly making Africans the beneficiaries of economic growth, job creation and consumption – thus delivering, as per the ANC slogan, 'a better life for all'. Political elites across the region have enjoyed long periods of relative stability in terms of their ability to govern with relative autonomy from domestic opposition. The Botswana Democratic Party (BDP) and ZANU-PF have governed without interruption since independence in 1966 and 1980 respectively. The ANC has governed South Africa unchallenged since 1994 and is likely to do so in the foreseeable future as well.

This political stability, which was only seriously challenged in Zimbabwe from the late 1990s onwards, has provided the region's leaders with ample opportunity to renegotiate relationships between the state, markets and civil society. Largely, however, elite-level accommodation between established capitalists and the incoming African political class has remained the order of the day, with majority populations still marginalized, if for somewhat different reasons now than before.[14] While entrenched structures of (white) capitalist power have weathered the storm of political transition rather effectively, all governments in the region have to some degree pursued policies of indigenization, or Africanization. African capitalist elites, whether they have taken advantage of a genuine opening of opportunities to compete on a more level playing field produced by independence and democracy or have merely relied on state cronyism in a parasitic fashion, have emerged as important actors in their own right, and local and multinational businesses have responded by accommodating their demands accordingly (Andreasson 2007a).

Linking regional trajectories to global developments, the changing patterns of exploitation and composition of regional capitalist elites are most appropriately examined in an international context where, following decades of disruption owing to struggles for national liberation and isolation due to apartheid, a new era of globalization has arrived. Economic globalization is obviously not a new phenomenon, in southern Africa or anywhere else (Arrighi 1996; Waltz 2000), and therefore any discussion of contemporary characteristics and effects of globalization in the region must be understood as part of a longer process of incorporation into an international system of capitalism. Some features of today's economic globalization, such as the drive for increasing deregulation, privatization and exposure to the volatility of global financial markets and trade, may differ (primarily in terms of technology) from bouts of globalization in the past (see Koelble and LiPuma 2006). Yet some aspects of this process are very similar to an earlier era in which the region's corporate giants – none more so than Anglo American and De Beers – placed southern Africa squarely on the global economic map and firmly in the minds of *haute finance* (see Innes 1984).[15]

This 'new' era of economic globalization provides both opportunities for and constraints on capitalist accumulation in the region, with the impact on development being generally negative. Any examination of the contemporary nature of capitalism in southern Africa must therefore be cognizant not only of the potentially transformative power of national liberation, the end of apartheid and an ongoing process of realigning the region with a global economy increasingly characterized by financialization.[16] It must also acknowledge the preservative power of the region's historical legacy, in particular the legacy of apartheid, which continues to shape the aspirations of capitalists and politicians alike, these professional categories clearly not being mutually exclusive (e.g. Adam et al. 1998; Andreasson 2006b).

Indeed, the difficulty in facilitating the emergence of a post-liberation 'patriotic bourgeoisie', the class foundation on which nationalist market advocates argue a genuine national developmental project can be built, features prominently in explanations of the difficulty in delivering on promises for broad-based development (Southall 2004). Emerging African elites have all too often been dependent on the ability to extract largesse and rents from established market actors by means of their increased post-liberation political power, as in South Africa and Zimbabwe, or reliant on traditional sources of authority and the diamond deposits that are exploited in collaboration with powerful multinationals like De Beers in Botswana. Even if capitalist development could mitigate some of the more debilitating consequences of extremely uneven development in southern Africa, just as the emergence of a national bourgeois development project produced rapid socio-economic development in several East Asian countries in the post-Second World War era, the particular nature of the new capitalist groupings in southern Africa, similar to a comprador class rather than a patriotic bourgeoisie (Andreasson 2007a: 277), is hardly comparable to the previous era of rapid capitalist development in the East Asian 'developmental states' (Andreasson 2007b).

Following an accommodationist path There are many reasons for the lack of transformation in southern Africa. They range from co-optation of incoming elites during transitions to independence, the ability of entrenched capital actors (and also traditional rulers in the case of Botswana) to continue exerting control, external pressures relating to the collapse of global communism which mitigated local challenges to market dogma, the turning of transformation strategies into elite enrichment schemes, to the lack of a coherent challenge to the fundamental logic of capitalism. Across southern Africa, and particularly in the three countries selected for examination here, the political transitions from colonial or minority rule (Botswana 1966, Zimbabwe 1980, South Africa 1994) can on the whole be characterized by a somewhat remarkable degree of continuity, rather than rupture and transformation, of relations between states, markets and civil societies.

The conservative nature of transition is perhaps least surprising in the case of Botswana, where a 'benign' imperial rule (relative to the experiences of the neighbouring countries) interacting with a traditional rural-based Tswana elite produced a (by regional standards) unremarkable path to independence (Picard 1985: 13–17). On the other hand, the post-independence period was in many ways quite remarkable by African post-independence standards generally, in terms of prudent economic management, consistent developmental policy-making and political stability that undoubtedly provided a significant improvement in living standards for many Batswana (Samatar 1999). All of these developments, however, did take place within the strict limits of an elitist and paternalistic political system deeply enmeshed in the regional realities of persistent inequality and marginalization of the poor (Good 1999).

The negotiated or 'elite' transition in South Africa has been described in detail by both liberal and socialist scholars (e.g. Waldmeir 1997; Bond 2000). Early contacts between white capital and the ANC in the 1980s initiated a transition that produced a new, majority-dominated political order while securing the property rights and economic influence of the privileged and at that time almost exclusively white minority (Marais 2001). What is less often acknowledged, however, is how the ANC's bourgeois leadership, always in uneasy alliance with communists and other radical organizations (Roux 1964; Benson 1966; Gumede 2007), promoted a relatively conservative, nationalist liberation struggle throughout the twentieth century, the logic of which mitigated any fundamental post-liberation socio-economic transformation for the poor majority (although the transformation was certainly in some aspects overwhelming for both white and black elites).

As argued forcefully in McKinley's (1997) biography of the ANC, the movement's ambivalence towards radical working-class politics, what McKinley (ibid.: 21) terms an 'accommodationist strategic approach to liberation', was evident even in the creation of the Freedom Charter. Proclaiming a commitment to democracy, equal rights, economic justice, equality, human rights, learning and peace, the spirit of the document inspired a generation of anti-apartheid activists.[17] However,

> [t]he ambiguity in the Charter's clauses meant that the ANC Alliance could claim that their strategic approach was simultaneously a predominantly nationalist anti-apartheid umbrella for all social forces and

a revolutionary struggle for radical socioeconomic transformation. The main problem was that the ANC's desired end, as expressed by Mandela, contained no requirement for the means needed to fulfil the second claim. (ibid.: 22)[18]

The notion of continuity in pre- and post-liberation relations between state and capital is perhaps more controversial in the case of Zimbabwe's transition, following Rhodesia's Unilateral Declaration of Independence (UDI) in 1965 and the 1970s war of national liberation resulting in an independent Zimbabwe by 1980. Yet, despite a major reorientation of spending priorities towards basic development (health and education) in the early years of independence (Dashwood 2000: 40–56), domestic and international capitalist interests were never seriously challenged by the government. To the degree that an indigenous (black) capitalist class emerged in Zimbabwe, it was generally closely tied to state patronage and co-optation by white capital (Bond 1998; Andreasson 2007a), a process not entirely dissimilar to the more counterproductive aspects of BEE in South Africa today (Southall 2004; Andreasson 2006b: 312–14).[19] While the post-liberation period in Zimbabwe has obviously been more volatile than has been the case in South Africa and, especially, Botswana, there is nevertheless a degree of continuity in state–market relations, carefully managed to adapt to and remain acceptable in new political circumstances, up until the turmoil of violent land reforms in the present decade, which has left Zimbabwe's economic and political future increasingly uncertain (see D. Moore 2007).

These continuities suggest that not only must the region's prevailing capitalist-dominated structures of power and influence be comprehensively challenged for genuine socio-economic transformation to be possible. They also suggest that (liberal) accounts of democratic transitions, where democracy creates opportunities for the marginalized to enjoy the benefits of capital accumulation, thereby distributing the benefits of development more widely (e.g. Olson 1982; Przeworski and Limongi 1993), are fundamentally flawed. This flaw is also implicit in former South African president Thabo Mbeki's conceptualization of the 'two economies' character of post-apartheid South Africa – one wealthy and white, the other poor and black – where it is assumed that bridging the divide between formal and informal economies will result in the development of the latter rather than its continued underdevelopment (Bond 2007b). Once regional transitions are recognized as being largely accommodationist in nature and predicated on variations of modernization theory assumptions about the relationship between growth, accumulation and development (see ibid.), it becomes possible to understand much of post-liberation politics in southern Africa as producing impediments to, rather than opportunities for, socio-economic transformation and emancipation.

The targets of development

If state–market relations have, with the notable exception of Zimbabwe's last decade, largely weathered the storms of transition in southern Africa, what has become of civil society, the African peoples themselves, in the post-liberation era? Africans remain in many ways at the margins, politically and economically as well as in intellectual debates on development, their needs and priorities generally defined by global and local elites who are accountable primarily to market forces as opposed to civil societies, and who are in some cases apparently ignorant of the history of exploitation in Africa and how it continues to affect its peoples. Speaking to an audience at the Cheikh Anta Diop University in Senegal in July 2007, French president Nicolas Sarkozy suggested that Africa's underdevelopment is a result of Africans having 'turned their back on progress':

> The tragedy of Africa is that the African has never really entered into history ... They have never really launched themselves into the future. The African peasant ... only knew the eternal renewal of time. In this imaginary world, where everything starts over and over again, there is room neither for human endeavour, nor for the idea progress. (McGreal 2007)

This reformulation of the standard colonial explanation of African backwardness (see Andreasson 2005a) and its dismissal of the very direct and brutal way in which Africa entered the history of the modern world (Rodney 1982) was met by then president Mbeki, leading proponent of the notion of an 'African Renaissance' (Bongma 2004), with approval in the form of a personal letter. According to Mbeki's letter, Africans are 'fortunate to count [Sarkozy] as a citizen of Africa, as a partner in the long struggle for a true African Renaissance' (Mbembe 2007).

Critics of South African 'sub-imperialism', or 'sub-hegemony' in Africa (Bond 2004a; Peet 2007: ch. 6), and the significant degree of co-optation of South African political elites by international financial institutions (IFIs) and by the West in general (Bond 2004b), will not be surprised by this endorsement of a well-established Western mischaracterization of

Africa's relationship to (Western) history. Judging the rural African as a passive spectator, best aided by benevolent top-down policy-making, rather than being actively solicited for his (and even less her) input on how needs can best be met, has been a persistent phenomenon in post-liberation southern Africa (Leysens 2006; Larmer 2007). From the South African government's active 'demobilization' of civil society and harsh responses to local pressure groups in the post-apartheid era (P. Naidoo 2007) to the Botswana government's removal of the San from their ancestral lands (Taylor and Mokhawa 2003) and the more extreme example of dragging the poor 'into history' with the Zimbabwe government's so-called 'Third *Chimurenga*' or 'struggle' for land, and against increasing political opposition to the ZANU-PF (Bracking 2005), there has been a rather one-sided attempt at imposing elite-driven visions of modernity and progress on Africans.

In addition to the problem of conservative and accommodationist transformations in southern Africa, the region's peoples have seen the potential for improvements in their lives diminished by a persistently elitist discourse on what liberation and development ought to entail. Despite relatively high levels of economic development (Botswana and South Africa are designated by the World Bank as upper-middle-income countries) and the continued ability of corporations and investors to profit from the region's wealth, little has been achieved in terms of improving on orthodox development indicators. Regional trajectories measured by indicators of health, inequality and poverty reduction have remained stagnant or worsened since the 1990s.[20] Yet the preoccupation of governments has remained how to create stable economic environments, i.e. sustaining policies that are acceptable by international business standards, and proving that southern Africa remains a place where companies can work closely with governments. An internal ANC discussion document described the situation thus:

> While on one hand [developing states] are called upon to starve and prettify themselves to compete on the 'catwalk' of attracting the limited amounts of foreign direct investment ... they are on the other hand reduced to bulimia by the vagaries of an extremely impetuous and whimsical market suitor! (ANC 1998)

Variations on the concept of a 'developmental state' have been articulated and pursued in Botswana and now apparently also South Africa, with the former generally considered Africa's 'success story' in this regard (see Samatar 1999).[21] Neoliberal reforms in South Africa and structural adjustment in Zimbabwe, the latter more obviously driven by external pressures, have been main features of government policy in the last two decades.

Yet much less critical attention has been focused on the issue of how to promote a greater sense of social cohesion, human and natural healing (i.e. reducing levels of violence and environmental degradation) and related issues of well-being, without attention to which no discussion of development becomes meaningful in any other sense than assuming that greater economic growth will in the end make possible increased attention to these 'soft' issues. Rather, the political discourse remains one of juxtaposing fairly orthodox liberal arguments for market-oriented economic reforms with corporatist or populist-socialist arguments for redistribution. In this kind of discourse, the peoples of the region, 'the poors' in Desai's (2002) analysis of community movement in post-apartheid South Africa, are often left without a meaningful voice beyond that of casting a vote in periodical elections for candidates whom they have had little direct influence in selecting in the first place. The elite orientation of policy-making in southern Africa has produced a state of 'virtual democracy' (Joseph 1999; Andreasson 2003), from which emanate policies aimed primarily at satisfying narrow economic interests rather than broadly developmental ones. Such policy-making will continue to exacerbate problems of uneven development, social breakdown and environmental degradation, which in turn further diminishes the likelihood of a better future for those most desperately in need of one.

For the region's capitalists and political elites it has been worthwhile to keep public economic debate focused on issues like foreign direct investment, aggregate economic growth that pays little attention to the distribution of that growth, corporate profitability and the degree to which national policy environments are deemed business-friendly, thus placating the ever-present and oft-employed business threat to 'exit'.[22] Serious debate on the role of capitalism in a liberated southern Africa, and the degree to which capital is required to contribute to socio-economic development and transformation, is fraught with difficulty and risk for capitalists and political elites alike, as the consequences of initial demands for economic justice and land reform spiralling out of control owing to a combination of irresponsible populist rhetoric, political opportunism, capitalist obfuscation and outright thuggery in Zimbabwe have shown. Evidence from South Africa suggests that where business has been willing to engage in debates with a wider range of societal stakeholders, the results have largely been rhetorical window-dressing *à la* Corporate

Social Responsibility (CSR) movement, which has yielded few concrete results and has not altered the control of national economies in favour of the poor (Fig 2005).

The result of an elite dialogue between governments and local and international capital on how to promote a growth-friendly policy environment that largely excludes societal actors from any effective input has been a renewed struggle for recognition and liberation from oppressive economic conditions by various social movements (Seddon and Zeilig 2005; Larmer 2007; Naidoo 2007). Such struggles are most obvious in South Africa and Zimbabwe, although the nature and dynamic of struggle in these two countries differ on account of the distinctly different state–society relations in each country. They are least obvious in Botswana, a result of greater post-independence political stability and a much less developed and autonomous civil society. While the struggle for rights and development in Zimbabwe has already engulfed the country in violence and state oppression, recent evidence of an escalation of violent protest in South Africa, from protests against lack of basic delivery of services in the Free State to clashes between anti-eviction activists and police in KwaZulu-Natal, and more recently also xenophobic violence against African immigrants (Booysen 2007; Neocosmos 2008), suggests that South Africa may, despite a democratic constitution and a government enjoying relatively high levels of legitimacy, fall prey to spiralling volatility if promises of delivery for the majority of poor inhabitants cannot be realized.

The increasingly unstable societal rift in these post-liberation societies points to a widening bifurcation of debates on socio-economic development and transformation. On one hand, there is the elite debate on market-driven or neoliberal versus developmental state or interventionist paths to development, predicated on growth and trickle-down effects in the former and growth with redistribution in the latter. These debates have been rehashed for several decades, and regional trajectories do not suggest that either approach, as each has at some point been pursued in the region, can resolve the fundamental problem of poverty and marginalization of the region's 'social majorities'.[23] On the other hand, renewed agitation among civil society groupings and related organizations is attempting to create grassroots debates and actions that pressure elites to include civil society in decisions on development in a meaningful way (Larmer 2007). At present, however, such movements are merely embryonic and quite weak in Botswana, unable (until very recently) to engage in any meaningful dialogue with a government intent on survival

33

by any means in Zimbabwe and too easily sidelined by well-entrenched capital interests and a sophisticated process of elite political co-optation in South Africa. Leysens's (2006) analysis of social movements among the poor in southern Africa suggests that they have so far not been very successful in promoting and achieving their goals. As protest grows, however, the ability of governments in southern Africa to maintain stability and some semblance of societal cohesion, without which any sustained improvements in well-being become impossible, will likely be increasingly dependent on the ability of governments to respond to the needs of civil society and to exercise a significant degree of autonomy from capitalist actors, for which the relentless perpetuation of accumulation and profit-making remains the key priority. At a tipping point, the region is not likely to sustain the societal fragmentation and natural exploitation that such accumulation entail even if that would be an obviously acceptable option for capital and presumably not an unacceptable option for the region's political elites.

The struggle continues

Following southern Africa's transitions from colonial rule to democracy, a sense of disappointment and despair remains among the region's poor and marginalized majorities, for whom liberation has brought precious little in terms of improvements to their daily lives. Indignities of colonial oppression and racist rule have faded from immediate memory, which is no doubt an important step on the road to psychological liberation, but economic opportunities and access to decent healthcare and housing, as well as the ability to live secure from violence, remain an elusive ideal for all too many. The persistence of extremely uneven development in southern Africa, and of a continued pandering to the very economic processes that produce that uneven development in the first place, ensures that privileged elites continue to monopolize the region's resources and most benefits of economic growth and accumulation. This situation will cast increasing doubt on the conventional wisdom in this not-yet-fully-discarded 'Washington Consensus' era that markets have to be accommodated at all costs and that government policies catering primarily to the interests of capital will provide benefits to all via a greater availability of private consumption and provision of public goods.

If governing elites in southern Africa cannot extricate themselves from the overwhelming temptations of the power and potential material rewards of political office (given the often too-easy transition from politics to business), a growing clash between states and societies is inevitable.

The desperate situation in Zimbabwe is clear evidence of this, as is the emerging populism and increasing social volatility caused by lack of service delivery and elite corruption in South Africa. While Botswana remains the region's 'success story', where a passive society offers little resistance to a government that maintains stability while not managing to reduce extreme socio-economic inequalities, increasing turmoil across its borders is bound to increase the risk of destabilization and increasing societal conflict over how the profits from the mineral resources on which the country so greatly depends are put to use.

Southern Africa thus remains a region of intense and seemingly un-interrupted exploitation, but also one where, following a post-liberation lull, social movements are re-emerging to challenge the leaders of former liberation movements who are now in government and who are desperately trying, although increasingly failing, to accommodate both market demands for neoliberal reforms and populist pressures for redistribution and genuine socio-economic transformation. These challenges to the post-liberation settlement (between states and capital) in southern Africa constitute a continuation of the historical struggle against capitalism that has been the main driver of social change in the modern era, and which is led by those without access to capital who wish to create a society in which the profit motive is no longer the central organizing principle. From the vantage point of the world's most powerful nations and IFIs, southern Africa remains on the fringes of the global economy. Its natural resources, however, remain valuable, and as a site of unabashed exploitation by global and local capital alike it, like many other developing regions, constitutes a key example of how future anti-capitalist movements with a global reach can unfold and produce new challenges to the status quo.

2 | The elusive developmental nexus

Turning and turning in the widening gyre
The falcon cannot hear the falconer;
Things fall apart; the centre cannot hold;
Mere anarchy is loosed upon the world,
The blood-dimmed tide is loosed, and everywhere
The ceremony of innocence is drowned;
The best lack all conviction, while the worst
Are full of passionate intensity. – William Butler Yeats

Institutions, actors and development

Yeats's unnerving vision of things falling apart has often been used as a metaphor for the fragile and ultimately dysfunctional nature of post-colonial African politics (see Andreasson 2005a), most notably in Chinua Achebe's classic post-colonial novel using Yeats's famous words as its title.[1] The notion of a widening gyre spiralling ever downward out of control, or an increasingly uncontrollable pendulum swing between developmental and predatory state behaviour prompted by government officials, businessmen and segments of civil society attempting to avoid 'things falling apart', becomes an apt metaphor for the formation of institutions, and of institutionalized interactions, within which these actors engage in the ostensible interests of long-term, mutually beneficial relations conducive to development. With the high stakes of this pursuit of development firmly in mind, this chapter outlines the historical context of interactions between states, markets and civil society within a broader comparative institutional literature on state–business relations and corporatism. Specifically the following two questions are considered: 1) what prompts state and market actors to collaborate, collude or clash with each other in the context of political and economic transitions;[2] and 2) under what circumstances may particular institutions and, more broadly, political and cultural environments become conducive to a developmental agenda that moves beyond the conventional strictures of orthodox development theory?

If the historical legacy of the southern African region, what I term its regional apartheid system,[3] provides a means to identify key actors driving capitalist, socio-economic and political developments, as well as their aims and relative strengths in shaping decision-making, then the region's *institutional configurations* provide an understanding of why these actors conduct business with each other on particular terms of agreement and how their (perceived) options to act are informed, shaped and at least partly constrained by those same institutional configurations. With reference to the democratic transitions in southern Africa, S. D. Taylor (2007) emphasizes the crucial impact of institutional configurations (themselves shaped by, and in turn shaping, particular kinds of state–business relations) in shaping political and economic trajectories. The economic transition in Zimbabwe was, according to Taylor (ibid.: 4), 'regarded as the archetype of business association influence', while in South Africa 'firms and groups, especially of big business, played a prominent role in the design of posttransition institutions'.

In addition to the well-documented role of domestic and international coalitional support bases in shaping policy trajectories over time (e.g. Gourevitch 1986), it is also important to recognize the importance of institutional arrangements by which key actors are constrained (North 1990; Doner 1992; Thelen and Steinmo 1992). Post-independence governments in southern Africa have all been constrained in policy-making by their respective economic, political and institutional legacies. Promises about fundamental transformation of established economic and political orders, for the benefit of newly enfranchised populations, have generally been tempered by underlying socio-economic power structures. Post-independence politics have in some significant aspects been characterized as much by compromise and continuity as by genuine change and transformation.

At the same time, however, it has been possible to observe important variance in developmental policy choices across the southern African region. Such variation is not simply the outcome of individual agency. Important as the leadership of a Seretse Khama as opposed to a Robert Mugabe may have been in terms of tilting the character of national politics in one direction or another, towards consolidation of democracy in Botswana as opposed to an increasingly stifling authoritarianism in Zimbabwe, these leaders as well as other pivotal actors exist in established socio-cultural contexts within which they are more likely to favour certain patterns of decision-making while discounting others. In other words, if the *kgotla* tradition in Botswana, whereby politicians meet with chiefs and villagers to explain and discuss policies, has aided that country's democratic consolidation, then the legacy of the *Chimurenga*, Zimbabwe's war of national liberation, is in part responsible for that country's democratic breakdown. It is thus possible to discern variation in the institutional arrangements and incentives that shape state–market relations, subsequent power configurations and ultimately policy choices. Specifically, by understanding how (institutional) relations between key state, market and societal actors emerge and are transformed over time, it is possible to explain how and why these countries are either moving closer to patterns of relations that, from a developmental perspective, are mutually beneficial to all significant actors and thus increasingly likely to produce what Evans (1989) describes as 'developmental states', or whether they are receding from that ideal to descend into praetorian politics and political decay (Huntington 1968), economically disastrous policies (Bates 1981), state collapse (Zartman 1995) and 'warlordism' (Reno 1998) – becoming, in Evans's (1989) terminology, 'predatory states'.[4]

These debates on development, whatever the regional or theoretical focus of each study, take place in the context of a broader literature on development in the developing world and how global political and economic realignments in the wake of the Second World War and the onset of decolonization shaped the fortunes of the world's previously colonized peoples. The key focus of Third World studies or development studies more generally has, as is outlined by U. Kothari (2005), been characterized by attempts, from various theoretical points of view and by means of different methodological approaches, to understand why some regions of the world have become increasingly 'modern', prosperous and stable (developed) while others have remained supposedly 'traditional', certainly poor and often unstable (predatory). The specific question, regarding why some have become rich while others remain poor, has been stated in various forms throughout the post-Second World War 'Era of Development' (see Rist 2002) by scholars such as Heilbroner (1963), Landes (1999) and Easterly (2001).[5] While their theoretical approaches and empirical explanations vary, and while the recognition that development of one region shapes the underdevelopment of another, and vice versa, by virtue of the interlinking of rich and poor regions in a global post-war economy as explained by Frank's (1966) thesis on the inevitably Janus-faced 'development of underdevelopment',[6] remains hotly contested, they are all fundamentally concerned with the persistence of global inequality.

In all these studies, moreover, the question of how states act to either facilitate or stifle development of local forms of capitalism and markets remains central. Whether market-led development is rejected outright in favour of socialist or other forms of anti-capitalist blueprints, or whether more or less regulated markets are preferred, it is acknowledged that the ways in which post-colonial states decide to engage with the capitalist market systems that do exist is of significant importance to future prospects for development, however construed. In terms of the latter concern about the degree to which markets should drive development, a consensus on what kind of institutional arrangements are most conducive to broad-based and sustainable development seems to be nowhere in sight given the radically different conceptualizations of the appropriate role for states versus markets in developing economies that are vigorously propagated by competing liberal and *étatiste* theories of growth and development in the political economy of development literature.[7]

Because the intent here is not primarily to add to or, even less profitably, attempt to resolve this state versus market impasse, the line of questioning pursued must move beyond this theoretical divide in the political economy literature. It is therefore necessary to ask not merely what the optimal balance between these actors might be, and consequently how relations between state and market actors can be improved to provide a better basis for the implementation of orthodox development policies, but to ask how a transformation of a state–market nexus is possible in order to make it more inclusive in the interests of promoting broad-based, sustainable development. Moreover, a new vision of what development entails will require a transformation not only of these actors' strategies of relating to each other, but indeed a transformation of the very ends to which they aspire. It is in such an environment that the notion of moving beyond development becomes possible. In the meantime, however, it is necessary to recall how state–business relations, and the potential shortcomings of such relations, are conventionally understood; this concerns the central problem of collusion, as dealt with in studies of the political economy of development (e.g. Krueger 1974; Bhagwati 1982; Olson 1982; Maxfield and Schneider 1997; Haggard 2000).

The pursuit of private versus public goods

A key concern across the spectrum of theoretical and ideological perspectives on development is that close collaboration between state and market actors, in the absence of transparent and genuinely reciprocal structures that can effectively channel private interests into public policies, can easily become collusion that is dysfunctional in terms of a diminishing likelihood that goods will be produced and become (publicly) available for actors beyond those immediately involved in producing and procuring the goods. Thus the key line of questioning to be considered for those seeking to understand how institutional arrangements can produce developmental states was poignantly posed in Maxfield and Schneider's (1997) seminal study of state–business relations in East Asia and South America:

> The general presumption is that when business and the state have close congenial relations, democratic ideals, economic efficiency, and social welfare will suffer. How can poorly paid officials defend the common weal when they come into close, lasting contact with capitalists who have keen appreciation of self-interest, flexible scruples, and vast resources? And if bureaucrats ... who mete out subsidies can be bought, why would rational capitalists invest in anything else? (ibid.: 3)

In the southern African context, many studies have outlined corrupt relationships between economic actors and governments, with the problem of former liberation movements making the transition to conventional politics and the conflicts of interests between public office and private interest that such politics generally entails clearly illustrated in Adam et al.'s (1998) *Comrades in Business*, which charts the transformation of the ANC from liberation movement to post-liberation governing party in Africa's most developed society (cf. Southall 2008). Similarly, N. Alexander's (2003) *An Ordinary Country* somewhat dejectedly outlines post-apartheid South Africa's move from a transition during which hopes for a better future are soon tempered by the turning of politicians to the politics of private interest (justified by reference to a Machiavellian nature of 'real world' politics) and the increasing obsession with making the most of the few opportunities that exist rather than aspiring to a fundamental restructuring of society to thereby create opportunities for the many. While the problem of democratically elected politicians becoming tempted by opportunities for enrichment, which is an endemic problem in neo-patrimonial, post-colonial African polities (Bayart et al. 1999; Chabal and Daloz 1999), is only one aspect of post-liberation politics dealt with by these authors, the notion of 'comrades in business' has become increasingly relevant in the South African context with, for example, the many controversies surrounding detrimental consequences of BEE policies in recent years (Southall 2004; Glaser 2007). 'It can be taken for granted that resignations from top civil service or cabinet positions are followed by individuals being taken up in the BEE world but today the deed is done before and without resignation' (Freund 2007: 667).

Maxfield and Schneider's (1997) analysis of state–business relations recognizes the (classical liberal) a priori, rational-choice assumption that self-interested actors will collude for private gains rather than collaborate (the benevolent form of close state–business relations) for public gains if given the opportunity to do so, while also acknowledging the potential role of institutional arrangements in shaping state–business collaboration that can exist for reasons beyond mere and immediate self-interest. While a more recent literature on CSR in developing countries suggests that some forms of enlightened self-interest (i.e. interest beyond immediate private gain) are increasingly important for business success (Painter-Morland 2006),[8] the history of state–business relations in Africa and other developing regions is rife with examples of collusion for private enrichment at the expense of public interest and needs. The mutually beneficial relationship between many segments of South African business and the apartheid regime is well documented (Lipton 1986; cf. Handley 2005: 228), if sometimes exaggerated (Nattrass 1999). In Rhodesia, corporatist relations between white business and the settler state were transformed into a largely accommodationist and collusive relationship between entrenched white business interests, the Zimbabwean state and an emerging African crony capitalist class promoted by that state (Bond 1998; Dashwood 2000; Brett 2005). Even in Botswana, generally considered the best example in Africa of collaborative state–business relations able to provide a foundation for long-term economic growth and socio-economic development (Samatar 1999), concerns about an increasing lack of transparency in these relations and increasing levels of state patronage more generally have tainted this 'African miracle' (I. Taylor 2003; Good 2005).

These problems, when considered against the predominant liberal account of how close and insufficiently transparent collaboration-cum-collusion between governments and business in East Asia played a significant role in triggering the late-1990s financial crisis (Pempel 1999; Haggard 2000) and how such collaboration will presumably be part of the explanation for the current global financial crisis, mean that those who wish to draw conclusions from the East Asian developmental trajectories for a southern African region in which local versions of the Washington Consensus are becoming an increasingly difficult policy proposition for governing parties to sell domestically[9] must explain how institutionalized interaction between states, businesses and, ideally, civil society can avoid the pitfalls of corruption and obfuscation to which they have been prone in developing societies that have experimented with forms of corporatist relations in the past (nowhere more obviously than in African states themselves). Considering how, and to what end(s), state–business relations can best be institutionalized is even more important considering that recent calls for greater cooperation between states and businesses do not reflect 'a newfound consensus about the necessity for institution-alizing state–private sector collaboration as a prerequisite to achieving national development and international competitiveness' (S. D. Taylor 2007: 1); in fact, this perspective is, as Taylor notes, 'not new at all' but has been prevalent in southern Africa since the end of the cold war and the onset of liberal economic reforms in the 1990s. Moreover, while the East Asian and, to a lesser degree, Latin American post-war examples of institutionalized state–business relations in the quest for development are held forth as good examples to follow as well as cautionary tales about how intimate state–business collaboration can become problematic, it is important to recognize that the experiences from East Asia and Latin America cannot simply be used to graft historical models on to African societies (see Andreasson 2007b).

> Africa, therefore, requires different questions [about how state–business collaboration emerges] from those of Latin America and Asia, where re-form coalitions have been abundant; Schneider and Maxfield, and others, can assume a degree of interaction in much of the developing world that is not yet commonplace in Africa. Yet the comparative literature on business–state relations, as well as the limited African experiences, does suggest that some degree of systematic cooperation is a necessary condition for development in capitalist systems. Thus, at a fundamental, a priori level, we need to understand in the African setting what gets cap-italists and bureaucrats together – or, far more typically, what prevents them from doing so – in the first place. (S. D. Taylor 2007: 5)

In the end, this literature concerns itself solely with the ways in which countries competing in an increasingly integrated and seamless global marketplace, or at least in what is described and understood as such, can most effectively orient themselves to meet global economic demands. These demands for a variety of economic and social policies intended to converge on what constitutes an acceptable level of 'business friendli-ness' at any particular point in time are considered as given (via powerful actors shaping the global economy) and therefore beyond the control of less powerful countries in the developing world, including emerging markets like South Africa.[10] In order to consider whether there are real alternatives to the current developmental paradigm, including currently acceptable variants of socio-economic organization, it is first necessary to understand the ways in which developing countries have attempted to institutionalize relations between key actors in public and private sectors in attempts to approximate models of successful development elsewhere.

When speaking of institutionalized relations, as opposed to 'organic' or 'free market' forms of interaction, between state and market actors, and the need to consciously foster stability in such relations for developmental purposes, it is generally the historical examples of 'late developers', from Germany and Japan to the post-war 'Asian tigers' and European social democracies, which have been most eagerly drawn upon by would-be modernizers, the 'late late developers' in the Third World (except where they have instead opted for development via the Soviet or Chinese state socialist planning path).[11] It is for this reason that corporatism in its many shapes has been of long-standing interest to both policy-makers and scholars interested in the relationship between socio-economic development, modernization and relations between states, markets and societies throughout the post-war Era of Development.

Developmental states and corporatism

Because the classical developmental state debates (e.g. Johnson 1982; R. Wade 1990) are notably state-centric in orientation, it is important to recognize that the ultimate effectiveness of states derives 'not from [their] own inherent capacity, but from the complexity and stability of [their] interaction with market players' (Samuels 1987: 262).[12]

> [T]he idea that the state can play a central role in economic development ... has a very long pedigree, stretching back to the mercantilist period at the dawn of capitalism, via the 19th-century critiques of free trade (Hamilton, List), to the period of 'late development' as analysed by Gerschenkron [1962] ... [T]he *locus classicus* of the modern [developmental state] concept was undoubtedly East Asia, and in particular the work of Amsden [1989] on South Korea and [R.] Wade [1990] on Taiwan. (Radice 2008: 1153)

Given the focus on stability in state–market interactions, much of the literature on developmental states has emphasized the importance of various kinds of corporatist arrangements (Evans 1989; Onis 1991; Schneider 2004). Given the intent of this study to attempt an understanding of how actors involved in shaping developmental efforts in southern Africa might reconceptualize the ways in which they understand what development entails and how it can best be pursued, it is necessary to first consider the ways in which African-style late development has generally relied on corporatism of one kind or another in structuring relations between states, markets and society.

The definition of corporatism, i.e. institutional arrangements shaping state–market–society relations, used here follows Grant's (1985) definition of *social*, as opposed to state, corporatism as

> a process of interest intermediation which involves the negotiation of policy between state agencies and interest organisations arising from the division of labour in society, where the policy agreements are implemented through the collaboration of the interest organisations and their ability to secure the compliance of their members. (ibid.: 3–4)[13]

Grant's definition differs in some important aspects from Schmitter's (1974) classical definition of corporatism.[14] Where Schmitter emphasizes the compulsory, non-competitive and hierarchical nature of the formal corporatist institutions, Grant's definition emphasizes the intermediating and collaborative characteristics of the corporatist *process*. It is in the context of a less hierarchical and rigid corporatism that any transformation of actors' identities, interests and aims is likely to occur. If state, business and societal actors' interests and strategies remain relatively static, there is then little use of speaking about possibilities for thinking beyond orthodox conceptualizations of development.

At the same time it is important to note that, following economic and political liberalization across Africa (Widner 1994; World Bank 1994; Bratton and van de Walle 1997) and the increasingly global nature of capital in the 1990s (Andrews 1994; Keohane and Milner 1996), the literature on corporatism gave way to an ascending literature on democratization (e.g. Sandbrook 2000; cf. Abrahamsen 2000). This shift replaced class-based analysis with pluralist conceptualizations of economic and political processes. Methodological individualism, as opposed to historically derived structural accounts, came to dominate thinking about interaction between competing economic interests, as well as the policy recommendations about how to best balance such interaction, of which Bates's (1981) seminal *Markets and States in Tropical Africa* was an important precursor. Nevertheless, the mainstream literature, which is concerned with orthodox conceptualizations of development, suggests that development is a function of particular policies (Rodrik 1996) as well as institutional conditions (Keefer and Knack 1995; Ndulu and O'Connell 1999). The policies most likely to enhance orthodox, growth-led development are those that encourage long-term investments in education (Romer 1986; Lucas 1988; Barro 1991) and infrastructure (Easterly and Rebelo 1993; Easterly and Levine 1997), suggesting that a proper understanding of and attention to institutional environments remains crucial for understanding where interaction between key societal actors may become developmental.

The emphasis on long-term policy planning and implementation requires stable institutional settings in which relevant actors can communicate and bargain regarding their respective interests and preferences, and where the setting and implementing of developmental policies depends on the ability of public officials to forgo 'predatory urges in favour of long-term benefits that may not necessarily accrue to the specific individuals who inhabit the state's space of power' (Kevane and Englebert 1999: 263).[15] The problem across Africa in the post-independence era, however, was that neo-patrimonial rule

> generally operated by conferring discretionary rents on favoured allies, giving little attention to the impact of rentier politics on economic growth, the efficiency of public services, or the quality of business regulation. The classic consequences, evident in country after country, included the disruption of markets, rising costs of doing business, urban bias, and increased protectionism. (Levy 2007: 500)[16]

Englebert (2000) links the ability to pursue development over the long term to legitimacy by arguing that state legitimacy is an important prerequisite for development and that African countries have performed so poorly compared to countries in other developing regions because of the more complete rupture with traditional, pre-colonial forms of legitimacy that resulted from the particular character of African colonialism. He argues in a similar fashion to Levy (2007) that

> the modern [African] state is reduced to a merely instrumental role, a set of resources that rulers use to foster their power: fiscal revenues are distributed to create networks of political support as rulers personally appropriate public funds to finance political allegiance; employment at the service of the state is used as a means of patronage; public investments follow political rather than economic rationales; and trade and pricing distortions are introduced to create rents and vested interests ... Bureaucracies turn into ghostly institutions. Eventually, the rule of law vacillates, as does the trust of citizens in their institutions. As respect for institutions diminishes, corruption spreads. Private agents, domestic and foreign, stay away from such volatile economic environments. Investments dry up, and both households and firms seek refuge in informal activities. Altogether, the economy stagnates while the very logic of the system makes it resistant to reform. This, in a nutshell, is the political dimension of economic stagnation in Africa. (Englebert 2000: 5–6)

Thus were established, for various reasons and via different routes, practices across African polities that reinforced the obstacles to pursuing long-term developmental perspectives and which exacerbated the tendency of government officials, as well as businesses engaging with these officials, to focus on short-term private gains alone.

At the same time, political and policy-making trends in post-colonial Africa generally reflect a preoccupation on the part of governing parties and rulers with avoiding destabilization and chaos that can be set in motion by centrifugal societal forces. Hence the commonplace justification of political and economic centralization, a mistrust of strong opposition in multiparty systems and a belief in the ability of neo-patrimonial distribution of government largesse to placate pivotal support groups (and sometimes also rivals) in society. One manifestation of this preoccupation with strategies and policies aiming at 'holding the centre', and avoiding 'things falling apart' (see Bates 2008), is the reliance on institutionalized relations between key actors in society – evident, for example, throughout southern Africa in terms of the region's evolving state–business relations.

Corporatism in southern Africa

The principal concern in corporatist attempts at mediating conflicts between societal interests relates to the danger of relying on pluralistic models of interest interaction alone in societies characterized by grave historical injustices, dual economies, extreme inequalities and a dire need for wholesale economic transformation. Political transitions in southern Africa have not produced the economic transformations that would break vicious cycles of marginalization and poverty experienced by people still unable to compete effectively for the relatively few economic opportunities that exist across the region's economies, which are all characterized by high levels of unemployment and large informal sectors. Therefore, corporatist forms of interest mediation are one important instrument that governments have considered in their attempts to gear economic activity towards development. While no corporatist arrangements in southern Africa approximate fully the well-developed post-Second World War social corporatism of Western democracies like Austria and Sweden, such arrangements have been institutionalized across the region, and there are also some important differences across countries in terms of the extent to which corporatism has been attempted and consolidated.[17] The following sketches of corporatist arrangements in South Africa, Zimbabwe and Botswana highlight attempts by state actors to form institutionalized relations with businesses and other (economic) stakeholders based on something more substantial than mere lobbying by corporate interests.

South Africa The literature on tripartite relations and corporatist arrangements in South Africa is substantial if sharply diminished in recent years (e.g. M. Prinsloo 1984; Bird and Schreiner 1992; Pretorius 1996; Habib 1997), and corporatist arrangements between governments and business have coexisted more or less efficiently with a long-established tradition of private lobbying of governments by the corporate sector. The great industrial magnates, such as Harry Oppenheimer of Anglo American, have always had access to key state actors on matters of economic policy-making (Lipton 1986; Handley 2005). In a landmark study of how the 'organic crisis' of latter-day apartheid capitalism prompted South African capital to push for economic and political reform, Saul and Gelb (1986) 'employed the concept "formative action" to interpret the efforts of business leaders to shape a political settlement that would reconsolidate corporate power' (Bassett 2008: 185). More recently, in the country's transition from apartheid to democracy, the Brenthurst Group, an important private sector lobby comprised of South Africa's leading corporate tycoons, and other established business leaders, remains influential. In 1994, the year of the ANC's accession to power, the Reconstruction and Development Programme (RDP) 'was presented by Mandela and Mbeki to Oppenheimer for approval' (Southall 2008: 292), although it constituted a more modest development framework than what the ANC had initially aimed for. In 1996 the Brenthurst Group consulted with the ANC government about the appointment of Trevor Manuel, who had, as the first minister of finance from the ANC's own ranks, previously received extensive courting of both local and international business communities and financial institutions (Bond 2001c), and the subsequent unveiling of the neoliberal Growth, Employment and Redistribution (GEAR) macroeconomic framework in the same year followed extensive government consultation with the business community (Bond 2000; Marais 2001). President Mbeki also established an international business working group where the presidency consults with international corporate magnates and financiers like Percy Barnevik and George Soros (Bond 2001c; Josefsson 2001). The ANC also launched the Network Lounge in 2002, to which corporations, parastatals and government departments 'paid a substantial sum to associate with the ANC elite', and the Progressive Forum in 2006, which offers businesses memberships which enable them to 'network with ANC policymakers' (Southall 2008: 287).[18] While these activities and forums facilitate lobbying of the ANC government by businesses, more formalized structures for (corporatist) bargaining have a long history in South Africa.

Pretorius (1996) traces corporatist thinking in South Africa back to 1930s Afrikaner nationalists and argues that South Africa moved steadily in a 'quasi-corporatist' (as opposed to a more formal corporatism *à la* western European social democracy) direction in the years leading up to the political transition of 1994. In 1960, Prime Minister Verwoerd established an Economic Advisory Council (EAC) which constituted 'a forum for discussion and more or less informal consultation and co-ordination between the State on one side and private enterprise inter-ests on the other' (Verwoerd, quoted in Pretorius 1994). President Botha reshaped and narrowed the scope of the EAC in 1985 'by replacing the representatives of organized business, agriculture and trade unions with corporate notables who were selected by the President himself' (Pretorius 1996: 265). The siege mentality created by increasing domestic unrest in the wake of the 1976 Soweto uprising and the international isolation of the apartheid regime throughout the 1980s helped convince both state and corporations of the need to work closely together in times of crisis and uncertainty, although this was clearly an arrangement about which major corporations came to have serious doubts well before politicians, and especially the security establishment, reached similar conclusions and consequently looked to regime-changing reforms. In addition to the corporatist interest representation of the 1980s, interest intermediation has continued in the 1990s, and, interestingly, 'the strengthening of corporatism came with the advent of a democratic regime' (ibid.: 263). Lodge (1999: 7) argues that the incoming ANC government continued the use of 'corporatist forums inherited from the National Party regime'. According to Habib (1997: 72), corporatism in South Africa emerged as a consequence of the 'distribution of capabilities that informed the political and economic settlement' in the country, which can be traced from the large industrial strikes in Durban in 1973 to the democratic transition of the early 1990s. Corporatist arrangements were seen as a desirable strategy by the ruling NP and entrenched economic elites in their at-tempts to co-opt the anti-apartheid opposition, but were also viewed in a positive light by some segments of this opposition itself, including labour organizations like the Congress of South African Trade Unions (COSATU), as they became integrated into the elite decision-making of the emerging new post-apartheid economic order.

Following the democratic transition, NEDLAC was established by an

Act of Parliament in 1994 to serve as a 'negotiating, not advisory, body, whose brief is to produce agreements, not recommendations, and with government being one of the three partners and not the only decision-maker' (J. Naidoo 1995; cf. Houston et al. 2001: ch. 2). NEDLAC provides the most concrete example in the 1990s of a corporatist institution for interest mediation in South Africa (and the region). Judgements about NEDLAC's efficiency have varied from the very pessimistic among analysts who are now outside government (Gelb 2001) to guardedly optimistic by then government officials (Aboobaker 2001) and NEDLAC insiders (Wilson 2001). Houston et al. (2001) conclude that the record of NEDLAC in fostering effective democratic participation in policy-making has been mixed. Overall,

> the nature of policy making in South Africa has clearly been transformed from a secretive and authoritarian approach to a more participatory approach. In this respect, NEDLAC has emerged as one of the key mechanisms for expanding the participation of organs of civil society in policy making. (ibid.: 71)

Pretorius (1996), however, shares T. M. Shaw's (1994) and Marais's (2001) concerns that the democratic transition in South Africa might simply have served to extend corporatist arrangements to elite representatives of the black majority, rather than promote genuine economic transformation. These concerns are echoed in Joseph's (1999) worries about the emergence of 'virtual democracies' that are lacking in vertical accountability between elected officials and the public, and in horizontal accountability between branches of government.[19]

Zimbabwe Zimbabwe's corporatist legacy originates in the colonial Rhodesian era and remains relevant into the Zimbabwean era (Brett 2005: 96).

> Even before the UDI period, the Rhodesian state took a major role in organizing business, adhering to an essentially corporatist strategy in which state-sanctioned monopoly groups were allowed substantial input into policymaking. (S. D. Taylor 2007: 104)

T. M. Shaw (1989) shows that the 1980 political transition was characterized by continuity rather than revolution 'at the level of economics', and that the corporatist legacy consists of 'exclusive and inclusive politico-economic structures which build upon continuities of both settler and "state capitalisms"' (ibid.: 150). New corporatist patterns emerged in the 1980s, revolving around relations between the ZANU-PF regime, white business (national capital, organized commercial interests and transnational corporations) and an assortment of domestic black interest groups, IFIs and other external agencies. Organizations representing mainly white capital, e.g. the Commercial Farmers' Union (CFU), the Confederation of Zimbabwe Industries (CZI), the Chamber of Mines and so on, were at the time 'in continuous contact-cum-dialogue with government ministries and parastatals over inputs, exports, labor, interests and exchange rates, and infrastructure' (ibid.: 153).

Constituting dominant business interests in Zimbabwe, the captains of industry and large-scale commercial farmers retained sufficient economic resources in the post-independence era to form a powerful bargaining bloc vis-à-vis the new black political elite, while emergent populist factions within the new corporatist arrangements pressed ever harder for state patronage and radical redistribution (ibid.; S. D. Taylor 2007). Anticipating Zimbabwe's current crisis as it has unfolded since the farm invasions that began in 2000 and preceded by the country's difficult path 'from corporatism to liberalization' in the 1990s (Brett 2005), Shaw prophetically questions the continued viability of maintaining corporatist structures inherited from settler rule in a post-independence era where government is expected to deliver on promises of broad-based development.

> The established patterns of settler agriculture and industry now coexist sometimes uncomfortably with new institutions of government and administration: how long can the super-imposed non-racial superstructure articulate with the inherited racist substructure? (T. M. Shaw 1989: 151)

The possibility for corporatist interest mediation tapered off in Zimbabwe as the country embarked on comprehensive structural adjustments with the acceptance of an Economic Structural Adjustment Programme (ESAP) in 1991; by the late 1990s such arrangements had collapsed completely (Bond and Manyanya 2002; Brett 2005). NEDLAC was considered a good model for interest mediation by Zimbabwean labour, but the National Economic Consultative Forum (NECF) was a 'non-starter' (Bond 2001c). The Zimbabwe Congress of Trade Unions (ZCTU), led by Morgan Tsvangirai, the man who would eventually became President Mugabe's first significant political challenger, called for the NECF. Envisioned as a true tripartite forum bringing a wide array of societal stakeholders together, the NECF initially included the ZCTU, the Zimbabwe National Chamber of Commerce (ZNCC), the CZI and other representatives of government, the private sector and civil society. Citing problems with labour representation, the ZCTU decided to boycott the NECF, and the ZNCC later withdrew its participation as well (*Financial Gazette*, 9 April 1998). According to Mhone (2001), bodies like the NECF designed for interaction between state, capital and societal actors were hampered by a tendency of government to make them biased in its favour through appointments of pro-government delegates. Thus labour became marginalized and the business sector weakened as bargaining power tilted decisively in the direction of the state; therefore business associations 'became *recipients* of policy rather than influential *shapers* of it' (S. D. Taylor 2007: 137) and so had to increasingly rely on informal lobbying when engaging state actors on economic policy issues.

Botswana Botswana's long tradition of accommodating corporate demands and relying on the private sector to facilitate economic growth and development originates in the state's limited capacity at independence. At the same time, the government has come to play a dominant role in the economy over time and has been active in fostering good relations with the private sector, thus enabling Botswana to safeguard its own developmental interests when striking deals with the private sector. An oft-cited example of such skilfulness on the part of the government was bringing De Beers to the country to prospect for mineral resources, and then managing to renegotiate the government's share of the resulting joint Debswana venture to an equal one (Stedman 1993; Samatar 1999). Subsequently bringing Hyundai and Volvo motor vehicle assembly to Botswana in the late 1990s became an additional, although short-lived, triumph for the government's marketing strategy. With diamonds remaining the bedrock of growth-led development in Botswana, the newly opened Diamond Trading Company, a joint venture between the government and De Beers, is the crowning achievement of attempts to bring diamond cutting and polishing to Botswana (paralleling similar developments in South Africa and Namibia) and is undoubtedly an important development in terms of adding value, job creation and diversification to the country's resource-led export growth (*Economist*, 19 March 2008). In addition to amenable relations between political and corporate elites of which these developments are indicators, Botswana has created a set of formal institutions designed to improve interactions between state, capital and societal actors.

Tripartite relations between government, business and labour have been developed in Botswana since the 1970s. The government has been proactive (and, according to its critics, rather high-handed) in developing stable and harmonious labour relations, especially in the vital mining industry. As a consequence of significant restrictions placed on the ability of unions to strike, industrial action has not been a significant factor in the post-independence era (I. Taylor 2003: 226). The 'major actors' in social dialogue are, according to the International Labour Organization (ILO 2002), the Botswana Federation of Trade Unions (BFTU), the Botswana Commission of Commerce, Industry and Manpower (BOCCIM) and the Ministry of Labour and Home Affairs. BOCCIM represents private companies and holds biennial conferences with government and representatives from workers' organizations and IFIs. Eventually these negotiations resulted in the establishment of a High-Level Consultative Council (HLCC), chaired by the president and comprising key state, capital and societal actors, which facilitates regularized interactions and stable relations between these actors on a sectoral basis (Land 2002). The effort to create effective interest mediation along corporatist lines in Botswana has been given serious attention but is also hampered by the weak financial and human resources of the BFTU and the fact that the country's National Employment, Manpower, and Incomes Council (NEMIC) provides only non-binding policy advice to the government. In general, Botswana's government has been considered 'committed to creating a climate of good industrial relations in order to attract Foreign Direct Investment (FDI) flows into the country' (ILO 2002).

Towards post-corporatism? Corporatist attempts at interest mediation have been consistently pursued in Botswana but have been hampered by a weak input from labour and civil society and by a tendency to emphasize informal ties between political and business elites. Corporatism in Zimbabwe has waned and eventually crumbled with the emergence of economic restructuring in the 1990s and the unfolding crisis of the 2000s. In South Africa corporatism remains a significant feature of interactions between the state, businesses and civil society, although economic liberalization in the post-apartheid era has placed increasing strains on such arrangements. Nevertheless, corporatism has had a more concrete presence in South Africa than in neighbouring countries (S. D. Taylor 2007; Handley 2008). Ultimately, the ability of corporatist frameworks to facilitate the emergence of developmental states, or at least policy trajectories conducive to development, remains contested.

The degree to which governments in the region have actually been committed to the various corporatist and quasi-corporatist forums and institutions they have created is difficult to estimate. Explanations put forth in the political economy literature for why such arrangements have either proved ineffective in competition with old-fashioned corporate lobbying or have simply stagnated as a result of overpowering states and dominant party pressures remain contested and inconclusive. Nevertheless, the region's corporatist experiments provide a useful backdrop against which to understand contemporary relations between governments, businesses, labour and civil society. The corporatist legacy furthermore points to both the limitations of attempting to understand how developmental trajectories emerge according to relatively formalistic notions of relations between key actors, and the potential for new forms of interaction and reconceptualizations of strategies and goals for the actors involved in shaping what may become a 'post-corporatist' southern Africa.

The developmental nexus

In addition to considering the nature of traditional institutional arrangements and their impact on development, it is important to recognize an intrinsic interdependence of the actors involved in shaping developmental policies if new visions of development aiming to break the current development impasse are to be found. The notion of interdependence is crucial to the thesis put forth in this study: it suggests that it is via a mutual interdependence of actors that we can best understand how approaches to development change in terms of concrete policy-making and, most importantly, how the understanding and conceptualization of development by different actors may also change as a result of interaction with each other and of changing historical and cultural contexts.

> [S]tate and market agents, despite the analytical distinction, evolve and exist symbiotically in practice, and ... the developmental outcome of the whole is distinguishable from the interests of particular state or market agents. States and markets are not discrete *things* as such. (Underhill and Zhang 2005: 5)

This, then, requires us to think about the logic of the space created as a result of states and markets interacting with each other as being essentially *integrative*, as opposed to being based on the *relational* logic from which standard treatment of such interactions in the historical institutionalist literature is derived (ibid.: 4).

Heeding the logic of integration, of actors' strategies, aims and ultimate goals, makes it imperative to understand how ideas and interests are diffused, shared and transformed by all relevant sets of actors involved in the pursuit of development, however it is defined, in any dynamic socio-economic setting. To merely assume an initial, or a given, interest of any particular actor, which that actor will then pursue and base his bargaining with other actors on, is insufficient. The southern African experience of major social, political and economic shifts associated with the regional transitions unfolding in the context of global economic transformation over the last several decades provides a good example of the importance of heeding this integrative logic. Established businesses have had to redefine themselves as new entrants, i.e. black/indigenous/ African businesses that sometimes have better links with governments, offer new challenges as competitors or as partners with established actors. In succeeding white minority rule, African governments have had to adapt their aspirations to the realities of post-independence, post-cold-war conditions. Allegiances of civil society movements may in the past have dovetailed with the aims of liberation movements, but do not necessarily do so now that those leading liberation have become ensconced in the powerful offices of state.

Analysing the rational agency of any actor (in terms of their impact on development) as discrete, or in contrast to and standing clearly *against* any other actor in this matrix of relations, is therefore unhelpful in terms of understanding why countries have been moving towards or away from whatever developmental ideal has been prevalent at a particular point in time. This notion of a non-discreteness of actors derives from Underhill and Zhang's (ibid.: 1) conceptual innovation in theorizing state–market relations, which stresses that interactions between states and markets (as they relate to processes of development) ought not to be understood as interactions between discrete entities, but rather as a set of complex and interdependent interactions between actors viewed as part of 'an integrated ensemble of governance', what they term the 'state–market condominium'. 'The central claim is that the state–market condominium is greater than its state–market/public–private parts and that the outcomes in terms of governance are significantly different from the preferences of either as identifiable agents' (ibid.: 1–2).

Adopting this perspective in studying how state–business relations affect socio-economic transformation and development in post-apartheid South Africa, the African country that has received by far the most attention in case studies of such a nature, Hamann et al. (2008) evaluate interactions between the state and mining and finance sectors in the context of BEE from the contrasting perspectives of 'collaborative governance' and 'power-based bargaining', where the concept of collaborative governance echoes some key insights of Underhill and Zhang's state–market condominium. Collaborative governance, or what is often referred to by the ANC as 'co-operative governance', is defined by two key characteristics: first, a reliance on 'multi-stakeholder initiatives, networks or partnerships for the purpose of policy-making and/or implementation'; second, an increasing expectation, on the part of governments and civil society, that businesses 'contribute to the provision of social goods' and that businesses themselves are actively seeking, with the (at least tacit) support of governments, to fulfil such expectations by promoting CSR (ibid.: 22). While collaborative governance defined in this way is clearly something that is institutionally much weaker than most forms of corporatist or tripartite relations as traditionally understood, it shares with the concept of the state–market condominium an expectation that 'the responsibility for policy-making, implementation, and the provision of social goods and services shifts from government to a more diffuse constellation of social actors, with a special role for business' (ibid.: 22).

The concept of collaborative governance, the state–market condominium or a more broadly defined site of interaction which, in the context of pursuing development, can be conceived of as constituting a 'developmental nexus' becomes directly relevant for existing debates on how southern African countries can best pursue the formation of developmental states (à la Asian tigers) and the substantial difficulties these countries face in attempting to approximate, never mind to replicate, such trajectories as they have previously unfolded in other developing regions (Andreasson 2007b). Indeed, the notion of a developmental nexus as a *site* of interaction necessitates some kind of formalized, institutionalized interaction among actors identified as key stakeholders in the developmental process. At the same time it is important to note that this is a site in more than just a spatial sense. It is also an *ideational* site where new ideas about how actors may interact and cooperate in the pursuit of new visions of development can emerge. Indeed, it is where new mindsets may become established and exercise some influence on policy-making and politics more generally. Whereas the state–market condominium may emerge as a consequence of a more or less organic interaction between state and market actors which produces new patterns of governance, the developmental nexus as it is defined and employed as a guiding conceptual framework in this study is at least partly dependent on formalized institutional arrangements capable of ensuring stability and also on some degree of predictability in the otherwise volatile socio-economic settings of southern Africa's unevenly developed, and in many respects deeply divided, societies.[20]

In contrast to the conceptualization of state and market actors as distinct, rational agents with their own exclusive, generally conflicting interests, as in, for example, Bates's (1981) influential account of public policy-making in tropical Africa or Lipton's (1986) account of the diverging interests of state and capital in the undoing of South African apartheid, the state–market condominium thesis makes possible a better conceptual understanding of how enduring relations emerge between state, market and societal actors over time and how the ebb and flow of such relations promote or hamper developmental policies as conventionally defined. As opposed to analysing the determinants of policy trajectories through traditional models of interest-group bargaining, the developmental nexus can accommodate a greater complexity of interactions, reconfigurations and fusions of different actors' interests as the concept of such a nexus comprises a broader and more diverse set of actors and recognizes that these actors' identities and their relationships with other relevant actors are constantly in flux. This is especially likely to be the case in the post-transition environments of divided and unevenly developed societies.

In the case of southern Africa several examples of such complexities and a general sense of flux are evident: entrenched white capital orienting itself away from domestic markets towards global markets as their previous ability to rely on relatively stable and privileged relations with their own governments is replaced by more adversarial relations with incoming African political elites and the states to which these African elites sometimes have better access; indigenous African entrepreneurial and 'comprador' elites forging beneficial relationships with government officials and lobbying successfully for government legislation increasingly responsive to their demands for greater access to market opportunities via indigenization and empowerment policies; government officials finding increasingly attractive opportunities to move from public office to lucrative positions in the private sector (the 'comrades in business' syndrome); multinational corporations operating in the region using their superior organizational skills and sheer advantage in size and resources to beat local corporations at the game of accommodating and adapting to new government directives relating to corporate responsibility, facilitation of government development objectives and the empowerment of indigenous African populations, and so on. The rapidly shifting policy environment in post-liberation southern Africa makes the notion of a 'developmental nexus', where key actors come and go and where the very ends of policy-making remain essentially contested, as exemplified by the debates surrounding GEAR and the National Democratic Revolution

(NDR) in South Africa and by the sharply divergent visions for Zimbabwe proposed by ZANU-PF and the MDC, preferable to that of traditional models of interest bargaining as a conceptual tool for analysing the region's and Africa's development impasse.

In this sense, the key issue here is how to best conceptualize and understand how collaborative rather than collusive relations become possible (see Maxfield and Schneider 1997), perhaps via a process akin to the iterative interactions between rational actors that Axelrod (1984) describes as 'the evolution of cooperation', or, somewhat similarly but in a perhaps less obvious way, to accounts of 'complex interdependence' in liberal institutionalist strands of international relations theory (Keohane and Nye 1977). It is at this juncture, the point where diverse sets of actors meet and bargain against an often changing socio-economic background with shifting elite and populist demands, that a developmental nexus takes shape and can not only facilitate and sustain mutually beneficial relations between actors, but can also make possible the very transformation of these actors' immediate aims and ultimate goals for interacting with each other in the first place. Such a nexus, and the resulting transformation of actors involved, can assume a positive as well as negative, a developmental or predatory, character.

For example, large multinational corporations might find that they have an interest in supporting the South African government's BEE policies if they perceive themselves to be in a better position to effectively implement or, by virtue of their foreign ownership, sidestep such policies in a way that domestic corporations are less likely to do, thus giving the multinationals a competitive advantage in adapting to current business regulations. While businesses that are still able to profit in Zimbabwe's extremely volatile and chaotic business environment, e.g. some international mining companies, are obviously distressed by the country's descent into dictatorship and the implications for their long-term operations in the country, it is also the case that these businesses have in some cases (perhaps unintentionally) benefited from the government's effective dismantling of unions and their ability to protect workers' rights. On the other hand, increasing unrest across the region resulting from a deterioration of living conditions for workers and the poor has given rise to new forms of community and civil society organization that look to visions for human emancipation beyond those on offer from the market and state-led development. A strengthening sense that Western forms of governance and market-driven development may not, after all, promise southern African countries a way out of the current impasse has led to political elites, whether Mugabe cynically 'Looking East' or Mbeki praising African communitarianism and *ubuntu*, and grassroots movements looking for ways in which southern African politics can be anchored in African values that can legitimize governments, thereby providing them with the stability rooted in societal cohesion that they need to pursue long-term development policies or, in some cases, dare to stake out new goals that are independent of the received wisdom imparted by Western governments, IFIs and the like. By accounting for the emergence of such a developmental nexus, then, it becomes possible to speak of a move beyond development as it is conventionally understood.

Beyond institutional orthodoxy

Assessing African prospects for development in the twenty-first century, Houngnikpo (2006) considers the ways in which a genuine 'new dawn' can be created by following through on previously derailed attempts to democratize organs of state and governance procedures across the continent. Writing against the backdrop of the abject failures in the wake of Africa's 'lost decade' (the 1980s), with the continent at its subsequent 'nadir' on the eve of a new century, he conveys a careful sense of optimism about the prospects for a new kind of politics in Africa. This guarded optimism stems from a notion that

> [i]nternal and external pressures seem to have brought to a halt to decades of Machiavellian personal rule marked by plots and faked coups, factionalisms, purges, rehabilitations, clientelism, corruption and mismanagement ... Against their will, African leaders had to introduce political and economic reforms ... Unfortunately, real changes have yet to occur because African democracy, when it does happen, is far from being genuine and cannot by itself right several decades of wrongs. (ibid.: 2)

Whether this optimism, which the author certainly tempers with a clear recognition of the obstacles remaining and the 'herculean tasks' still to be performed if African countries are to turn the corner on decades of developmental failures, is at all justified, the analysis correctly identifies the need for a new kind of politics in Africa, one that can escape from the well-established trap of neo-patrimonial politics in all its destructive manifestations. His analysis also focuses on another important issue, the need for 'genuineness' in African rule, which is something similar to Englebert's (2000) concept of (state) legitimacy. As Englebert argues, 'low-legitimacy states are not unique to Africa, but their concentration in the continent is unique among all regions of the world and accounts in part for the differential in economic performance between Africa and the rest of the world' (ibid.: 6).

Whereas Houngnikpo's analysis is limited by a focus on how African countries can improve well-being by, essentially, democratizing existing structures of the state and of economic policy-making – yet another version of the 'good governance' argument applied to Africa (cf. Abrahamsen 2000; Kapoor 2008: 29–33)[21] – and although Englebert's argument about the link between legitimacy and development is ultimately limited by the very conventional, economic-growth-and-good-governance-defined understanding of development on which his analysis rests (Englebert 2000: 4), the argument put forth in this book relies partly on both Houngnikpo's argument for a fundamental democratization of institutions and Englebert's argument for the legitimacy of states as springboards from which to eventually articulate a radical revisioning of what development in Africa ought to entail and how it can best be accomplished.

Because the goal here is to enquire as to how Africa's developmental dilemma can be resolved – indeed, be somehow transcended – while at the same time the very pressing material, social and spiritual needs of people left destitute by the combined forces of corrupt misrule and capitalism's 'creative destruction' (Schumpeter 1947) can be cared for, it is necessary to further rethink how institutional arrangements designed with the aim of facilitating orthodox, growth-led development can be made to accommodate aims beyond this dominant conceptualization of what development is and indeed ought to be. Envisioning institutional arrangements or relations more broadly defined between states, markets and societal actors which can effectively move beyond (material) self-interest is difficult, and all mainstream theoretical approaches to development are to some significant degree predicated on such interests guiding the actors involved. Moreover, any arguments about pursuing new goals, and about forging new kinds of relations between these actors, cannot leave aside material needs and self-interest or they will inevitably be deemed utopian, indeed impossible, before such ideas have any chance of percolating into policy-making arenas. If the goal here is not only to speak of ideas, important as they are in themselves,[22] but also to attempt an assessment of how different understandings of development can bring forth new social and political spaces where the predominant development discourse can be reconceptualized so that underdevelopment, i.e. poverty, and the unsustainable nature of current growth and accumulation-led development strategies can be confronted, then real-life politics and economics of development must remain part of the analysis.

What is needed here, beyond an empirical analysis of the elusive nature of the developmental nexus in southern African countries, is a re-examination of ideas about the sociocultural context of institutional design (e.g. as it impacts on state–business relations), and of politics in Africa more generally – ideas that somehow went out of fashion with the ascendancy of behavioural and then rational-choice approaches to development in Africa in the post-war era (see Kapoor 2008: ch. 2).[23] Moreover, as assumptions of global convergence on models of 'best practice' (as in the African good governance debate) came to dominate public and scholarly debates on development and about the political and social requisites thereof, any suggestions that the particular cultures and traditions of African societies and the legacy of pre-colonial rule could serve as an important context in which to anchor heterodox visions for improvements to conditions of life in Africa have come to be seen as a backwards-striving, anachronistic and reactionary romanticizing of an irretrievable past, or worse.[24] Surely, as the common form of criticism would have it, African leaders do not need to be supplied with additional arguments for why they should resist what is received wisdom about how to promote sustainable development, which entails democratization along Western liberal lines and economic policies supporting growth-led development, no matter what adjustment are needed or what the impact on African societal cohesion is.

There is a resistance, then, to suggestions that, for example, social stability might in some cases trump liberal freedoms, that legitimacy may in some cases be more securely anchored in traditional forms of rule, whether secular or religious in nature, than in modern and perhaps more democratic ones, and that not all forms of deference to authority and acceptance of social hierarchies may be counterproductive to the improvement of conditions in African societies suffering from the combined pressures of domestic social disintegration and global economic subordination. Similar ideas underpin Huntington's (1968) seminal study of the importance of political order and the potential danger of change, which, although considered by its critics to be tainted by the (ideological) cold war context in which it was written, still stands as an important reminder of the potentially disastrous effects in newly post-colonial countries of rapidly rising popular expectations when those expectations are combined with state institutions incapable of effectively meeting them – expectations that the states themselves have often created or exacerbated. After all, African societies have incurred significant costs as a result of the many ill-fated attempts to graft on to them either liberal or socialist models of modernization and development that originated elsewhere under very different circumstances, i.e. in the Western Industrial Revolution and later in the state communism of the Soviet Union and its allies.

Of course, relying on tradition does not mean only acceptance of authority and an emphasis on stability over freedom. Other, perhaps more egalitarian and proto-democratic forms of tradition are also important. Much of the current literature on social movements in southern Africa relies on visions for bottom-up development that entail a localization of decision-making power, an emphasis on ongoing deliberation, an appreciation of local knowledge as an important source of solutions to local needs that markets and state planning have often failed to properly address (e.g. Moyo and Yeros 2005; Gibson 2006; Prempeh 2006). From these points of view, globalization is not only about how the global economy, as it is shaped by the world's most powerful economic actors, produces various pressures for reform and convergence to which marginalized countries have to adapt. Globalization also offers regions across the global South new opportunities for interaction with each other and for considering how the traditional values, institutions and politics indigenous to these regions – values, institutions and politics that, crucially, are distinct from those Western trajectories of industrialization and development that have in the past always been considered the appropriate models for development in the Third World – can be adapted to suit local conditions and needs today.

As but one example, India and Africa traditionally share many similar problems of development relating to their respective colonial heritages, deep (rural) poverty, the marginalization of women and relative lack of urbanization and industrialization. With regard to what may (loosely) be termed 'philosophies of development', the historical link between the person of Gandhi and South Africa is not only controversial (Swan 1985) but also potentially useful in terms of how 'neo-Gandhian movements' may influence thinking about new directions in southern Africa's post-corporatist era. According to Sitas (2008), who 'discerns the influence of Gandhi in a range of liberation philosophies', from Nkrumah's 'consciencism' and Nyerere's 'utopianism' to Cabral and Mandela, there are 'five elements' inherent in such movements:

> social voluntarism; a cooperativism that can be seen in the concept of
> ubuntu; a guiding principle for collective action, which emphasises
> that the means of struggle are as important as its ends; a rejection of

calculative approaches; and a rejection of the terms of engagement as defined by the oppressor. (ibid.)

The importance of social voluntarism is obvious in the new social movement literature, and how it can be mobilized in a post-structural adjustment age characterized by worsening marginalization of the poor and wholesale social fragmentation remains a key question for that literature to address. 'Cooperativism' as part of a new African politics anchored in a communitarian philosophy of *ubuntu* offers the possibility for new ways of thinking, a thinking that may in light of the focus in recent decades on development-as-modernization come across as positively radical (although in fact hearkening back to many inherently traditional ways), to become socially embedded and therefore politically feasible and sustainable. The emphasis on collective action, a rejection of 'calculative approaches' and a rejection of 'terms of engagement' with questions of development as defined by Western proponents of state-led or market-led development throughout the Era of Development combines to create the space in which all actors can learn, by actually beginning the practice, to engage with each other on new terms and for new ends.

Following on the post-war Era of Development (Rist 2002), in which not only the 'really existing' socialist visions for development and emancipation of the Third World failed and became discredited, but the Keynesian and neoliberal market strategies have also failed to produce broad-based development and consolidated democracies worldwide – witness the perennial plight of Collier's (2007) 'the bottom billion'[25] and the reassertion of authoritarian rule from Russia to Venezuela and Zimbabwe – it seems evident that mainstream theories of development, whether socialist or liberal, offer few prospects for any leap beyond development. Southern Africa and regions facing similar challenges require a basis for theorizing about development from which a radically different set of relations and goals can be articulated. Scholars, activists, politicians and others concerned about development and long-term stability must consider anew what theoretical foundations are best suited for deriving arguments about how, in practice, state, market and societal actors will be able to break out of the status quo. Their rational, generally short-term and self-interested, relations with each other can scarcely provide an impetus for thinking about means and goals of socio-economic organization that differ from those predominant in the current era, in which development and modernization have remained imperative, but always elusive, concepts towards which the so-called underdeveloped societies must strive, or at least be seen to strive. Thinking anew about how an eclectic range of theories usually labelled post-development theories can, in conscious and ongoing dialogue with more orthodox critiques of development, contribute to such an effort is the challenge to which the next chapter is devoted.

3 | Beyond development

Our society has been captured by a rapacious individualism which is corroding our social cohesion, which is repudiating the value and practice of human solidarity, and which totally rejects the fundamental precept of Ubuntu. – Thabo Mbeki

We believe that in the long run the special contribution to the world by Africa will be in the field of human relationships. – Steve Biko

A modern predicament

Speaking at the eighth annual Steve Biko Memorial Lecture in Cape Town in September 2007, South Africa's president Thabo Mbeki provided a sombre and rather frank assessment of disturbing levels of fragmentation and dysfunction in post-apartheid society. According to Mbeki, the problem of 'rapacious and venal individualism' – which the neoliberal policies of his government have been accused of exacerbating (e.g. Bond 2000; Marais 2001) – will be resolved only by a rediscovery of 'African identity' and the building of a society that is 'new not only in its economic arrangements, but also in terms of the values it upholds', namely the 'Ubuntu value system' (Mbeki 2007: 16–17).[1] The notion that development entails more than socio-economic (i.e. material) change is thus keenly felt and recognized at the highest level of political office.

The sentiments expressed by President Mbeki and Steve Biko, the founder of South Africa's Black Consciousness Movement (BCM), who died in 1977 following a beating in police custody, suggest an established mode of thinking which holds that the way in which South Africa has developed, indeed how it has become Africa's most Westernized and modern state, has produced serious social ills that impede development of human potential and emancipation anchored in African values and tradition. Most obvious among these ills are rates of murder and sexual violence that are among the highest in the world and the world's greatest number of people suffering from HIV/AIDS. These crises of criminality and disease are both cause and consequence of a deteriorating societal fabric, as much as a result of underdevelopment.[2] Indeed, it is a crisis of late modernity enveloping southern Africa, similar to crises of rupturing social fabrics playing themselves out in both developed and developing countries worldwide, albeit in varying ways and with different degrees of severity. Nevertheless, prominent debates on how to pursue development in southern Africa tend to leave questions regarding culture, identity, individualism, community and belonging aside, in favour of paying attention to more easily measurable (and operationalizable) issues, such as how to promote economic growth, greater economic redistribution and the political means by which access to the productive output of the region's economies can be broadened.

Across the ideological spectrum, from radical and socialist to liberal and reactionary, the key debate on southern Africa's future revolves around the question of how, given the region's difficult socio-economic circumstances and a highly competitive and rather unforgiving global economy, development can most effectively be pursued. Regional particularities, such as the need to pursue development within the framework of the NDR and BEE in South Africa, the politics of indigenization alongside a breakdown of state–society relations in Zimbabwe and an urgent need to promote development with diversification in Botswana, provide in each country debates on development with their own distinct character. Still, the debate is first and foremost about how regional productive capabilities can be enhanced and harnessed more efficiently, so that the region's overwhelmingly poor inhabitants can increase their consumption and thereby improve their (material) well-being (e.g. Lee 2003; Hentz 2005; S. D. Taylor 2007). This is seen as particularly urgent in the context of increasing hardships associated with the strictures of structural adjustment policies (whether externally imposed or home-grown), little success with broadening the benefits of economic growth and the devastating HIV/AIDS epidemic. In their most basic and powerful manifestations, southern African debates on development remain safely anchored in the orthodox conceptualization of development predicated on ever-increasing economic growth, material accumulation and consumption that has defined both liberal and socialist paradigms since the Industrial Revolution and which, since the end of the Second World War and the onset of the cold war, has constituted the Era of Development (Rist 2002).[3]

Given the very urgent material needs of southern Africa's inhabitants – ranging most obviously from access to adequate nutrition and medical care to decent housing, education and employment – it is not surprising that scholarly critiques of fundamental problems inherent in orthodox understandings and pursuits of development, in this case post-development theory, have not featured prominently in African debates, either at the level of elite policy-making or in civil society (Matthews 2004).

Instead, there exists and generally remains unchallenged a disturbing, counterproductive and therefore dangerous cognitive dissonance in debates on development in contemporary Africa. In its simplest form, this dissonance stems from the lack, or even dismissal, among politicians, policy-makers and social commentators alike, of a sophisticated analysis and comprehension of the particular historical, social, political and economic contexts in which development has successfully been pursued in the past, most notably in the West and later among East Asia's so-called tigers. This has resulted in a failure to properly appreciate how southern Africa has arrived at modernity, albeit an alternative modernity to that in either the West or East Asia, via a different route to that taken in these other regions (see Ferguson 2006).

Few, if any, of the important factors facilitating developmental states in East Asia, i.e. national and social cohesion, a favourable global strategic and economic environment and stable state–business–labour relations (Woo-Cumings 1999), are present in southern Africa today, although Botswana's stable relations between government, business and labour, in part a consequence of its weak civil society, constitute an important exception. This suggests that countries in the region do not, at present, possess the basic foundations on which development along the lines of the developmental state can be built (Andreasson 2007b). But politicians choose to proceed by simply declaring a goal and the pursuit thereof, without considering explicitly whether it is likely or even possible that that goal can be arrived at given existing conditions. At a more fundamental level, there is little if any serious consideration given to the notion that even a 'successful' implementation of orthodox development strategies, whether of a state-interventionist or market-oriented kind, producing a sustained trajectory of economic growth and increases in aggregate levels of production and consumption, may in fact exacerbate already disturbing levels of stress placed on social, environmental and cultural/spiritual dimensions of contemporary southern African societies.[4]

Thus contributions of post-development theory to debates on development have been largely ignored by politicians and scholars alike in southern Africa. Matthews (2004: 377) notes that no African scholar is linked prominently with the post-development school of thought; indeed, 'the African situation has not featured prominently in discussions by [post-development] theorists'.[5] Thus Lunn (2009: 941) is overly optimistic in terms of what remains marginal (so-called postmodern and post-structural) academic developments having an influence on political processes and public policy when asserting that 'the "impasse" in development theory between neoclassical economics and neo-Marxist political economy has now been superseded'. Given the hypothesis that post-development theory identifies serious shortcomings and contradictions inherent in mainstream liberal and socialist blueprints for development, however, it is useful to examine ways in which post-development thinking can contribute to genuine and sustainable improvements in well-being. To do so, this chapter proceeds as follows.

First, central tenets of post-development theory and their relevance to debates on development in Africa are outlined. Main criticisms of post-development theory are identified and the need to make post-development theory more directly relevant to political and economic processes in southern Africa explained. Second, the 'Afro-pessimist' scenario is examined. This is the scenario where, given current conditions in southern Africa, all paths to development are exhausted and proven unworkable, thus giving rise to a dangerous mix of despair, cynicism and fatalism regarding the region's future among both its local inhabitants and external actors with an interest in the region's affairs. Within the context of this pessimistic and disabling scenario, the concerns of post-development may seem utopian at best, containing little of concrete value to contemporary political processes and the immediate (material) interests of key political and economic actors driving regional developments and the region's poor majorities desperately in need of improvements in their living conditions. Third, an examination of post-development in the context of *ubuntu* is undertaken, where *ubuntu* has been harnessed by both politicians and civil society in southern Africa to represent a community-centred, traditionally anchored approach to social and spiritual well-being on which any workable solution to politics in the post-colonial era of an anticipated African Renaissance must be based. Linking post-development with *ubuntu* provides a theoretical and conceptual means to transcend the mental cul-de-sac of Afro-pessimism and a pragmatic means of aligning a fundamental criticism of the orthodox development project as pursued throughout the modern era with the social, political and economic realities of contemporary southern Africa. The chapter concludes by considering prospects for basing a new 'South–South' dialogue on development in the twenty-first century on post-development thinking. While such an ideologically pluralistic and inclusive dialogue might seem far-fetched given the great enthusiasm with which leaders and peoples across the global South embrace orthodox development thinking and the industrial processes of production and consumption as a means to that development, it is argued that post-development theory contains potential solutions for those interested in contributing to a future in which dependency on the Western experience, notably its legacy of industrial production and divisive economic and political ideologies, is overcome in favour of a holistic approach to improving well-being in which indigenous tradition and knowledge play a central role.

Post-development theory redux

The key assertion of post-development theory is that development as it is conceptualized and pursued within an orthodox, modern framework is not sustainable, that it produces a range of deleterious effects on mankind, society and nature, and that the promise that a Western-style mass-consumption lifestyle can be achieved for a majority of the world's population is simply a 'deceitful mirage' (Rahnema 1997a: x; cf. Pieterse 1998: 360). Considering Pieterse's (1999: 70–1) definition of development as 'applied modernity', as a 'politics of measurement' (where the measurements do not add up), Rist appropriately defines the central problem with development as follows:

> 'Development' consists of a set of practices, sometimes appearing to conflict with one another, which require – for the reproduction of society – the general transformation and destruction of the natural environment and of social relations. Its aim is to increase the production of commodities (goods and services) geared, by way of exchange, to effective demand. (Rist 2002: 13)

As it stands, the promise of development thus allows for the destructive effects of growth-led, industrial development to continue unabated and for a dangerously unequal and blatantly unjust status quo, in terms of the global order as it has been shaped in the wake of the Industrial Revolution and throughout the post-colonial era, to be maintained. It is unequal and unjust because the benefits of such development remain relatively concentrated and narrow while the poor bear the brunt of costs associated with this developmental trajectory, whether these are costs associated with increasing economic volatility prompted by financial mobility and speculation (Koelble and LiPuma 2006) or the environmental degradation which, according to a recent Intergovernmental Panel of Climate Change report, is mainly contributed to by the wealthy North while affecting poor countries in the South by far the worst (Revkin 2007).

While the promises held out by agents of development, from governments to non-governmental organizations (NGOs) and multinationals, to the world's poor fail to materialize time and time again for a variety of complex reasons, the notion that 'development for all' must be possible remains a desperate article of faith.

> [T]he spectacular enrichment of the well-offs fuels hopes of a possible re-distribution among those left out in the cold. People cling to these hopes all the more tightly in that some advance signs seem to be visible ... In essence, however, the scenario barely changes: some 'develop', others are left out. Whereas the main dividing line has so far run between North and South, it is now establishing itself within each nation-state ... To avoid having to admit that 'development' can never become general, a pretence is made of believing that it is simply far away. (Rist 2002: 238–9)

This is 'development as eschatology', whereby a 'utopian end-goal' is necessarily posited to sufficiently motivate people in their pursuit of that distant goal, while at the same time that utopian goal is 'inevitably exclusionary' as only those who follow the prescribed path to it will be de-livered (see Andreasson 2005b) – i.e. Derrida's 'aporetic structure', where 'two mutually opposed principles [utopia and exclusivity] are essential to the stability of a concept [development] ... but they simultaneously destabilise that concept' (Parfitt 2009: 644).

Because achieving a *general* state of development for the world's poor constitutes a formidable task,[6] including huge obstacles such as lack of state capacity, corruption, mismanagement and even the selfish nature of man as *Homo oeconomicus*, never mind a global economy constituted so that it is geared towards narrow enrichment rather than broad-based redistribution, it is not difficult to see that it will take a great deal of time to achieve that developmental objective if it is possible at all.[7] Nowhere is a general state of development as distant as it is in Africa (and South Asia). But as long as it is far away, rather than impossible to achieve within global economic and political frameworks as currently constituted, then arguments in favour of a radical reconceptualization of development, and of what it means to transform human and natural well-being, can be dismissed as being unrealistic, irresponsible and all too eager to throw the proverbial baby (the limited success with development) out with the bathwater (the many failed and outright counterproductive developmen-tal projects worldwide). In this situation, the insistence on 'keeping hope alive' by insisting that there is no acceptable alternative to development produces an intellectual environment conducive to strengthening argu-ments in favour of the status quo while marginalizing alternatives.

The core criticism of development by post-development theory revolves around the key premise that assumptions underpinning the orthodox concept of development are fundamentally flawed. Following structuralism and the Dependency School, post-development theory holds that success with development in some parts of the world, and always for a small minority of the global population, is directly linked with and indeed a contributing factor to underdevelopment elsewhere (Baran 1957; Frank 1966; Wallerstein 1974). From this point of view, problems of underdevelopment are not merely a consequence of failing to adopt policies that have been successful elsewhere; *contra* the conceptualization in liberal international relations theory in, for example, studies of international trade or interstate relations more generally (e.g. Keohane and Nye 1977), development is seldom if ever a positive-sum game. Following 'traditionalists' – sometimes but not always representative of what Ziai (2004) terms 'neo-populism' – who emphasize the destruction of local cultures and identities by modernization grafted on to traditional societies by Western countries seeking to promote their own economic and political interests, post-development thinkers are wary of modern secular hubris and argue that developmental policies that are not, or cannot become, anchored in local and national cultures to thereby gain a necessary level of legitimacy are bound to fail. Along with environmentalists, post-development also recognizes the impossibility of combining rapacious use of natural resources with a sustainable future. And like communitarian political philosophers, post-development is sceptical of individualism as *the* organizing principle of society.

What is unique about the post-development perspective in terms of its engagement with the political economy of development literature is an insistence on the futility of merely pursuing reform within an existing development paradigm, and of the global economy and political systems on which that paradigm rests, and of the impossibility of achieving development by simply promoting a radical shift from one modern system (capitalist) to another (socialist). Nor is 'delinking', a severing of deeply exploitative economic and social ties between the West and developing regions (Amin 1990), considered a panacea. Rather it is the suggestion that modern civilization in its entirety must be rethought, that an entirely different way of thinking about what it means 'to develop' can be pursued, which constitutes the unique theoretical contribution of post-development. This is also why the task set out by post-development theory is bound to be a very difficult one, especially in terms of producing a shift in economic and political practice as opposed to merely affecting a modest shift in academic discourse regarding these issues.[8]

In both its socialist and liberal ideological guise – the two progressive currents of modern thought opposed to conservatism of various kinds – development predicated on increasing economic growth, material accumulation, technological innovation and mass consumption fails to take account of the amount of ever-increasing human activity and disposal of resources that our biosphere can sustain, i.e. of the limits to development as it is normally understood.[9] From pollution by industrial emissions to deforestation, depletion of natural resources and increasingly rapid extinction of species, the evidence of an increasingly unmanageable stress on the environment is everywhere visible, most obviously so in those more rapidly developing countries of the world, such as Brazil, Russia, India and China (the 'BRIC' nations), where industrial development is harnessed with ever-increasing urgency so as to narrow the gap in material well-being between less and more developed regions of the world. And developmental success on one hand creates new problems on the other.

A competitive advantage in growing soybeans and supplying ethanol as a 'green' biofuel to the world market depletes the Amazon rainforest in Brazil. Increasing industrial production, fuelled by what is uniformly considered successful economic growth (ignoring negative externalities), in China and India produces intensified competition for oil and other basic industrial inputs worldwide, with the poorest countries even less able than in the past to secure access to such resources on affordable terms. The increasing prosperity of growing middle classes across the global South entails rapidly increasing per capita usage (and also waste) of clean water, with the result that those who remain very poor, and number many millions more than the new middle classes, see their access to clean water decline.[10] As a consequence, water may well replace oil as the natural resource most likely to trigger conflict in the future. The post-development critique of this Era of Development and of the idea of progress, however, i.e. the modern project in its entirety (e.g. Illich 1970; Shanin 1997),[11] goes far beyond merely a green critique of the environmentally disastrous effects of industrial development, which still forms the basis of any large-scale attempt to lift developing regions out of poverty.

In addition to the problem of large-scale development running up against real natural limits, post-development thinkers have emphasized the damage to local cultures, and to the ways in which human beings relate to each other and to the natural world of which they of course are an integral part, in an age of increasing commodification, individualism, competition and, consequently, alienation (Nandy 1987; Shiva 1989; Escobar 1995).[12] In addition to economic exploitation leading to

71

impoverishment of Africa and Africa's incorporation into the global economy on very unfavourable terms (Rodney 1982; Bond 2006), its peoples have long suffered from social and spiritual degradation rooted in the long-standing demeaning of Africans and their history by the racist prejudices and cultural chauvinism by which the continent's subjugation was justified.[13] This form of mental enslavement has produced a debilitating legacy, in Africa as well as in its diaspora, which, for the sake of development and emancipation, will be as important to overcome as Africa's economic dependency and political dysfunction (Fanon 1986 [1952]; Memmi 2003 [1974]; cf. Andreasson 2005a: 974). On this important point post-development theory differs from the Marxist critique of the modern world order, in particular the Marxist notions of immiseration and alienation under capitalism, in that it does not offer a solution based simply on a reorganization of the mode of production whereby the developmental dilemma of our capitalist age will be transcended – for Marxists, the advent of a socialist mode of production and ensuing communist society (see Rist 2002: 121).

Whereas the Marxist scenario *progresses* from inevitable class conflict to the transcending of capitalism, post-development theory posits a wholly open-ended scenario where any combination of dynamics and incentives engendered by pre-modern, capitalist and socialist modes of socio-economic organization may combine to offer new alternatives to the status quo. Here it is important to note that, socially and politically speaking, a sustainable outcome of a transition from the current Era of Development could be 'regressive' in terms of drawing on tradition and pre-modern sentiments – i.e. 'remedying' modernism by recovering 'lost sensibilities' and traditional knowledge (Fals-Borda 1985, cited in Pieterse 1999: 74–5) – as well as 'progressive' in terms of fulfilling the modernist and universalist dream of a secular world in which the basic tenets of Enlightenment philosophy prevail and all *individuals* are *equal* (this is, however, not necessarily a world in which human diversity in all its political and economic forms, let alone its cultural and religious ones, can survive). This open-endedness suggests the possibility of a plurality of (post) modernities where Africa constitutes but one, distinctly hybrid, modernity (Ferguson 2006; cf. Geschiere 1997; Piot 1999; Deutch et al. 2002).[14]

> [W]e have become accustomed to ... industrial workers with so-called extended family structures, or transnational business executives who fear witches, or white-collar workers who fly in jet airplanes to visit their matrilineal clan elders. Anthropologists ... no longer regard such juxtapositions

as entailing any 'contradiction' or 'lag'. Modern Africa is today understood as a place of bricolage and creative invention, where bits and pieces of what used to be called 'Western modernity' are picked up, combined with local resources, and put back together. (Ferguson 2006: 183)

Africa *is* different from the West, albeit also modern. It is just that such difference has long been misunderstood as an 'anachronistic relic; as somehow not really of the present; as a symptom of backwardness and incomplete development – in short, as "tradition"' (ibid.: 184).

Post-development theory also does not insist that a better life will necessarily mean improvements on measurements such as life expectancy, purchasing power and education – the basic components of the United Nations Development Programme's (UNDP) Human Development Index (HDI).[15] It may well be that in contexts where for a variety of reasons this is not possible or permitted by circumstances beyond the immediate control of suffering peoples themselves – e.g. an increasingly commodified and privatized world in which 'development space' is steadily shrinking (R. H. Wade 2003; cf. Andreasson 2006a) – a better life may simply mean a more *bearable* life. That is, a bearable life in the sense of an ability by people suffering from, for example, a lack of proper nutrition, healthcare and education – a lack, therefore, of the means by which to pursue greater aspirations in life as according to Sen's (1999) concept of 'freedom *to*' – to somehow accommodate themselves to the suffering they have to endure in the knowledge that it will not be alleviated in the foreseeable future. In such a situation, aspirations to emancipation are (at least in this world) reduced to fostering an ability merely to cope.

The somewhat disturbing analogy here is of course with the practice of palliative care, i.e. easing symptoms without curing an underlying cause; hence a subject matter to be approached with great care and delicacy. One of the most forceful criticisms levelled against post-development theory is that its proponents, in their careless or studied disregard for mainstream notions of development and of poor people's common material needs and desires (a refrigerator, a car or a television set, even some nicer clothes for the children to wear), become not only oblivious to reasonable human needs but risk falling into a nihilist trap where indisputable suffering is dismissed as the mere inability among those suffering to bite down and cope with their situation and to transcend their 'false consciousness' about being marginalized by reorienting their priorities and desires away from the lure of modernity towards a simpler, more 'genuine' traditional life. Given this risk that some post-development thinkers may indeed have fallen for, the notion of recognizing, let alone cultivating, an 'art of suffering', as that notion has been present in meditations on human existence from the Stoics to Gandhi as a means of coping with underdevelopment and an unjust global order, is perhaps the most controversial contention of post-development (cf. Illich 1976; Esteva 1995). There is indeed a fine line between a notion of how to best accommodate suffering that may be inevitable and a cynical neglect of genuine alternatives or even a fatalist capitulation in the face of immense obstacles, Saul's (2003: 190) 'pessimism of the intellect', that condemns people to a fate that is unacceptable in the view of any standard argument regarding (global) justice. Any such notions of reconciling oneself to suffering, or even emphasizing the idea of coping mechanisms, are of course also anathema to the Promethean idea of Progress and therefore play no role whatsoever in orthodox debates on development.

Post-development theory and its critics Given that the post-development critique of development casts doubt not merely on dominant modes of political and economic thinking as they shape policy-making on development but also questions the very philosophical and cultural basis on which our understanding of development rests, i.e. rationality, progress, modernity (the Western trajectory), it has been roundly criticized on several grounds. Because of an antipathy towards much of that which is generally celebrated as modern, post-development scholars are suspected of harbouring longings for the confines of traditional societies, with all the grave implications that such tradition supposedly entails for individual rights, the rights of women, our collective ability to generate scientific knowledge and many other things besides. From this point of view, post-development constitutes a reactionary ideological force.

Because post-development does not merely critique modernity with a view to improving it but argues that the modern paradigm is inherently flawed and dangerous as key aspects of it are simply irredeemable, the post-development sentiment shows some affinity with what, according to Habermas's (1996: 38, 42) critique of postmodernism as 'a new conservatism' or even 'Antimodernity', is a 'neo-conservative' fear of 'hedonism', 'lack of social identification' and 'incapacity for obedience' (but which also echoes some of the concerns underlying the decidedly modern approach in Huntington's [1968] *Political Order in Changing Societies*). While there are aspects of post-development that fit this description it is important to recognize that the way in which post-development is engaged with in this study does not simply replicate postmodern or post-structural critiques of modernity. Rather it emphasizes how both post-development and political economy approaches to development in Africa can benefit from interaction with each other and thus move forward in symbiosis. In that sense, this critique of modernity avoids the 'simplistic dichotomies' of modernity versus tradition and science versus indigenous knowledge which fail to understand that 'opposition to modernization has been a *part* of modern experience' (Pieterse 1999: 73).

Post-development theory is also criticized for not producing credible or feasible alternatives to existing development frameworks; in other words, it is not a constructive theory. This accusation resembles a prominent criticism of Marx's vision of a better world, i.e. that it is long on the problems with the current capitalist system and short on solutions and the details of alternative visions (for Marx, communism). If the industrialization-based route to development is problematic and unsustainable, then what are leaders of developing countries and the poor peoples who constitute a majority of the world's population, including the great majority of Africans, to do? They could, presumably, wait for appropriately sustainable technologies to be developed in advanced countries and then, via a process of diffusion, adopt those technologies according to local needs. The socio-economic marginalization of Africa suggests, however, that this will continue to be difficult and therefore an unlikely trajectory on which to place one's bets for achieving development. Moreover, how can scholars, who themselves constitute a privileged group in society, quarrelling about abstract understandings of development, possibly suggest what the needs and aspirations of poor and often desperate people ought to be? This line of argumentation basically rejects post-development theory on grounds of being irresponsible because it offers no alternative route to development for people suffering greatly from material deprivation and that in some cases post-development theory, in some of its more radical manifestations, is also misanthropic and even nihilistic.[16] Environmentalists, often concerned with the problem of overpopulation, are also subjected to similar accusations of misanthropy.

The critique of post-colonialism, with which post-development is not synonymous but shares some important affinities as well as an intellectual heritage, more generally by predominantly Western scholars interested in Africa, so-called Africanists, emphasizes similar concerns.

[Post]colonialism is regarded as too theoretical and too preoccupied with textuality and discourse to have anything meaningful to contribute … The study of African politics, particularly in its Anglophone version, has constituted itself as a largely empirical discipline, dedicated to assisting and facilitating [Africa's] economic and political development ... since the 1980s perceptions of the 'African crisis' have led to calls that scholarship should be dedicated first and foremost to solving that crisis. To this end, postcolonialism is deemed ineffective ... perceived to be a cultural product of the West ... [and] perceived as politically passive, and perhaps ultimately politically conservative. (Abrahamsen 2003: 190)

Pieterse's (1998, 2000) critique of post-development theory has perhaps been the most influential. It describes post-development as a 'radical reaction to the impasse of development theory and policy', a reaction based on '[p]erplexity and extreme disaffection with business-as-usual and standard development rhetoric and practice' (Pieterse 1998: 360). The general thrust of post-development as articulated by Escobar (1995), one of its most prominent advocates, contains 'exaggerated claims sustained by weak examples ... His perspective on actual development is flimsy and confused, with more rhetoric than logic'; in the end, post-development 'reflects both a hunger for a new era and a nostalgia for the politics of romanticism, glorification of the local, grassroots, community with conservative overtones' (Pieterse 1998: 364). Of course, this 'hunger' can also be interpreted as a willingness to look ahead and think anew about how to improve on existing socio-economic arrangements, just as it can be understood as a 'nostalgic' awareness of the importance of looking back (as much as the notion of a 'backward' orientation seems to violate the spirit of progress), fully conscious of the importance of historical experience and tradition in providing solid foundations for the future.

A brief but succinct critique of post-development by Storey (2000: 42–4) argues that post-development fails on four specific fronts: 1) it promotes an overly generalized view of what development actually is and it neglects real developmental achievements such as increases in life expectancies worldwide; 2) it fails to demonstrate that a state of existence 'beyond development' is either feasible or indeed desirable for the world's poor, and furthermore fails to properly engage with the fact that so many people in the world actually want what development is understood to offer; 3) the social movements upon which are based most post-development arguments for how social change can be achieved may in many cases be reactionary and authoritarian, nor do they always 'occupy a space outside' capitalist structures and developmental ideology; 4) these often fragmented and narrowly focused social movements and related groups are in most cases 'no match' for the power wielded by global capital and other actors seeking to maintain status quo in terms of global socio-economic organization and approaches to development.

These are important criticisms, which in some cases have brought much-needed attention to flaws and instances of carelessness in the arguments put forth by post-development thinkers. Moreover, these astute critics had, by the turn of the last century, largely managed to dismantle the radical aspirations of post-development theorists and to effectively marginalize their potential input in wider debates on development and the question of alternatives. This was a feat well recognized by those who now wish to carefully bring back into the debate some key notions of post-development theory, and who recognize that the first generation of post-development scholars perhaps let caution to the wind in an attempt to bravely undermine a hegemonic ideology, thereby leaving themselves open to sharp criticism and in need of refinement of their ambitious claims and daring arguments (see Ziai 2004). It is therefore crucial to explain what is different about current scholarly debates on the notion of moving beyond development, debates that continue to engage critically with a hegemonic development paradigm and which retain some of the core criticisms put forth by an earlier generation of post-development thinkers.

The first point to make in response to the critics of post-development theory is to note that while a total rejection of development has been articulated in some post-development writings (Esteva 1985; Rahnema 1997b), this radical position is not the only one encompassed by post-development theory. Ziai (2004) identifies two main strands of post-development theory: one he labels 'sceptical' and the other 'neo-populist'. While neo-populism lends itself to a less nuanced, and sometimes exaggerated, criticism of development – it is indeed an 'anti-development' position – and is also prone to romanticize notions of tradition and community, the 'sceptical' approach lends itself to a more nuanced criticism of development that may facilitate the emergence of a 'radical democratic' approach in the field of development studies, where a fundamental criticism of development remains cognizant of the political and economic power structures within which any constructive debate on radical alternatives to the status quo must be located. This sceptical strand of post-development theory, which is the one most directly relevant to the argument developed here, does not require a politics in which development as traditionally understood can play no part, nor does it unquestioningly embrace tradition, community and the local as necessarily opposed to modernity, individualism and globalization.

'The idea, then, in spite of "development", is to organize and invent new ways of life – between modernization, with its sufferings *but also some advantages*, and a tradition from which people may derive inspiration while knowing that *it can never be revived*' (Rist 2002: 244, emphases added).

A similar recognition of the mixed if ultimately disappointing legacy of orthodox development is echoed by Hoogvelt (2001: 172): '[p]ostdevelopment ... is different from anti-development ... in that it does not deny globalization or modernity, but wants to find some ways of living with it and imaginatively transcending it'.

Second, while post-development faces a challenge in linking arguments about the problems of development to a concrete strategy for change, and whereas it is true that translating post-development theory into actual politics is quite difficult given powerful vested interests in business and politics that are not interested in such ideas, it does not follow that post-development theory has nothing to offer. Simply put, the degree of difficulty in promoting a point of view is not indicative of its inherent value, correctness or ultimate utility. After all, 'it is the human ability and compulsion to envisage the good society that enables and motivates us to bring about positive change' (Parfitt 2009: 643), suggesting that developments at the ideational level may well end up having practical implications. Institutions such as slavery, colonialism and even the market, all at some time supported by powerful interests, have been challenged (the first two successfully) by what were at one time radical arguments that in the end produced significant change, for better or worse, in both political and economic spheres. Development as an ideology and organizing principle of social change has had a great influence on peoples worldwide and should post-development arguments take root, first at the levels of heterodox scholarship and traditionally oriented social movements and then perhaps at the level of conventional politics, they will then undoubtedly have a profound impact on societal change similar to that of radical ideas in the past. In the end, mainstream thinking on development in Africa has so far not been able to significantly dent the debilitating effects of a pervasive Afro-pessimism that pervades the international view and often also that of Africans themselves regarding Africa's overall disappointing post-independence trajectories.

The 'Afro-pessimist' scenario

The Minister's eyes were like egg yolks, an aftereffect of some of the many illnesses, malaria especially, endemic in his country. There was also an irrefutable sadness in his eyes. He spoke in a slow and creaking voice, the voice of hope about to expire. Flame trees, coconut palms, and a ballpoint-blue Atlantic composed the background. None of it seemed beautiful, though. (Kaplan 1994: 44)

The failure of many state-led development projects, some Keynesian and others socialist, and the stagnation of African economies and polities more generally in post-independence Africa (Sandbrook 1985; van de Walle 2001), coupled with the onset of the deeply debilitating 1980s debt crisis (Parfitt and Riley 1989), made scholarship on Africa and development in the 1990s prone to severe criticism of the politics that produced such miserable failure. While the responsibility of external actors in Africa's unravelling was generally acknowledged, it was on Africa's own leaders and institutions that the critics focused (e.g. Zartman 1995; Reno 1998; Ayittey 1999). The nature of African states received notable attention, being described as 'criminalized' (Bayart et al. 1999) and even 'vampire states' (Frimpong-Ansah 1992). In terms of economic reforms intended to promote economic development, African states have been the major obstacle (van de Walle 2001). Implicit in all these arguments is the notion that African attempts at development have failed on a comprehensive range of issues, and on all ideological and political fronts. Negative influences of both external and domestic actors have undermined post-independence political systems and consequently also the possibilities for sustained economic development and democratization. Where genuine efforts have been made to promote development, by African governments themselves and in partnership with helpful international partners, they have in the face of the enormous obstacles created by social and political instability, patronage, authoritarianism and corruption fallen hopelessly short of what is needed.

Seemingly endemic corruption has caused outrage not only among external donors, Western governments eager to lecture Africans on the need for good governance and progressive social forces on the continent itself (see Abrahamsen 2000). Standard texts on African politics consider neo-patrimonialism to be a key aspect of African politics, indeed a phenomenon endemic in African cultures (Hyden 2005). Even African leaders with a poor record in these matters have expressed exasperation with the tangled web of conflict, mismanagement and crisis management in which they and their subjects alike seem caught. Speaking to the ZANU-PF Central Committee in Harare in 2004, Zimbabwe's president Robert Mugabe lashed out at those who subvert the cause of economic transformation and indigenization in an effort to enrich themselves (a problem appropriately recognized, albeit in denial of his own government's contribution thereto).

> We have seen the effects of corruption and how it erodes and collapses [people's] welfare because of ill-gotten affluence. We have all seen how riches that come easily through devious ways translate into arrogant flamboyance and wastefulness ... [W]e thought these men were leading business luminaries of our country! They have cheated us and deserve their punishment ... Some have sought to defeat [the government's anti-corruption] campaign by pleading the cause of indigenization. Let them remember that indigenization does not, and shall never, mean empowering crooks who cut business corners and thrive on dirty deals. Certainly, it does not mean putting your shameless indigenous finger into the national till. (Mugabe 2004)

Some discontents have taken this type of criticism farther and have, like Etounga-Manguelle (2000), placed ultimate blame for Africa's misery on African culture: given its 'progress resistant' culture, Africa needs to undergo a 'cultural adjustment programme' so as to become compatible with modernity and the structural adjustment programmes that have been devised for it. The idea of African culture being ultimately incapable of facilitating development or indeed sustaining modernity strikes at the heart of any post-development notion of harnessing indigenous knowledge and aligning political and economic programmes for change with the cultural parameters of African societies. If the inherent characteristics of African culture are thus deficient, then any solution to Africa's problems must necessarily originate elsewhere and be imposed or at the very least guided by external actors such as the Western governments and institutions that have devised, promoted and often led the implementation of Africa's many structural adjustment programmes (Andreasson 2005a). Clearly this line of reasoning does not entertain the notion, emphasized by Kothari (1990: 49–50, cited in Matthews 2004: 380), that a wealth of indigenous (and imported) cultural and religious traditions in, for example, India constitute a source of inspiration on which those seeking to devise new solutions to long-standing problems with underdevelopment can draw. If this is the case then the cultural and religious diversity of Africa, the unique cultural hybrid of indigenous, Muslim and Christian origins which Mazrui (1986) labels Africa's 'triple heritage', presumably amounts to something similarly positive from which novel ideas providing better solutions can be derived.

It is somewhat curious that very little of the voluminous literature on Africa's post-independence failures, whether focusing on how Western countries have employed neocolonial linkages in continued exploitation of Africa (Bracking and Harrison 2003; Bond 2006; Bush 2007) or the failure of African countries to properly embrace modernization and the economic and political reforms necessary to succeed in a capitalist world order (World Bank 1981; Mistry 2004), has considered whether it could be the orthodox notion of development which is problematic rather than simply concluding that it is African states and societies, i.e. Africans themselves, that have failed. Indeed, Afro-pessimism suggests that there is in the end little that can be done with respect to Africa's development impasse. Such an overly cynical and ultimately defeatist attitude is popularized and vulgarized in accounts like Kaplan's (1994) 'The coming anarchy', which, ironically, shares concerns about scarcity, crime, overpopulation, disease and the environment with post-development thinkers. This pessimistic and often resigned attitude towards the continent produces serious side effects in terms of legitimizing existing prejudices about Africans, exacerbating donor fatigue, discouraging international investment and, given Africa's deep and supposedly self-inflicted deprivations, the need to treat Africans with respect and decency in affairs both public and private (see Ferguson 2006: 189–91).

Most importantly, Afro-pessimism suggests that there is little in terms of Africa's own history, its cultural and social legacy, to be retrieved and built upon for the purposes of overcoming the development impasse that has produced misery across the continent in the post-independence era. This state of affairs constitutes a serious handicap for Africa as a whole. It has long been recognized that developmental trajectories across the Western world, specifically in terms of the development of capitalism, have diverged according to cultural settings; hence the rise of Anglo-Saxon and social democratic versions of the modern capitalist state (Dore 2000; Hall and Soskice 2001). More fundamentally, the rise of the East Asian tigers recognizes the importance of anchoring development in a historical context and a cultural legacy very different from those of the West. Debates on development in China and India, countries that remain to a significant degree rural and impoverished, similarly recognize the importance of each country's civilizational legacy in producing a modern form of development, or at least a globally competitive form of capitalism.

While the previously alluded to open-endedness and possibility of plural modernities suggests a variety of ways to innovate, theoretically and empirically, and negotiate the complexities and pressures of modernity, it also harbours danger for those societies that would stake out an alternative modern existence and form of governance from those conventionally accepted as 'successful'. Ferguson (2006: 178) notes that the teleological nature of development means that countries deemed underdeveloped today are not at 'the bottom' of a global hierarchy of states and societies but are simply at 'the beginning' of the developmental timeline; existing in a 'not yet shadow land of [developed] societies' already realized history', they still have the hope of catching up and, belatedly, arriving at the table of developed states as equals. If these countries are no longer assumed to be 'behind' and still attempting to catch up, however, but have indeed arrived at modernity like the rest of the world, albeit an alternative modernity to that in, say, the West and East Asia, then there is a risk that what may still be considered their inferior or dysfunctional status becomes permanent. Once the trajectory of these African societies is considered to have come to an end with the arrival at modernity, then their character is no longer a matter of *telos*, with the opportunity for further improvement, but of *status*, which implies permanence and finality. So if African modernity is deemed inferior, then African peoples will find themselves no longer on the path towards equality but stranded in a largely fixed hierarchy of peoples, states and cultures (ibid.: 188–90).

> Africans denied the status of [equality in] modernity increasingly come to be seen, and may even ... come to see themselves, not as 'less developed' but simply as less ... they are increasingly understood as naturally, perhaps even racially, *beneath* [the West]. (ibid.: 189–90)

For Africa, however, the importance and potential usefulness of a non-Western legacy are much less evident in mainstream thinking on development. Instead a much more straightforward debate on how Africa can most easily import an appropriate Western set of attitudes, ranging from the intellectual and cultural to the political and economic, is generally accepted as an appropriate point of intellectual departure. In part this reflects a sense, sometimes expressed as a historically informed regret and other times as an aggressively articulated prejudice, that Africa lacks a proper history of civilization, thus making it necessary for its peoples to acquire the useful tools bequeathed by civilization from elsewhere.[17] While it is certainly true that Africa's history differs in many important respects to that of Europe, India and China, and while it is also true that no country or region has developed in isolation from important cultural, technological and scientific advances elsewhere, the development-as-modernization discourse becomes so focused on what has worked elsewhere that it neglects the importance of finding what may be conducive to a better future in African experiences and values themselves. Post-development challenges this mindset by making the simple assumption that the quest for a way forward out of the current quagmire begins at home.

Modernity, alienation and *ubuntu*

Following on from the post-development critique of development and the need to somehow resolve Africa's development impasse, two key arguments must be considered. The first argument is that nothing short of a genuinely communal effort, i.e. society in dialogue and in awareness of its constituent parts and common interests, to reimagine and where necessary reinvent goals and aspirations of southern African societies must be embarked upon before any lasting transformation of these societies can be achieved or even properly contemplated. An emphasis on the region's political economy alone will not suffice. Debates on how to reform politics and economies must be anchored in a greater societal debate about what the headlong rush to embrace orthodox development policies has meant for societal cohesion and the sustainability of social and natural environments alike.[18] On the whole, mainstream indicators of development such as trends in the HDI are pointing down across southern Africa while levels of societal fragmentation produced and exemplified by violent crime, xenophobia and HIV/AIDS have been on the rise. Simply focusing on political issues and processes, such as whether the ANC will remain a hegemonic force and what role ZANU-PF will play when Mugabe is no longer president, and economic policy, whether ASGISA might produce better macroeconomic outcomes than GEAR and how the indigenization of businesses in Zimbabwe will affect economic growth, without also addressing the enormous rupture caused in southern African societies by the settler colonial system and the compromised transitions that followed in its wake is an exercise bound to produce temporary solutions at best. It cannot be the basis for transcending core problems afflicting the region today.

The second argument is that two types of alienation must be resolved in order to move beyond development as it is commonly understood: alienation of man from nature – a theological and philosophical issue, with roots in the Book of Genesis and Descartes and thus, by extension, emblematic of modern industrial civilization – and alienation of human beings from society in general as well as each other, whether understood in terms of Marx's 'alienation' or Durkheim's 'anomie'.[19] Clearly these

83

two forms of alienation are related, as implied by the need for developing a holistic view of development and the ways in which societies will need to reorient themselves to offer genuine alternatives to the contemporary impasse.

That is to say, man alienated from nature and from the society in which he exists prevents the emergence of a holistic conceptualization of the problems that will increasingly feature as key concerns in any constructive debate on development, given that countries in developing regions pay a disproportionately high proportion of the costs associated with both global environmental degradation and societal fragmentation. The uprooting of traditional societies such as the San of the Kalahari to make way for tourism and mining in Botswana, the widespread poaching and destruction of wildlife in the wake of land invasions and the violent expulsion of urban dwellers from their homes during the Zimbabwean government's ruthless Operation Murambatsvina ('drive out trash') and the very high levels of industrial pollution, stress on natural habitats and increasingly violent government response to popular protest against the lack of service delivery in South Africa are all deeply problematic manifestations of an underlying malaise that reinforces the importance of rethinking matters of both environment and human relations and the need to approach these issues holistically. The alienation of human beings from each other, which inevitably produces fragmentation, instability and ultimately violence, is symptomatic of a social-Darwinian competition-above-all society that is disembedded from local culture and social cohesion and which in the case of southern Africa runs counter to communitarian understandings of human nature, including moral and social obligations and responsibilities embodied in the traditional concept and philosophy of *ubuntu*.

The problem in terms of these two forms of alienation is that the modern development paradigm neglects precisely that which needs to be resolved. Modern development concerns itself with institutions, politics and economics, but it does not in any meaningful way engage with greater social debates on how human beings may aspire to a *different* kind of good life from the one prescribed by conventional development. The alienation of mankind from nature is central to the modern notion of man moulding and inevitably exploiting his environment for his own needs. This goes far beyond simply recognizing that devising ways to grow better crops and reduce exposure to malaria is a good thing in terms of improving living conditions; it also entails an ever-increasing exploitation of resources, both natural and human, in the quest for enrichment and advantage – Tawney's (1921) 'acquisitive society' run amok. The alienation of human beings from each other is also a key foundation upon which modern development rests. The rational and self-interested individual as *Homo oeconomicus* and the question of how to most effectively unleash his potential as manifest in development and progress in the wake of Schumpeterian 'creative destruction' form the basis for all modern development policy frameworks, from the Keynesian to the neoliberal. This fundamental problem with the origins and nature of orthodox development suggests that any new thinking on how to proceed would benefit from anchoring that thinking in a different sociocultural framework. In the southern African context, that framework is *ubuntu*.

The ubuntu value system The concept of *ubuntu* stems from the traditional African aphorism *umuntu ngumuntu ngabantu* (isiZulu) or *motho ke motho ka batho* (seSotho), which essentially means 'a person is a person through other persons'. The central concept of *ubuntu* translates as 'humanity', 'humanness' or even 'humaneness'; importantly, it is not merely a factual description of human nature but also constitutes a rule of conduct and social ethic (Louw 2001: 15; cf. Ramose 2003b). In terms of societal relations, *ubuntu* can be understood as

> a metaphor that describes the significance of group solidarity, on survival issues, that is so central to the survival of African communities, who as a result the poverty and deprivation have to survive through brotherly group care and not individual self-reliance. (Mbigi and Maree 1995: 1)

Moreover, the notion of 'personhood' in *ubuntu* entails a process of *becoming* a person; personhood is not automatically granted (i.e. not all human beings are persons) but dependent on a recognition of and acting in a way that is commensurate with recognizing the humanness of others (Louw 2001: 17).

Although the concept of *ubuntu* is African in origin (and related to the concept of 'Afrocentricity')[20] and its focus is on an essentially communal humanity, it does not promote essentialization of difference and exclusion. Attempts to justify social exclusion, as in some forms of nationalism and xenophobia, are not commensurate with a proper understanding and usage of *ubuntu* as it 'is not necessarily limited by biological ancestry, nationality or actual place of residence' (van Binsbergen 2001: 60). Nor does the strong emphasis on community and consensus, which is an issue of great significance for the nature of political and economic reform in post-liberation southern Africa, mean that adherence to *ubuntu* must

85

deteriorate into what Sono (1994, cited in Louw 2001: 19) describes as 'tyrannical custom' and 'totalitarian communalism'. This is obviously one potential consequence of an instrumental misuse of *ubuntu* by elites wishing to justify repression of opposition and dissent, a danger that must be recognized given post-colonial Africa's recurrent problems with erosion of democratic principles and the emergence of authoritarian and dictatorial regimes.

Despite its strong emphasis on solidarity and community, Bhengu (1996) suggests that *ubuntu* constitutes the 'essence' of (African) democracy. Moreover,

> [*u*]*buntu* as an effort to reach consensus or agreement should thus not be confused with outmoded and suspect cravings for (an oppressive) universal sameness, often associated with so-called teleological or 'modernistic' attempts at the final resolution of differences (cf. Ramose 1999: 131, 132; van der Merwe 1996: 12). True Ubuntu takes plurality seriously. While it constitutes personhood *through other persons*, it appreciates the fact that 'other persons' are so called, precisely because we can ultimately never quite 'stand in their shoes' or 'see through their eyes'. When Ubuntuists read 'solidarity' and 'consensus', s/he therefore also reads 'alterity', 'autonomy', and 'co-operation' (note: not 'co-optation'). (Louw 2001: 21)

The origins of *ubuntu* in the thought and traditions of pre-modern southern African village life means that the concept has in some instances become a philosophical tool for Africanist scholars wishing to reconstruct (or invent) an 'unadulterated' form of African village life as it supposedly existed before European conquest (van Binsbergen 2001: 53).

> The self-proclaimed experts on *ubuntu* form a globally-informed, Southern African intellectual elite who, remote in place and social practice from the *emic* expressions at the village level which they seek to capture, have officially coined the concept of *ubuntu* as a cornerstone Southern African self-reflexive ethnography. (ibid.: 70)

The concept of *ubuntu* has also been appropriated in a wide variety of literatures beyond its usage in African philosophy, ranging from research on management and business practices in Africa (Karsten and Illa 2005) to South Africa's Truth and Reconciliation Commission (Murithi 2006). *Ubuntu* has also become an issue in relation to government policy. At the suggestion of President Mbeki, South Africa's National Heritage Council convened its first National Imbizo on Ubuntu and Nation-building in

South Africa (*imbizo* is a gathering, a forum for interaction and dialogue) to debate 'the notion of Ubuntu and how it should filter into the policies of government'.[21] Indeed, the concept has been evoked as the philosophical underpinning of the 'African Renaissance' as promoted by Mbeki (Vale and Maseko 1998; van Kessel 2001), with that renaissance in turn informing continent-wide policy initiatives such as the New Economic Partnership for Africa's Development (NEPAD) (Bongma 2004).[22]

While this widespread usage of *ubuntu* indicates a great desire and need to find alternatives to the Western logic of modernity as a foundation for post-liberation southern African societies, it is at the same time necessary to note that the great majority of southern Africans today do not live in or have the experience of a culture where *ubuntu* constitutes a central organizing principle. The way of life that is derived from the concept of *ubuntu* 'is not within easy reach of the globalised urban population that has become standard in Southern Africa. Outside contemporary village contexts, it is only selectively and superficially communicated to the Southern African population at large' (van Binsbergen 2001: 61).

According to van Binsbergen (ibid.), *ubuntu* is therefore most usefully understood as a means, social as well as philosophical in nature, by which people can retrieve a sense of belonging and comprehension in an environment where a variety of cultural, political and economic pressures relating to the impact of globalization and underdevelopment on southern African societies have produced dangerous levels of stress and dysfunction, what in some cases can be described as a 'profound existential crisis'. In this sense *ubuntu* constitutes 'the creation of a moral community of people concerned about the present and future of Southern Africa', and the fact that this community will have to be retrieved, indeed reconstructed, from a past with which many southern Africans are no longer directly connected to then be adapted to the reality of globalization (as no culture can now be successfully maintained in isolation from outside influences) means that an excessive emphasis on the philosophical and historical purity or authenticity of the concept is unnecessary:

> [I]t does not really matter whether the ethnological and linguistic underpinnings of *ubuntu* philosophy are empirically and epistemologically impeccable ... [given that *ubuntu* is] an exhortative instrument at the service of modern urban society at large ... [seeking] to address fundamental ills in the make-up of urban, globalised Southern Africa. (ibid.: 73)

If this understanding of *ubuntu* prevails and can become the philosophical and cultural context in which discourse on development is anchored and legitimized, we can then see how *ubuntu* as a culture-specific concept in a regional context is compatible with post-development theory as an intellectual process of looking back at tradition and experience as well as looking ahead, embracing new but also 'culturally compatible' ways of thinking in the search for alternatives to development as traditionally understood.[23] In the end, the revival of traditional concepts such as *ubuntu* will be strengthened if they can be linked to broader international debates on the global economic organization, social justice and how to resolve the dilemma of continued poverty and marginalization for the many combined with ever-increasing wealth for the few – the development impasse for which orthodox development has so far not provided a solution.[24]

Concluding thoughts on a 'South–South' dialogue moving beyond development

Thoughts like these originating in scholarly debates on post-development, and specifically the question of how to move 'beyond development' for the sake of improving the lives of people and the environment in which they exist, have so far been received sometimes politely, but often in a hostile manner and never enthusiastically, by the mainstream development community. Nor have the main tenets of post-development theory been in any significant way translated into policy-making in developing countries. The idea of moving beyond development may seem hopelessly ephemeral when contrasted with a well-established and accepted modernist worldview informing and justifying powerful economic and political interests that promote politics and business as usual.

How, then, could an emerging 'South–South' dialogue on development in the twenty-first century possibly become based on or at least influenced by post-development thinking? Recent writings on how to foster a new debate on development between southern Africa and other regions in the global South do not explicitly argue for a post-development approach (e.g. Neocosmos 2006b). Research by the UNDP's Special Unit for South–South Cooperation and by the United Nations Industrial Development Organization (UNIDO) concentrates primarily on how to best facilitate orthodox development policies.[25] While former Malaysian president Mahathir and other Asian leaders have urged Africa to 'look East' for a more appropriate model for development,[26] Mugabe's announcement of a Look East policy for Zimbabwe, the motivations for which are generously interpreted by Youde (2007), has generally been interpreted as nothing more than a desperate attempt by the Zimbabwean regime to curry favour with its financial backers, most notably China, in the wake of its increasing international isolation (Mashingaidze 2006: 71).

Given the great enthusiasm with which developing countries embrace orthodox development thinking and the industrial processes of production and consumption as a means to that development, an ideologically pluralistic and inclusive dialogue that can accommodate and engage with the contentions of post-development theory might seem far-fetched. On the other hand, given the manifest failures of the Era of Development and the clearly detrimental effects that many policies from the right and the left that intend to bring about development are having on poor communities with little ability to shield themselves from the overwhelming disruptions caused in the name of modernization, could the ideas informed by post-development theory not in the end find reception among leaders as well as peoples looking for a way out of the current development impasse? Do the social majorities worst affected by failures of modern development and the elites purporting to represent them, elites that are themselves increasingly vulnerable to popular discontent because of continued failure to deliver development, really have much to lose by taking seriously the post-development critique of development and the implications for socio-economic organization thereof?

Since post-development entails a major departure from the thinking about both means and ends as they have been traditionally conceptualized within the development paradigm, the most important question here is whether a post-development turn in elite and popular political discourse, and eventually in policy-making processes, risks producing a worsening of conditions for the poor by turning attention away from tangible aims of orthodox development. That this should not become the case remains a key consideration and responsibility for those articulating a move beyond development. In the end, post-development theory constitutes a sufficiently coherent and comprehensive intellectual project for those who wish to steer the debate on development in a different direction, towards a future where the traditions, values and experiences of peoples in the global South are prioritized. The immediate task ahead is how to translate the promise of post-development into a politics of change.

TWO | **Comparative regional trajectories**

4 | Botswana: paternalism and the developmental state

The road to political expediency and populism may be lined with cheering crowds; but in the end, we can not escape the cold hard facts of our limitations as a developing country. As sure as the merry-maker must account for his excesses with a splitting hangover the morning after, an even harsher punishment awaits a nation that spends unwisely in pursuit of immediate gratification rather than sustainable development. – Festus Mogae[1]

In an enthusiastic assessment of Botswana's developmental achievements, and of the important role played by a consciously public-service-minded Kalanga ethnic minority elite that has defied the stereotype of self-serving and rapacious elites in Africa, Werbner (2004) hints at an 'Asian tiger' link underpinning the government's contemporary vision for the country's future.

> Possibly inspired originally by the former president Quett Masire's trips to the Pacific Rim and the Tiger Economies, Botswana at last has an ideological manifesto of its own for the country's big picture. It is a public vision for the future of the country as a whole, put forward under state sponsorship by a panel of eminent citizens in a position paper, Vision 2016 (Republic of Botswana 1997). (Werbner 2004: 17)

The notion of a 'big vision' for the country's future fits well with the commonly expressed understanding of Botswana as a country quite remarkable in Africa on account of its class relations and cohesion, its genuine appreciation of tradition and social stability and its sense of national unity in forging ahead with a coherent strategy for its future development. It is a vision of developing and maintaining a stable democracy rooted in African tradition on a volatile continent associated more often with misrule and state failure than with democratic consolidation. It is the aspiration that a country on the margins of the global economy can manage to play a significant role (in this case in the global diamond industry) and also to invest the revenues of the national patrimony in its future rather than let them fuel ethnic divisions, corruption and conflict as has been commonplace in many other African countries rich in natural resources. It is, ultimately, an idea of a country that can serve as an example of how even a poor people in an inhospitable geographic and political environment can develop and prosper. It is this vision, whatever its shortcomings so far, which Botswana's post-independence leaders and civil servants have managed to pursue relatively successfully. They have done so in a region fraught with political instability, social fragmentation and a deep legacy of uneven development rooted in the settler societies surrounding this sparsely populated country, which emerged as a British protectorate very much on the margins of but always influenced by colonial southern Africa.[2]

Somehow the rural cattle-owning elites who in 1962, some four years prior to independence, formed the BDP, which has governed ever since independence, have managed not only to consolidate democracy and early developmental gains, but have also understood their own future in a greater context of the developmental state as it has emerged elsewhere, notably among the so-called Asian tigers. Like the post-colonial ruling classes in these states, the elites of Botswana have also relied on advantages bestowed upon them by finding themselves governors of an (at independence) largely historically and ethnically cohesive state with strong linkages between pre- and post-colonial forms of rule (see Englebert 2000) and a populace largely accepting of a relatively paternalistic style of government (Maundeni 2004). If Botswana's post-independence trajectory is a success story, it is also one of prudence, moderation and indeed (social) conservatism as compared to the class forces leading liberation movements and transitions to independence (or majority rule) elsewhere in the region, in Mozambique and Angola as well as in Zimbabwe, Namibia and South Africa.[3]

> In contrast to South Africa and Rhodesia where African nationalist protesters spearheaded the demand for reforms, the old and new Tswana state elites were in full command in pre- and post-protectorate Botswana, and sought limited democratisation and modernisation. (Maundeni 2001: 125)[4]

Similarly, Good and Taylor (2008: 753) argue that '[t]he goal of both colonial and national sides ... was far less democracy than continuity in the ... economy and in gaining legitimacy and stability for government'. These factors have, in turn, enabled the government to minimize or, according to its critics (Good 1999; I. Taylor 2003), to suppress potentially fragmenting phenomena, from class or ethnically based confrontation to labour and social movement agitation. In doing so they have facilitated a climate in which relatively autonomous bureaucrats in key government departments are able to pursue long-term developmental strategies and ensure amiable relations with important multinational corporations, bringing much-needed human and capital resources, thus playing an important role in initiating and sustaining the country's impressive record of economic growth (cf. Lewis 1993; Morrison 1993).

The key question, then, is what the consequences of Botswana's socio-cultural heritage and post-independence developmental trajectory are for thinking beyond development as currently constituted. That is, to imagine how outcomes more in tune with Botswana's vision for itself as a successful country that can embrace both tradition and modernity can best be promoted. The aim of considering this question of alternatives to Botswana's current trajectory (which also implies that it is not as unproblematic a trajectory as its main proponents would have it) is not simply to produce an assessment of Botswana's record on development, including the serious challenges to its future posed by the HIV/AIDS epidemic, very high levels of socio-economic inequality and lack of economic diversification. The literature on Botswana's development referenced elsewhere in this chapter has already produced nuanced and insightful commentaries on this matter. Rather, the core issue to be examined is to what degree the pursuit of development in Botswana rests on sociocultural foundations that can enable its decision-makers to chart a course for the future that might allow the country to escape some of the worst problems associated with societal conflict, economic hardship, cultural fragmentation and political instability that plague its neighbouring countries to various degrees.

Most importantly, this chapter considers whether Botswana can escape the all too convenient resort to excessively paternalistic, or even authoritarian, politics that can seem to dominant-party regimes a natural and legitimate option when faced with domestic discontent (Southall 1994; Giliomee 1998; van de Walle 2003; Lodge 2004) – in Botswana's case discontent stemming from persistent inequality and unemployment as well as external economic and political pressures, including fallout from the ongoing crisis in Zimbabwe. If this can be avoided, Botswana's leaders, in coordination with what is commonly but problematically understood as a weak civil society and acquiescent labour movement (Maundeni 2004), may instead be able to draw upon its traditionally derived legitimacy and a widespread sense of social belonging to devise renewed methods for coping with modernity and the demands of development.

With these considerations in mind, the case of Botswana will be examined as follows. The examination begins with an outline of Botswana's development 'miracle' as conventionally understood. From this outline follows an explanation of this exceptional trajectory where the miracle narrative revolves around a set of arguments emphasizing the importance of the country's leadership in fostering transparent and efficient governance, thereby allowing it to channel revenue from its immense diamond deposits into developmental projects and to achieve high levels of economic growth over the long term. From this discussion of Botswana's alleged exceptionality follows a consideration of paternalism in Botswana and whether, contrary to most accounts of its negative effects on African regimes and governance, such a conservative social force can be harnessed for beneficial ends by allowing key decision-makers opportunities to make difficult decisions and to consider new ways of engaging with both markets and civil society while at the same time maintaining a sufficiently high degree of legitimacy necessary to avoid societal disruption that would impede plans for transformation over the long term. A final section looks at the 'social foundations' in Botswana, and how they can be linked, conceptually if not immediately in terms of policy, to post-development ideas about social harmony, holistic notions of development (including cultural and spiritual dimensions) and a serious appreciation of indigenous social and political traditions as an important catalyst for redefining what development and progress in Botswana ought to entail. The chapter concludes with an assessment of Botswana's potential for moving beyond development or for at least becoming a genuinely exemplary model of African development in the twenty-first century.

Botswana's miracle: the post-independence development trajectory

Samatar's (1999) designation of Botswana as Africa's 'miracle' has become a commonplace verdict on the country's post-independence developmental trajectory (e.g. Picard 1985; Holm and Molutsi 1989; Harvey and Lewis 1990; Stedman 1993; Dale 1995; Werbner 2004; cf. Good and Taylor 2008: 752).[5] That verdict has also become the focus of many subsequent critiques of what are perceived as notable shortcomings with Botswana's development, particularly the failure to diversify the economy away from a heavy reliance on diamond exports and to ensure a broader distribution of wealth (Good 2005; Hillbom 2008) as well as a tendency to paternalistic, or even authoritarian, rule by the dominant BDP (Good and Taylor 2008). Nevertheless, being one of the world's poorest and least developed countries at the time of independence in 1966, Botswana has since experienced rapid economic growth, averaging 10.7 per cent in the years 1974–92 (Samatar 1999: 65), making Botswana the world's fastest-growing economy in the two decades following its independence, and the emergence of a stable and overall democratic polity (see Hillbom 2008: 192).

> There are very few examples of rapid economic development within a democratic context ... Botswana and Mauritius are two countries that have achieved sustained levels of economic growth rivalling those of the East Asian newly industrialising countries (NICs), while maintaining democratic institutions and procedures. (Carroll and Carroll 1997: 464–5)

As a consequence Botswana experienced from 1970 to 1990 the world's highest absolute increase on the UNDP's HDI (Werbner 2004: 17–18), a measure that constitutes the dominant quantitative indicator of development as conventionally defined. This is an achievement that has since been seriously undermined, with HDI scores consequently plummeting as they have done elsewhere in southern Africa, by the country's unrelenting HIV/AIDS epidemic, which is one of the most severe anywhere in the world (I. Taylor 2004; Thurlow 2007). Botswana's achievements remain impressive on other measures. Its gross national income (GNI) per capita of $US5,480 as estimated by the World Bank is by far the highest in sub-Saharan Africa (excepting the GNI of Equatorial Guinea and Gabon, which are extremely skewed by these countries' oil exports); along with Benin, Namibia and South Africa, Freedom House awards Botswana the highest score for political rights and civil liberties; on Transparency International's Corruption Perceptions Index Botswana remains Africa's least corrupt country; the Heritage Foundation's Index of Economic Freedom, which measures levels of property rights protection and the freedom of movement for labour, capital and goods, ranks Botswana alongside Norway and the Czech Republic and far ahead of any other African nation; and South Africa is the only country in sub-Saharan Africa ranked higher than Botswana on the World Economic Forum's Global Competitiveness Index.[6] While these measures are all potentially contestable in terms of their ideological underpinnings as well as what these rankings tell us about the well-being and prospects for the majority of people in these countries, the combined picture is clearly one of Botswana as a country that has prospered relative to other African countries.

These social, political and economic developments are, even when

97

considering the ongoing HIV/AIDS epidemic and the damaging consequences thereof, seen as particularly impressive considering the near-total lack of industry, physical infrastructure and human capital at independence.

> Even by the very low standards of Sub-Saharan Africa, Botswana was neglected during the colonial period. In the vital bases for economic growth – physical infrastructure and skilled people – neglect was almost total until ten years before independence. The increase in expenditure in the last decade of colonial rule was too little and much too late to have made much difference by 1966, especially as much of that spending simply transferred public administration to a site inside the country. (Harvey and Lewis 1990: 25)[7]

Furthermore the country's independence coincided with a four-year drought, half of its recurrent expenditures had to be provided by Britain and the country was surrounded by hostile regimes in South Africa, South-West Africa (now Namibia) and Rhodesia (now Zimbabwe) (ibid.: 1). This was hardly an environment in which a newly independent Botswana would be expected to thrive and develop. Indeed, the country 'was caught within perhaps the ultimate unfavourable structural setting for democratization, not only in geographic, but also in economic and political terms' (Good and Taylor 2008: 750).

Diamond-reliant development Following the discovery by De Beers of enormous mineral deposits at Orapa in 1967 and at Jwaneng in 1976 (Harvey and Lewis 1990: 119–20) collaboration between the government and De Beers resulted in a transformation of Botswana's economy with diamond exports skyrocketing from 14.8 per cent of total exports in 1970 to 84.8 per cent by 1987 (ibid.: 121).

> Greatly increased government revenue supported massive expenditures on new physical and social infrastructure as well as support for economic policies, which sustained the private market and the growth of private investment in agriculture and other sectors. Roads, water supplies, health services, and education, provided where none existed before, resulted in an improvement of the quality of life for most citizens. (Parson 1993: 66)

Reliance on diamonds to fuel Botswana's economic growth and development remains very high; over the past decade, diamonds have contributed on average 38.4 per cent to gross domestic product (GDP) and have constituted 75 per cent of total exports (Basdevant 2008: 3).

The lack of diversification away from dependence on diamonds remains a great concern. Although diamond production is expected to increase from 32 million carats in 2005 to 44 million carats in 2017, the country's diamond deposits could be depleted by 2029, which would result in a very sharp reduction in fiscal revenue (ibid.: 4–5). The current depression in global prices and demand for diamonds, however, have forced an end to production at some of the country's mines and a drastic reduction in output, suggesting that the plans for expanding production and revenue will be at the mercy of a currently rapidly changing global market.

There are, however, plans for a 'second diamond revolution', aiming to develop an independent diamond marketing process outside the current system, whereby all diamonds in Botswana are marketed through the De Beers system and in direct competition with diamond marketing centres in Antwerp, Tel Aviv and Dubai. As De Beers now controls less than 50 per cent of the global diamond market (down from 80 per cent in previous decades), Botswana's government is interested in competing directly on the world market to create 'viable and sustainable' markets that can survive in a future where the country's major mines (Jwaneng and Orapa), having produced the bulk of the country's diamond wealth for over three decades, will decline. Centred on the establishment of Botswana's Diamond Trading Centre and the agreement by De Beers to aggregate its international diamond production in the country, this anticipated second stage in Botswana's diamond-based economy is also intended to promote much-needed economic diversification by helping to develop 'supporting activities' such as banking, insurance and IT services as part of the capital city's Diamond Hub (Mosinyi 2008).

Beef exports have been Botswana's 'only significant agricultural export' and were recognized already in the 1920s as likely to be the country's only comparative advantage (until the discovery of diamonds), meaning that agriculture was never likely to generate significant employment, and have in any case declined steadily in importance from constituting about 85 per cent of exports at independence to about 2 per cent today (Hillbom 2008: 198). Various projects aiming at diversifying the economy beyond the dependence on diamond exports have been rewarded with little success. While contributing only a modest 5 per cent to GDP, tourism has become a rapidly growing and increasingly important component of Botswana's economy (Kaynak and Marandu 2006). The magnificent national parks and game reserves in the north and west of Botswana attract wealthy tourists from around the world, making Maun International Airport the country's busiest ahead of the far larger one in the capital Gaborone. Manufacturing has on the other hand remained stagnant over the last few decades and now, at about 4 per cent of GDP, contributes less to the economy than does tourism (Hillbom 2008: 196). Textile industries established in the Selebi-Phikwe region, Gaborone and Francistown have not survived. Hyundai and Volvo assembly plants set up with the establishment of the Motor Company of Botswana in 1993 to assemble vehicles for the South African market have since left for South Africa, in part because of South African labour and government opposition to cross-border competition (McGowan and Ahwireng-Obeng 1998: 182–3; *Economist*, 18 November 1999). On balance, diversification of the diamond-dependent economy must at present be considered a failure as the 'contemporary economy is thus not substantially more diversified than was the case at independence' (Hillbom 2008: 196), with Good and Taylor (2008: 760) suggesting that 'structural transformation and economic diversification have never been truly attempted'.

The lack of any significant domestic capacity for developing the country required Botswana's independence leaders to forge close alliances with external actors from the outset. Kenneth Matambo, managing director of the Botswana Development Corporation (BDC), which was established in 1970 to facilitate industrial development and partnerships between government and the private sector, emphasizes an early recognition on the part of government that an almost non-existent private sector at the time of independence meant that engagement with international business, as well as facilitation by the state of an environment that was accommodating to these businesses, would be required to spur development in the country (Matambo 2001; cf. Tsie 1996: 606).[8] As the country lacked capacity to prospect for minerals and to develop a mineral industry by its own means once deposits were found, De Beers became an early and dominant industrial presence in Botswana by initially gaining a majority share in the diamond mining company Debswana, a joint venture with the Botswana government that eventually became a fifty/fifty partnership (Taylor and Mokhawa 2003: 263).[9]

The case of a small indigenous political elite dependent on foreign capital (and expatriate administrators and businessmen) is hardly a novelty in post-independence Africa. What is remarkable in the case of Botswana is how the post-independence leadership could negotiate a beneficial deal with a multinational corporation like De Beers, which was accomplished by recognizing the substantial bargaining power the discovery of great mining prospects entailed, thereby allowing the government to prioritize state–business collaboration and long-term public goods provisions over short-term collusion and private gains, as has been the case in other mineral-rich African countries following independence. In fact, Dunning's (2005) study of the effects of resource dependence on economic performance and political stability in developing countries concludes that Botswana's 'exceptionalism' can be explained by its 'uncommon', meaning stable, cordial and mutually beneficial relationship with De Beers.

Ultimately it is the relative 'backwardness' of Botswana at independence and its seemingly vulnerable position in a volatile region which make the country's qualified success ever since so interesting to Africanists and development scholars eager to find examples of success, however tenuous, in post-colonial Africa. The Afro-pessimist case often seems all too easy to make and substantiate – witness the voluminous commentary regarding Zimbabwe's current economic meltdown and descent into dictatorship and what are considered the disappointing responses of African leaders thereto. That analytical pessimism, however, also obscures those socio-political drivers of relative success that are important to identify and comprehend if scholarship on the political economy and development of Africa is to accomplish more than a mere cataloguing of Africa's decline and instead come to an understanding of how that decline may be reversed or at the very least alleviated. In terms of explaining Botswana's seemingly counter-intuitive achievements, case studies have generally attributed the country's positive developments to a mix of 'good fortune' (the discovery of diamonds), an efficient civil service combined with a cohesive traditional culture in which civil servants have been able to act autonomously in the interests of the public good, competent negotiating skills employed in negotiations with multinational corporations and international aid donors and prudent management of state revenues by the governing BDP (Harvey and Lewis 1990; Stedman 1993; Samatar 1999; Werbner 2004).

This review of Botswana's transformation from a quiet colonial backwater to a rapidly growing and modernizing state with the distinction among African states of being considered a comparatively free and stable democracy explains, in general terms, how the government has pursued a fairly conventional path of development (albeit with few options available at the outset and the odds seemingly therefore against success) by mixing accommodation of business interests with strategic state intervention to facilitate economic growth that has then been prudently invested, so as to maintain an overall stable macroeconomic environment, in the commonly prioritized areas of education, infrastructure and so on. What it does not shed any particular light on is whether the nature of Botswana's society and leadership class as it has emerged out of its colonial past is somehow exceptional and can therefore explain why Botswana has succeeded where most other African states have so far failed. It is to this question, which is crucial for evaluating whether alternatives to orthodox development strategies are viable and can be translated into actual politics in southern Africa, that the analysis now turns. This is where the case study departs from simply investigating the characteristics of Botswana's political economy and whether recent economic decision-making and trajectories suggest improvements or stagnation in terms of conventional measures of development (e.g. GDP and HDI) to instead consider matters of tradition and culture in those particular areas where they affect government policies and developmental trajectories.

Explaining Botswana's exceptionality

In their evaluation of foundations for development in Botswana, Beaulier and Subrick (2006: 104) identify Weber's (1968 [1922]) three sources of legitimacy as crucial to understanding Botswana's success. These sources are: a) tradition, as evident in a strong linkage between pre- and post-colonial tradition underpinning rule by chiefs and the BDP respectively; b) rational-legal authority, as manifested in the post-independence leadership's respect for basic constitutional and democratic rules as well as their prudent approach to policy-making (most obviously the case when compared with other African states); and c) a charismatic leader, embodied in Sir Seretse Khama, Botswana's founding father, who remains a symbol of national political leadership anchored in tradition as well as a modernizing outlook (Beaulier and Subrick 2006: 109).[10]

Samatar (1999: 4–5) identifies the competent nature of Botswana's 'class leadership' and its 'state apparatus' as key drivers of the country's success.[11] The success of class leadership is according to Samatar to a significant degree dependent on how a 'hegemonic project', here the 'vision' for Botswana as imagined by its modernizing political leaders and administrators (Werbner 2004: 17), becomes 'organically linked' with popular welfare. This linking between an (elite) class project and popular welfare is what Jessop (1990) understands as a 'one nation strategy' and which clearly resembles the ways in which hegemonic projects were pursued by autonomous class leaderships among the East Asian tigers, where, at least initially, there was little room for popular input and contestation of policy by civil society and labour.

While Botswana's government has always maintained that its leadership is wholly democratic, pointing to both traditional institutions like the *kgotla* and modern ones such as multiparty elections, it is important to be mindful of the fact that there are obvious echoes in Botswana of the East Asian model (without emulating the East Asian success with industrialization and diversification). These include the major role played by the state in its export-dependent economy, its pivotal partnership with strategically important corporations (i.e. De Beers), its at least quasi-corporatist nature of tripartite relations between government, business and labour, and the fact that the impressive post-war trajectories of the Asian tigers would obviously have been a source of inspiration for a newly independent state like Botswana when attempting to secure its self-determination and to sustain growth with which to finance a comprehensive plan for modernization of an economically and technologically backward nation. The discovery of huge mineral deposits adds an interesting twist to Botswana's relative success with development in that such mineral wealth by no means guarantees economic growth and development upon which a stable political system can be built – consider, for instance, the Democratic Republic of Congo and Sierra Leone (Hillbom 2008: 201–2).[12]

An early commitment to democratic rule, enhanced by the surviving *kgotla* tradition, which encourages dialogue and negotiation between rulers and their people, relatively unique to Tswana (and Sotho) culture (Schapera 1952: 64),[13] and a civil service based on meritocracy, seems to have paid good dividends in terms of future developmental outcomes (Acemoglu et al. 2003; Beaulier and Subrick 2006). It is in this environment that what Maundeni (2001) terms an 'indigenous [Tswana] initiator state culture', which he contrasts favourably with the neighbouring Shona culture giving rise to the modern Zimbabwean state, has emerged. Key to this 'initiator culture' is a historical acceptance of the centrality of the state and the fact that no parallel religious institutions rivalled that state, meaning that 'there was no fragmentation of social power' (ibid.: 109). What emerged in Botswana is a situation where society, i.e. the elite-defined culture of the dominant Tswana, has remained strong in the face of colonialism and modernization and where the post-independence state has also become a strong autonomous actor and driver of development.

The existence of both a strong state and a strong society – not necessarily strong in the modern sense of an active role for civil society organizations, but in the traditional sense of displaying coherency and a significant degree of historical continuity (Maundeni 2004) – contradicts Migdal's (1988) contention that strong societies, generally dominated by tribal authority, prevent strong and effective states from emerging. It also casts doubt on the argument that strong states necessarily suppress strong societies; this was clearly not the case in terms of the rapid socio-economic development among the Asian tigers, whatever the limitations of that Asian model for the emergence of democratic rights (Samatar 1999: 6).[14] Thus an environment existed in which it was possible to subordinate cultural and religious affairs to the needs of a modernizing state, while at the same time not threatening the legitimacy of that state, as has often been the case in societies where it would have been perceived as a modern imposition on traditional ways of governing society and of mediating between people, rulers and gods. This is contrary to most cases in Africa, where the populace would have been considered alienated in the extreme from post-independence states with modernizing aspirations, as in that conflict between modernists and communitarians that forms the basis for Mamdani's (1996) analysis of this fundamental predicament bedevilling post-colonial African societies.

This, then, is not merely an explanation for success that emphasizes the bureaucratic and technocratic attributes of the modern state as per conventional (Western) development theory, but an explanation that focuses on how Botswana's leaders have drawn on existing sociocultural foundations on which an acceptable and functioning state can be built. As an explanation for Botswana's post-independence trajectory this perspective avoids placing excessive emphasis on the institutional and legal basis of modern Botswana's political system. It also moves away from a purely rationalistic understanding of the self-interest of key actors in state and business (labour and civil society organizations playing a less central role in any such explanation in the case of Botswana) as an explanation for why both 'resource curse' and 'Dutch disease' have been avoided, corruption tempered and stability in state–business relations maintained. The political economy analysis of Botswana's post-independence trajectory remains integral while anchored in the sociocultural context of tradition as chiefdom, paternalism and the inherent openness and mutual respect symbolized by the *kgotla*.

The socio-politically dominant cattle-owning elite's connections with the rural areas in which a majority of Batswana live, and which remain the focal point of Batswana identity and sense of national belonging (Nyamnjoh 2004: 40), have been crucial for the retention of culturally meaningful links between state and society. This is despite the fact that a traditionally very unequal distribution of cattle ownership has sustained socio-economic inequality in the modern era following a decline in the cattle industry as an overall contributor to the national economy (Picard 1985: 23–4; cf. Colclough and McCarthy 1980).[15] Societal stability and the absence of a sharply divisive past along overt racial lines as in neighbouring South Africa and Zimbabwe enabled Botswana's leaders to reduce risk aversion among its partners in the private sector. Early industrial policies also aimed at producing an investment-friendly climate (Samatar 1999: 136–45).[16] As the divisive legacy of settler colonialism weighs less heavily on the Batswana, a greater degree of flexibility in charting a favourable course in terms of economic policy-making in the post-independence era has been possible. 'Thus, through developmental nationalism, financial incentives, and developmental policies, the Botswana state was able to promote economic development for thirty-four years' (Maundeni 2001: 129).

The fact that Botswana did not, given its relative independence from IFIs, liberalize its economy owing to external pressures, but did so instead on its own initiative, is another important factor in explaining post-independence stability. 'The impetus for [liberalization] came from Batswana, the Ministry of Finance, the Bank of Botswana, and the private sector organizations, especially BOCCIM' (BIDPA Official 2001). The absence of armed conflict, or indeed a war of liberation as preceded independence in Namibia and Zimbabwe, or the severe societal upheaval and conflict that brought about the demise of apartheid in South Africa, paved the way for Botswana's relatively stable post-independence relations between state, market and societal actors. Hence the important long-term perspectives on cooperation between these actors were from the very outset more likely to be established in Botswana than in neighbouring countries.

Botswana's Ministry of Finance and Development Planning (MFDP) is considered the 'epicenter of the state apparatus' and the main institution directing the country's development programmes, where the insulation and professional character of the civil service operating within a highly coordinated planning structure are essential components of the MFDP's acknowledged efficiency (Samatar 1999: 9–10).[17] Public institutions in Botswana enjoy a high reputation for efficiency and reliance on meritocracy that enhances their ability to work effectively with businesses and other economic stakeholders and 'the presidential protection given the [MFDP] to plan and direct the economy is exceptional' (Holm and Darnolf 2000: 139). In this regard, Harvey and Lewis (1990: 9–10) emphasize the 'high quality' of Botswana's independence leadership by noting that Presidents Khama and Masire (the vice-president at independence) were skilled economists and administrators, rather than freedom fighters, providing a key link between technocrats in the civil service and political leadership in cabinet and parliament.

> The political system is dominated by (and policy is set in the interest of) a coalition of wealthy, well educated, cattle-owning political elites who are committed to rapid economic growth in the framework of a largely free enterprise system. This coalition of traditional leaders, teachers, junior state functionaries, and wealthy farmers was joined by more senior administrators in the 1970s. (Samatar 1999: 67)

Furthermore, given Botswana's domestic stability and the accountability fostered by democratic governance, it was possible to appoint and keep qualified people in the civil service without losing them to international organizations or other forms of political exile (voluntary or not), as has commonly been the case elsewhere in Africa. The influence of cattlemen in post-independence Botswana politics 'had the advantage that those responsible for major decisions about the economy were steeped in commercial experience' (Harvey and Lewis 1990: 10). The resulting good reputation for professionalism, efficiency and reliability has helped reduce uncertainty about the country's domestic environment and thus lengthen the time horizons employed by state and capital actors when negotiating with each other. Botswana's political economy has on the whole been characterized by a lesser degree of antagonistic relations between state and capital actors than has been the case elsewhere in southern Africa.[18] While government has not been able to diversify the economy to the degree it has hoped for, economic growth has continued and resources have been channelled comparatively efficiently into developmental projects.

A heavy reliance on expatriate skills has, however, remained a feature of the post-independence era and has over time become a salient and controversial political issue as demands among Batswana for an increasing share in the country's economic activities have increased (BIDPA Official 2001). While recognizing that the pressures are not as intense as in other African countries with significant economic involvement by 'foreigners' (however defined), there are according to Matthew Wright (2001) of the Bank of Botswana increasing concerns about rent-seeking effects of increasing pressures for indigenization (or Africanization) of the economy. Although public debate on the need to economically and professionally empower Botswana's citizens (and the means of doing so) has not reached the same level of urgency and resentment as have debates on BEE in South Africa, populist pressures for transformation have (as in South Africa) become embroiled in a set of complex issues that have increased in prominence since the 1980s. These issues concern the meaning of belonging and of being indigenous, i.e. questions about what criteria ought to determine who is a Motswana with equal citizenship rights and what groups (if any) should be prioritized in Botswana's multi-ethnic society, in which interests of the Tswana majority dominate (Nyamnjoh 2007).

These explanations for Botswana's success, which focus on the country's embedded state apparatus and resilient, traditional societal structures, are clearly controversial. While political moderation and prudent policy-making may have ensured stability, this moderation and prudence may also be the reason why a genuine structural transformation of Botswana's society and economy has never taken place. Inherent conservatism on the part of Botswana's rulers and throughout society may reduce incentives to tackle the high levels of inequality and poverty that remain and may also make politicians and the public too tolerant of anti-democratic tendencies. Indeed, the question of whether paternalism has served independent Botswana well, or whether it has morphed into a creeping authoritarianism that threatens to undermine the very basis for the country's success, remains unresolved.

Benevolent paternalism or creeping authoritarianism?

As has already been noted, Botswana's record remains disputed, by those who consider the country's post-independence trajectory a remarkable success (e.g. Samatar 1999; Maundeni 2001; Werbner 2004) and those who consider Botswana's achievements tainted or even overshadowed by elitist tendencies, intolerance of criticism and a creeping authoritarianism (e.g. I. Taylor 2003; Good 2005). There is, however, no disputing the fact that politics in Botswana have always been shaped by traditional and conservative societal forces. These forces have contributed to a political environment in which there are notable hierarchical relations between elites and the poor. These are relations between patrons who have social duties and obligations that come with their high status and clients who, while they are subordinate, nevertheless expect their interests and needs to be acknowledged, in the *kgotla* as well as in policy outcomes that in the end tend to be accepted whatever their content. The generally deferential nature of civil society organizations, however, and the at times high-handed nature of the state, cannot on their own account for the relative absence throughout Botswana's post-independence era of strong popular opposition and protest against BDP rule and persistent socio-economic inequalities and general hardships.

Botswana

Defending Botswana's civil society against accusations of it being weak and thus unable to play any useful role in demanding democratic accountability from the country's ruling class, Maundeni (2004) stresses the traditional appreciation of 'civility', i.e. a preference for debate and consensus rather than open confrontation, as an inherent strength of civil society which has contributed positively to the country's stability and democracy. Against I. Taylor's (2003: 221) contention that the ruling BDP has 'exhibited highly undemocratic tendencies to portray ... organs of civil society it deems beyond its control as foreign stooges, and has not been shy of playing the race card against any foreign supporters of civil society' (quoted in Maundeni 2004: 620), Maundeni argues that

> [t]he main reason why Botswana's civil society is often considered 'weak' is because it has staged very few violent clashes with the government leading to reversal of policies, the hallmark of a strong Western civil society. This Eurocentric way of measuring the strength of civil society seems to be inappropriate for Botswana politics, where lengthy debates are common and confrontations are unusual. (ibid.: 620)

It is not easy to adjudicate between these two competing readings of Botswana's civil society. On one hand, I. Taylor (2003) runs the risk of assuming that a state–society dynamic which does not conform to a Western-style (i.e. pluralistic and confrontational) democratic politics must be deficient or deviant. On the other hand, Maundeni (2004) must be equally careful so as not to misunderstand a preference for avoiding confrontation as evidence of a fundamentally content populace. Apparent contentment may instead be a consequence of fear – a reluctance to speak up in a paternalistic-cum-intolerant environment where such action may meet not only with disagreement, but with ostracism and punitive sanction (whether social, political, economic, judicial).[19]

Acquiescence on the part of the public in this particular context, i.e. vis-à-vis a state remarkably restrained in dealing with opposition as compared to other well-entrenched regimes in Africa, does seem to indicate some significant and enduring support for the BDP and of recognition by the public of the developmental project that the BDP has embarked upon as fundamentally legitimate. There are examples of popular unrest in modern-day Botswana and of harsh state responses thereto. In early 1995, public protest (primarily by students) turned into rioting in the wake of the 1994 elections and a cabinet reshuffle that involved the controversial reappointment of minsters forced to resign some years earlier. This public backlash triggered a harsh response by the state. Confrontation over the next couple of days between protesters, some of them armed, and armed police and military units deploying both helicopters and tear gas resulted in several arrests, beatings and the death of one young man (Good 1996: 69–72). Outrageous and objectionable as this series of incidents may have been, they constitute the exception proving the rule of generally peaceful state–society relations in Botswana, even in situations where strong disagreement may exist. The state in Botswana cannot in any way be compared to the Zimbabwean state and the ruthlessness (including mass murder in the case of the Matabeleland massacres in the early 1980s) it has been willing to deploy against its own citizens. The few examples of serious state–society confrontation in Botswana are also of a mild variety compared to the several clashes that have broken out in recent years in South Africa's townships, between police and impoverished citizens protesting against the government's lack of basic service delivery (Atkinson 2007; Booysen 2007).

One of the explanations for this relatively benign state of affairs centres on the particular nature of hierarchical relations between ruling elites and the general population – referred to pejoratively in the Africanist and development studies literature as patron–client relations – as they have emerged in Botswana, where there is a higher degree of continuity between pre- and post-colonial forms of rule, particularly in terms of the social basis of that rule, than has been the case in Zimbabwe and South Africa, where the rupture between the pre- and post-colonial has been more evident.

> Patron–client relationships contribute to routinisation and legitimation of coercive dependence by projecting a form of *benevolent paternalism*; they facilitate *the establishment of moral authority of obedience and stifle a sense of injustice*. They tend to freeze the emergence of class conflict and enshrine as natural the existing hierarchy of domination and subordination. (Fatton 1990: 460, quoted in Tsie 1996: 605; emphases added)[20]

It is precisely because such patron–client relationships tend to foster an acceptance of a historically derived status quo which generally entails inequality and some form of oppression, whether relatively 'mild' or outright violent, that the vast majority of studies examining such relationships, usually labelled under the rubric 'neo-patrimonialism' (see Erdmann and Engel 2006), consider them fundamentally problematic for Africa's developmental prospects and for democratization (Eisenstadt 1973; Le Vine 1980; Callaghy 1988; Bratton and van de Walle 1994).[21] And it is indeed the case that no relationship between state and civil society that is blatantly unjust, oppressive, violent or otherwise causing those left outside to suffer can be construed as being positive for development, let alone for creating an environment in which decision-makers are receptive to different ideas about what development might entail and to notions of how societies could rethink development altogether so as to arrive at more propitious ways of improving well-being.

Accusations suggesting that Botswana's BDP is being complicit in a creeping sort of authoritarianism generally emphasize what is perceived as an 'illiberal authoritarianism and presidentialism ... characterized by an elitist top-down structure of government' (Good and Taylor 2008: 751), with Söderbaum (2008: 330) going so far as to describe patrimonialism in Botswana as 'pathological'. When confronted with criticism or opposition, government is prone to employ a self-serving 'paternalist rhetoric', as exemplified by President Khama's lecturing of trade unionists on the tenth anniversary of independence:

> [Y]ou are first and foremost Batswana and your first responsibility is to assist in the development of the country. If you exercise your freedom to bargain for higher wages without restraint, you will be deliberately avoiding this responsibility. (Sir Seretse Khama, quoted in Good and Taylor 2008: 762)

Examples of serious shortcomings supposedly generated by this political environment include one-party dominance and the weakening of accountability created by such a state of affairs; policies deliberately aiming at keeping political opposition, labour and civil society weak; an excessive control of and interference in media outlets; and, as already noted, a sometimes sharp intolerance of overt forms of criticism of the government, especially when such criticism is articulated by representatives of NGOs or other foreign voices. Moreover, persistent social and cultural prejudice against the nomadic San (or Basarwa) minority has resulted in their continued marginalization and alleged ill treatment, as in the case of their forced relocation away from their traditional hunting grounds in the Central Kalahari Game Reserve (ostensibly to provide them with access to modern amenities such as education and healthcare) to pave the way for mining and tourism interests (I. Taylor 2003).[22]

None of these criticisms of Botswana's government can be taken lightly given the evidence provided. Although such matters may seem of small importance compared to the very grave and violent forms of oppression existing elsewhere, they are nevertheless serious issues that give rise to important questions about the quality of what is generally deemed

Africa's best democracy and the difficulties inherent in promoting and consolidating democratic values and democratic governance in any society where paternalism and patron–client relations legitimized by reference to tradition are powerful social forces. In such cases it can become far too tempting and convenient for authoritarian leaders to instrumentally appeal to tradition, so as to escape being held accountable for their actions and having to acquiesce in demands for reform.

A contemporary example of a glaring disregard for accountability and popular welfare excused by reference to tradition can be found in Swaziland, where King Mswati III, presiding over one of the world's most impoverished nations, which is also racked by the world's highest HIV/AIDS prevalence rate, appropriates large portions of the national budget to lavish on official luxury and remains contemptuous of popular demands for democratic reform. As the country recently celebrated its fortieth anniversary of independence and the king's fortieth birthday by inaugurating another round of lavish government spending, government spokesman Percy Simelane argued that

> [p]overty has been with us for many years. We cannot then sit by the roadside and weep just because the country is faced with poverty. We have made great strides as a country that gives us pleasure in celebrating 40 years of independence and the king's birthday. (Bearak 2008)

As with the contrast between relatively restrained state responses to popular protest in Botswana and harsh repression in Zimbabwe, the example of misrule and blatant disregard for well-being masquerading as the upholding of tradition in Swaziland stands in clear contrast to a restrained form of paternalism in Botswana anchored in a genuine concern about democratic accountability and competent governance (whatever the actual shortcomings may be).

If, on the other hand, a case can be made that the consequences of a particular form of patron–client relationship such as it has emerged in Botswana is not the cause of overt forms of oppression, even though it might entail minor violations of democratic ideals, then it becomes much easier to actually recognize positive aspects of such a delicate arrangement, however disparaged it may be in the mainstream literature on democracy, good governance and development. Arguments for a benevolent paternalism are seldom explicitly made by scholars who have found Botswana's post-independence achievements impressive. That would after all be tantamount to condoning a departure from accepted standards of good governance and the promotion of (liberal) democracy

Botswana

which generally constitute a set of non-negotiable ideals towards which all developing countries should strive. It is, however, not difficult to see how a country like Botswana, which faces immense challenges, could benefit from having its state apparatus, and the state's wider relations with market actors and society, anchored in such a socio-political context.

Key to the argument that a somehow benign form of patron–client relationship comes with some actual benefits is Fatton's (1990: 460) observation that a benevolent form of paternalism (however that is defined) makes people able to cope under difficult circumstances that are not likely to let up in the short term, no matter what choices are made by government officials. This idea echoes the argument promoted by some post-development thinkers, e.g. Illich (1976) and Esteva (1995), that when people who are suffering but yet feel 'at home' in a particular societal context, as opposed to feeling alienated by a modernization process that has eroded traditional notions of legitimacy and belonging, they can find it easier to accept their situation and thus to endure.[23] While finding solace in tradition and harnessing a sense of belonging as a means to endure hardship can hardly be the end point of any enquiry into development in Botswana or anywhere else, it can well be argued that such a sense of endurance will lengthen time horizons. This process of buying time then provides at least the chance that those who are genuinely motivated to find solutions to current predicaments can come up with ideas that may in the end provide solutions acceptable to all.

If this is the case, then it is precisely this embedded paternalism which has allowed Botswana's government to enjoy stability and autonomy, both characteristics of the political and economic climate of post-independence Botswana that have been noted by so many different commentators as key to the country's relative success. A benevolent form of paternalistic democracy becomes the societal glue which gives the government breathing space, allowing it to keep to its course when arguably many other countries facing a similar combination of problems – persistent inequality and poverty, an HIV/AIDS crisis, difficulties in achieving economic diversification and the threat of instability spilling across national borders – would likely descend into chaos and democratic breakdown. Whether Botswana's paternalistic form of democracy is the price the country has had to pay for its stability is a question that will be left open here. What now must be asked is whether genuine alternatives to a developmental course that seems to offer diminishing returns can be charted, indeed envisioned, from within the social and political status quo of contemporary Botswana.

Sociocultural foundations for rethinking development

Having examined Botswana's 'miracle', the socio-political and economic underpinnings of its exceptional post-independence trajectory and its particular form of paternalistic democracy, we must now ask what Botswana's rulers, in concert with businesses and civil society, might build on to take post-development seriously and move beyond development as currently constituted. Current debates on development in Botswana, both within government and in dialogue between government and its main societal stakeholders (i.e. business and, to a lesser degree, labour and civil society), do not suggest any significant move to fundamentally rethink what development entails or whether it can, *contra* Rist (2002) and other critics of the modern development paradigm, ever be realized in its current form. There is no strong challenge from civil society whereby clear alternatives to mainstream understandings of development as essentially the continued reliance on natural resource extraction, integration into the global economy on the basis of enhancing competitiveness and more FDI to fund ongoing modernization projects and service delivery are being articulated.

Grassroots movements with linkages to organizations elsewhere in the global South and in the West that promote alternatives to conventional development strategies, such as Abahlali baseMjondolo (the shack dwellers' movement) and the Anti-Privatisation Forum in South Africa,[24] have no comparable presence or profile in Botswana. The Friedrich Ebert Stiftung, which promotes 'the involvement of Non-State Actors into the process of shaping policy and democracy' in Botswana, states that

> democracy has largely been the domain of the State. Consultations with society are held in traditional *'Kgotla'*-meetings, a direct interaction between State and citizens. Dialogue and effective involvement of organised Non-State Actors have been exceptional or purely formalistic in the past. (Friedrich Ebert Stiftung 2007)

The crucial difficulty here in terms of considering how alternative understandings of development could be translated into actual politics is that there is no consensus on whether Botswana is a genuine success story or not. The pessimistic view holds that it is precisely this trajectory of pursuing conventional development policies which, while continuing to earn the country accolades from IFIs and Western governments concerned with adherence to a broadly liberal formula, prevents Botswana from resolving its problems with everything from diamond-dependent growth to poverty and extreme socio-economic inequality. In this case,

alternatives to conventional development do not emerge in public discourse because those (in civil society) who would push for alternatives are
kept marginalized and thus lacking the ability to influence government
because of these very policies that the government is pursuing. The positive point of view, however, holds that it is precisely because of the policy
trajectory embarked upon at independence that Botswana has become
successful relative to most other African countries and that existing policies should therefore be retained and enhanced rather than replaced. In
this case, it is not clear that alternatives are needed if Botswana after all
is doing well by comparison with other African states and therefore the
risks of embracing a wholly different thinking about development might
outweigh the costs of continuing apace within the current framework.
In either case, thinking beyond development is not likely to demand the
attention and interest of policy-makers.

While the combination of what Samatar (1999) identified as a strong
traditional society and a strong state has provided Botswana with stability
and societal cohesion in the face of persisting problems with inequality
and poverty, it is difficult to see how Botswana, just like any other country
in the region beset by the problems constituting the legacy of a regional
apartheid system, will be able to transcend this trajectory. As is clear from
the analysis in this chapter, Botswana's independence era can certainly be
considered a success in parts when set against the record of neighbouring states or of Africa as a whole. Steady economic growth, low levels of
corruption and instability, the functional multiparty system and so on are
achievements that ought not to be belittled. But while it may well be the
case that such a trajectory can be maintained for the foreseeable future,
it does not offer hope for any substantial socio-economic transformation
that would increase the well-being of the majority of those who are seriously marginalized and living well below the poverty line. Those left largely
untouched by the real and significant developments that have occurred
may still in the long run benefit from living in a society where the state
has sufficient capacity and financial resources to maintain delivery in
terms of schooling, healthcare (despite the enormous strains on health
services caused by the HIV/AIDS epidemic) and an overall level of stability and security that is not even remotely approximated in many other
African societies. There is, however, little scope on the basis of politics
as usual in Botswana that the poor will see their lives genuinely transformed and that a political environment will emerge wherein they are
genuinely included and thereby transformed from being merely people
on the margins to whom the government attempts to 'bring development'

into active citizens whose local needs and aspirations are recognized in the very processes of public policy-making.

As suggested by Maundeni (2004) it is, moreover, not in the 'nature' of civil society in Botswana to act in a confrontational manner vis-à-vis government. And if civil society is reluctant to do so on issues pertaining to the quality of democratic governance, why would novel conceptions of development or the seemingly abstract exercise of attempting to re-envision what development means altogether be any more likely to spur civil society into action? And why would key state and market actors who are in charge of the process of development as currently constituted be interested in any radical shift in direction, either at the conceptual level or in terms of actual policy-making? It is in the context of this state of affairs that one must consider the difficult task of articulating ways in which post-development critiques of current trajectories in southern Africa can become rooted in the aspirations of social movements, incentive structures of businesses and the affairs of state.

Considering all these potential impediments to any significant change of course it is nevertheless the case that if a change in thinking about development is to emerge in Botswana, it would likely have to come from within government channels. If civil society is unlikely or unable to lead and business lacks sufficient incentive to do so, then government will have to continue its role as the prime catalyst for change. While such a scenario suggests the usual top-down process of effecting policy change, it would nevertheless be the case that any such rethinking of development would have to be rooted in appeals to social and political tradition in order to be deemed legitimate and thereby politically feasible over the long term. To this end, a traditional forum like the *kgotla*, especially if rejuvenated and made more inclusive and effective than it has tended to be in modern times (Sebudubudu and Osei-Hwedie 2006: 44–5), would serve an important function by lending a sense of traditional legitimacy to any departure from the current trajectory. It would also place any such change within a framework of consultation, thus displaying that mutual sense of 'civility' between state and citizens which has been so important in ensuring the state's ability to lead and where necessary to make decisions autonomously while at the same time maintaining social cohesion (Maundeni 2004). It is a conservative kind of transformation, then, which is most likely to emerge in Botswana, and also one that fits well with the conservative aspects of post-development thinking which emphasize tradition, hierarchy, order, belonging and community. While such change might not be 'organic' in the sense of it emerging from the bottom up and via multiple channels relating back to societal custom and organization, but would rather be state-led and top-down, it would have the benefit, if successful, of appealing to the very traditions and practices of a deferential yet traditionally minded society.

Any move beyond development as currently constituted, taking into account core post-development tenets such as popular inclusivity, a holistic conceptualization of development-as-well-being and a rejection of development as growth- and accumulation-based modernization, could once it is anchored in a popular/traditionalist context then presumably be vetted in consultations with other stakeholders, via the various quasi-corporatist arrangements that do exist, such as businesses that have substantial engagement with Botswana and therefore also an incentive to promote long-term stability and acceptance of their role as dominant players in the country's economy. In one sense this process suggests no real difference from that of the normal course of moving from policy formation to implementation. What would arguably be different when considering not just a tweaking of policy within the existing develop-ment paradigm, but rather a radical departure from current policy and a rethinking of ultimate goals, is that whereas any successful policy would need to gain some modicum of acceptance by key government allies (such as influential businesses), a paradigm shift in the pursuit of development would constitute a challenge to vested interests (primarily among the ruling class and in the private sector) so serious that in order to be considered in any way feasible it would have to draw explicitly on accepted tradition and a sense of legitimate popular demand (whether or not it is manifested in actual organized pressure by civil society or government). And this is especially the case if the intention behind that change is to overcome the many stresses placed on traditional societies by modern development.

One advantage here, alluded to in the preceding section on paternal-ism and drawing on the traditional concept of *ubuntu* as it is understood across the region (see Chapter 3), may be the preference for social unity that is a more obvious feature of contemporary politics in Botswana than is the case in either South Africa or Zimbabwe, where modern antagonisms have produced a greater rupture with tradition and a greater acceptance of confrontational politics. If a politics of change could be justified (how-ever paradoxically) by reference to the importance of embedding policy in tradition and striving for unity and cohesion, then a comprehensive re-evaluation and reconceptualization of what development in Botswana ought to mean could be perceived not as a radical and therefore risky departure from established norms but rather accepted as a genuine effort to maintain Botswana's exceptionality in the face of global modernizing forces threatening to undermine the country's traditional way of life.[25] The potential inherent in the idea of anchoring a politics of change in a greater aspiration to maintain tradition is underscored by the fact that the value placed on adherence to social mores promoting unity and cohesion in Botswana has roots in values that go deeper than mere politics and class-based expediency.

> Tswana state religion defined morality in social and political terms. Evil was considered mainly social and political. A doer of evil was one who violated the social taboos and the political unity of the society ... (Schapera 1953; Setiloane 1976; Alverson 1978). Evil is the destroyer of social living; it undermines a person because it ruptures his moral embeddedness in the existence of other people. (Maundeni 2001: 110)

Such an understanding of personhood, 'in the existence of other people', is a direct derivation of *ubuntu*, the idea that 'a person is a person through other persons' (*motho ke motho ka batho* in seTswana). *A Long Term Vision for Botswana*, a government document outlining the government's Vision 2016 development framework, similarly recognizes *ubuntu* as an underlying principle of the politics of development in Botswana. It suggests that the principle of *Botho* is to be added to the four 'national principles' underlining all development plans of Botswana, namely Democracy, Development, Self-Reliance and Unity.

> [*Botho*] refers to one of the tenets of African culture – the concept of a person who has a well-rounded character, who is well-mannered, courteous and disciplined, and realises his or her full potential both as an individual and as a part of the community to which he or she belongs. *Botho* defines a process for earning respect by first giving it, and to gain empowerment by empowering others. It encourages people to applaud rather than resent those who succeed. It disapproves of anti-social, disgraceful, inhuman and criminal behaviour, and encourages social justice for all. (Botswana Vision 2016 Council 2004)

Moreover, '[t]he five principles are derived from Botswana's cultural heritage, and are designed to promote social harmony, or *kagisano*' (ibid.). These principles constitute the 'broader context' for national development based on four key objectives: sustained development, rapid economic growth, economic independence and social justice. Just as there is a clear connection here between the concept of *Botho* and that of *ubuntu* as it is used more generally throughout southern Africa, the notion of social harmony or *kagisano* as outlined in this government vision is the same social force from which Maundeni (2004) derives the emphasis on and importance of 'civility' in public life and politics. An environment in which a premium is placed on social unity and cohesion will likely be receptive to Rist's (2002: 244) notion of a future beyond development as currently understood, a future in which the drawbacks of modernization, such as alienation and social fragmentation, are mitigated by a continued engagement with a living tradition that remains an important guiding principle but not a cause of atavistic compulsion on the part of either rulers or people.

Whatever the difficulties inherent in promoting a move beyond development in Botswana may be (as in any country hard pressed by acute problems of underdevelopment and attendant suffering they are significant), it is also clear that the social stability and general legitimacy enjoyed by a government characterized by both democratic and paternalistic tendencies provide the country with a foundation on which to base any departure from conventional development thinking that is very different from the social context in which any future reconceptualization of development in neighbouring Zimbabwe may emerge, which is the topic to be addressed in the following chapter.

5 | Zimbabwe: the failing state revisited

We will never allow an event like an election to reverse our independence, our sovereignty, our sweat and all that we fought for ... all that our comrades died fighting for. – Robert Mugabe[1]

A violent birth

When considering post-transition trajectories in southern Africa, developments in Zimbabwe stand in stark contrast to those in neighbouring Botswana. If Botswana's unremarkable and by regional comparison very peaceful transition to independence set the tone for a politics characterized by stability and democratic consolidation resting on the *kgotla* tradition and a modernizing, meritocratic civil service, then post-independence politics in Zimbabwe provides a vivid example of the difficulty in stabilizing and consolidating an independent polity forged in the crucible of deeply rooted racial oppression, violent confrontation and the attainment of independence via a national war of liberation. If the emphasis in Botswana has been on consensus, deference and a kind of democratic pragmatism in shaping the post-independence polity within a broader historical and cultural context of benevolent paternalism, then the trend in Zimbabwe has been towards confrontational politics, persistent (ethnic and racial) divisions and increasingly authoritarian rule.

In Zimbabwe it is the *Chimurenga* ('struggle' in chiShona), those great upheavals pregnant with the forceful and now politically expedient symbolism of a popular rising against external foes – against colonial rule in the late nineteenth century, the Rhodesian state during the 1970s and, with the inception of the land invasions in 2000, what the government considers vestiges of (white/settler) neocolonial oppression – which has underpinned social movements and political trajectories since the days of British South Africa Company rule (Ranger 2004; Kriger 2006). Add to the symbolism of the *Chimurenga* the violent force of the early 1980s *Gukurahundi* operations ('the early rain which washes away the chaff before the spring rains'), during which time the North Korean-trained Fifth Brigade deployed by Robert Mugabe's ruling Zimbabwe African National Union (ZANU) rooted out rebellious forces from the Zimbabwe People's Revolutionary Army (ZIPRA) concentrated in Matabeleland and loyal to Joshua Nkomo's Zimbabwe African People's Union (ZAPU) at the expense of tens of thousands of mostly civilian lives (Ndlovu-Gatsheni 2003), and the image of Zimbabwe is indeed one of a nation born in conflict and bloodshed.[2]

This imagery, effectively turning the symbols of Shona priests into state symbols, was consciously deployed by ZANU to legitimize the party and its claim to being the sole representative of the people.

> Peasants use [the term *Gukurahundi*] with terror and awe. *Gukurahundi* occurs during crop seasons and destroys crops, weeds, huts and forests, the good and the bad, including people and beasts. ZANU deliberately sought to link its revolutionary policy with such fearsome association. (Sithole 1997: 131–2, quoted in Maundeni 2001: 126)

Meredith's (2002) journalistic dramatization of Mugabe's Zimbabwe is emblematic of this vision,[3] quoting Mugabe while a commander of the Zimbabwe African National Liberation Army (ZANLA) as a would-be Mao Zedong ('political power grows out of the barrel of a gun') liberating his country by force of arms and cathartic violence:

> Our votes must go together with our guns. After all, any vote we shall have, shall have been the product of the gun. The gun which produces the vote should remain its security officer – its guarantor. The people's votes and the people's guns are always inseparable twins. (Mugabe, quoted in ibid.)

Some thirty years later, at what is likely the nadir of Zimbabwe's descent into ruin, Western media, aghast at the scale of socio-economic collapse and the desperation with which President Mugabe and the ruling ZANU-PF (a result of the forceful merger of ZANU and ZAPU, the ruling party is itself a consequence of the *Gukurahundi* violence) are clinging to power, quote the ageing liberation hero as ever dismissive of the legitimacy of popular democratic will as compared to the legitimacy of force: 'We fought for this country, and a lot of blood was shed ... We are not going to give up our country because of a mere X. How can a ballpoint fight with a gun?' (Raath and Philp 2008). This irreverent challenge to a more or less universalized discourse on democracy, whereby even the most ruthless of regimes will couch their actions in terms of democracy or aspirations thereto (e.g. 'self-determination'), Mugabe's nonchalant dismissal of the ballot box seems somehow as chilling, if not more so, than the brutal actions of his regime. When combined, this blatant disregard for the democratic aspirations of its people and the callousness with which state violence is deployed to suppress Zimbabweans as the national economy ceases to function seem to portend the very 'end of modernity' (see Worby 2003).

Considering, then, the contrast between the local contexts in which independence was achieved and between subsequent trajectories in Botswana and Zimbabwe, it is useful to recollect the sharp distinction made by Maundeni (2001) between Tswana and Shona 'state cultures' and his description of the importance of 'civility' in politics as symbolized by the traditional Tswana emphasis on consensus-seeking as captured by the adage *ntwa kgolo ke a molomo* ('conflicts are best solved through discussion' in seTswana) (Maundeni 2004: 621). By contrast, in Zimbabwe, a more heterogeneous collection of entities prior to colonization than Botswana ever was, the onset of colonization in the late nineteenth century produced and exacerbated significant rivalries between various African peoples (e.g. Shona, Ndebele and Kalanga) which played an important part in weakening resistance during the First *Chimurenga* against the recently arrived European settlers (Maundeni 2001: 121–2; cf. Beach 1986). The subsequent co-optation during the 1930s of some traditional chiefs and elected Africans representing an educated segment of the population on to newly created native boards cemented divisions between those Africans resisting such co-optation, instead turning to African nationalism, and those who participated in these structures and were later labelled 'sell-outs' (ibid.: 123; cf. Weinrich 1971). Hence a well-established history of confrontation and political schism between segments of the African population in Zimbabwe before independence that, in terms of continued antagonisms between white and black, nationalist and moderate African, etc., continued unresolved into the post-independence era.

These historical, cultural and political differences between Botswana and Zimbabwe suggest that we cannot simply locate the reasons for diverging post-independence trajectories in the strategies producing two different routes to that independence (peaceful in Botswana, violent in Zimbabwe). Those reasons must also be sought in the nature of colonialism in each territory (i.e. settler colonial rule in Zimbabwe and indirect rule in Botswana) and, importantly, in their pre-colonial structures of rule.[4] Indeed, our understanding of developmental trajectories in these two countries and of the prospects for moving beyond their respective impasses must take into consideration different origins and contexts of each country's contemporary developmental dilemma.

Following on from the empirical analysis of Botswana in the previous chapter, the examination in this chapter of post-independence Zimbabwe and its prospects for transcending a history of instability and ever-deepening crisis to move beyond well-worn public discourses on development proceeds as follows. First, the transition to independence and subsequent consolidation of ZANU's power throughout the 1980s is outlined, suggesting that the early developmental achievements of the state that have since been positively contrasted with the general decline of the 1990s were in fact always subordinated to a violent project of consolidating party power. Second, the era of structural adjustment and indigenization of the economy in the 1990s is explained as a continuing attempt to maintain the ruling party's vital patronage networks, which then unravels completely by the end of the decade, leaving remnants of a genuine developmental discourse eclipsed by a new kind of survivalist discourse underpinned by increasingly oppressive state action. Third, the era of land invasions and the fierce competition for power between ZANU-PF and the MDC is examined in the context of the government's violent scorched-earth policy, where a final breakdown in societal and economic structures, exemplified by famine and hyperinflation, suggests that a radical break with Mugabe's rule is inevitable and might thereby open up space for new directions. Fourth, the chapter ends with a consideration of the potentialities inherent in this 'opening up' made possible by the current crisis. What are the prospects for a new politics emerging out of the current ruins of Zimbabwe, and can the protracted stand-off between opposing parties be construed as a window of opportunity out of which a discourse moving Zimbabwe beyond development as it has currently been conceived of can emerge?

Independence and consolidation of power: an ongoing struggle

Although Zimbabwe has become a byword for African failure, for the all too typical case of African popular aspirations to freedom and development being thwarted by corrupt and violent dictators,[5] the country's descent was by no means foreordained. There were, according to mainstream opinion among commentators on Zimbabwean independence, important reasons to believe that things should have turned out better.

> When it attained its independence in 1980, there were high hopes expressed for Zimbabwe's political and economic future. It was amongst the top four more industrialized countries in Sub-Saharan Africa; it possessed a more diversified economy than most countries; ... it had a better human resource base than most; and it had a middle-income status. Comparatively speaking, therefore, Zimbabwe had better prospects of making a head start in economic and political development than most countries on the continent. (Sachikonye 2002: 13)

Zimbabwe did indeed emerge into the independence era with a (by

African standards) developed and diversified economy but it is also the case that a century of colonial rule had firmly established a dual and extremely unevenly developed economy institutionalized along racial lines (Bond 1998). Policies ensuring white domination and maintenance of racial inequalities were key features of colonial, Southern Rhodesian and Rhodesian governments alike.[6] Independence was achieved following a lengthy and brutal war of independence, the legacy of which remains controversial and contested (Ranger 2004), and following which Zimbabwe's government faced immediate challenges relating to the need to accommodate established economic interests, responding to popular pressures for transformation and consolidating ZANU rule in the face of ongoing political disputes with Nkomo's ZAPU and the white minority. Transforming the economy and ownership of the land so that Zimbabwe's black majority (constituting about 95 per cent of the population at independence and more than 98 per cent today) could be brought into the mainstream, gearing economic growth towards broad-based development and fostering peace and stability in a divided society, as suggested by Mugabe's guiding principles of 'Reconciliation, Reconstruction and Resettlement', became key tasks for the government as official proclamations made clear its aspirations to developmental and progressive politics (Yates 1980).

The 1980s, particularly the years 1980–86, saw the Zimbabwean government pursuing what were generally considered by international and local observers alike to be genuine developmental policies. Improved public services extended access to education and healthcare to a majority of Zimbabweans, notably in rural areas (Dashwood 2000). These developments were perhaps possible and likely to be pursued only at a time when Zimbabwe's rulers felt some sense of obligation towards its liberated people and where collusion with entrenched business interests and an emerging black crony-capitalist class had not yet degenerated into a wholesale pursuit of private gains by means of increasingly predatory policies. This was a time when Zimbabwe outperformed the rest of sub-Saharan Africa on all social welfare indicators (ibid.: 41–3),[7] reflecting key policy goals established by the government following independence: the consolidation of state power, creating conditions of peace and national unity; embarking on a vigorous resettlement, reconstruction and rehabilitation programme; and laying down the political, economic and social bases for the transition to socialism (ibid.: 20). While it is doubtful that a transition to socialism was ever feasible or earnestly pursued (see Bond 1998), the general developmental thrust in the first decade of independence was in accordance with the belief that comprehensive improvements in the basic living conditions of Zimbabweans were necessary for structural transformation of the national economy to be possible. 'The [government's] stance was pro-poor, pro-redistribution; very explicitly so' (Mhone 2001). In an ironic twist, the developmental inroads and provision of public goods during the 1980s led to an increase in the working, middle and professional classes that in the 1990s would become the main proponents of improved democratic governance (Sachikonye 2002: 16).

From liberation to accommodation As was the case with most African liberation movements during the cold war the official rhetoric about development and progress in Zimbabwe had a distinct ideological pedigree. Despite the adoption during the 1970s of 'scientific socialist' principles by both Mugabe's ZANU and Nkomo's ZAPU, however, the direction of economic management in the post-independence era was by no means predetermined. Socialist rhetoric clashed with 'raw capitalist reality' (Bond 1998: 15), and although Zimbabweans had suffered fifteen years of violent struggle and warfare, the post-independence leadership initially determined that racial reconciliation would be necessary for sustained development and stability (Dashwood 2000: 20). Thus the government had to balance sharply divergent pressures: demands on the one hand by (white) business interests for some continuity in policy and for protection of private property rights (hence tempering plans for wholesale redistribution in the name of development) and on the other hand an urgent need to achieve some significant redistribution and redirection of resources to thereby enhance opportunities for the majority of poor Zimbabweans.

Notwithstanding the socialist rhetoric and an increased attention to the needs of poor Zimbabweans as witnessed by improvements in provisions of healthcare and educational attainment, Bond (1998) notes that an entrenched former settler elite and an emergent black bourgeoisie continued to enjoy the fruits of the exploitative arrangements of the past (cf. Dansereau and Zamponi 2005; Andreasson 2007a). Economic policy-making was therefore in the post-independence era more correctly characterized by some significant degree of continuity rather than radical change.

Indeed Zimbabwe perseveres long after independence as a semi-peripheral neo-colony – witness its profound reliance on exports of primary commodities, extreme differentiations in domestic income and wealth (which remained among the most skewed in the world), and Zimbabwe's wholesale adoption of the economic and social policies of international financiers. However, this reality was somewhat veiled during the 1980s by the combination of radical-populist rhetoric from government ... and the steady hand of a strong and visible national capitalist class (especially in manufacturing and agriculture). The notion that a socialist experiment was underway in the years after independence, all evidence to the contrary notwithstanding, served both groups well. (Bond 1998: 152)

This co-optation of the liberation movement by established financial and business interests had already been predicted in the latter days of the Rhodesian regime.

After national liberation, the petitbourgeois leadership can abandon its alliance with the workers and peasants and emerge as the new ruling class, by gaining certain concessions from both foreign and local capital and, in fact, forming a new alliance with these forces which they will need to stay in power. Of course, lip service commitment, a la Kenya, to the masses, will be made. (Murapa 1977: 28, quoted in Bond 2001a: 62)

By the end of the 1980s, however, President Mugabe himself had increasingly come to doubt the wisdom of accommodating business interests. He voiced concern about pro-market forces within ZANU-PF, about a 'very powerful bourgeois group [championing] the cause of international finance and national private capital ... opposed to the development and growth of a socialist and egalitarian society in Zimbabwe' (Mugabe 1989: 358). This group of people – including then ministers Bernard Chidzero (Finance), Kumbirayi Kangai (Industry and Commerce), Tichaendepi Masaya (Finance) and Kombo Moyana (Reserve Bank) – had of course emerged under the patronage of Mugabe himself (Bond 1998: 201). It is, furthermore, an irony that such doubts were articulated by the president only two years before the country embarked on its own version of structural adjustment, the legacy of which has been so controversial across Africa and which would end up shaping the crisis to come in important ways.

While the above constitutes a relatively non-controversial and commonly accepted summary of Zimbabwe's advanced level of socioeconomic development as compared to other African states at the time of independence, as well as its early successes with development, it neglects the violent road to independence and the consequences thereof. For all its potential advantages vis-à-vis many other African countries at independence, Zimbabwe was born through violent struggle and that struggle has never really abated in the minds and actions of its rulers. The notion of an ongoing struggle, symbolized by the frequently (mis-) appropriated slogan *A luta continua* ('the struggle continues'; initially the rallying cry for the struggle against Portuguese colonial rule in Mozambique) by those calling for perpetual revolution throughout southern Africa,[8] is at the root of the problem with Zimbabwe's violent and predatory post-independence trajectory (as is the case in South Africa). Continued references throughout the post-independence era to politics as an 'anti-colonial' *struggle* (which was almost by necessity a violent one while minority regimes still ruled southern African nations by force), often in a context where such rhetoric is deployed to justify the marginalization of groups in society representing a genuine and potentially persuasive opposition to the conduct of post-independence governments, have sometimes resulted in the justification of intolerance of opposition, the abuse of power by government officials and an increasingly authoritarian means of governing. Southall (2003) has argued that the difficulty of liberation movements adapting to their new roles as governing political parties in post-transition dispensations plays an important role in the difficulty of consolidating democratic transitions throughout southern Africa, and thereby also in exacerbating elitist tendencies and thwarting development.

An early turn to violence

> Regime power in Zimbabwe has always been buttressed by coercion, chillingly symbolized in ZANU-PF's trademark emblem, the fist. The political elite take as articles of faith the assumptions that violence was effective in delivering independence and that repression is the party's most effective weapon for countering real and imagined threats. (Bratton and Masunungure 2008: 50)

Somewhat paradoxically the early developmental trend coexisted with generally anti-democratic behaviour and ongoing repression, sometimes intensely violent, of political opposition by the government. The harshly authoritarian means by which the ZANU-dominated regime pursued consolidation of state power, which culminated in the brutal repression of political dissidents (primarily Ndebele ZAPU supporters in Matabeleland and Midlands), presaged the government's future willingness to blatantly cast aside democratic principles when faced with political opposition. Hammar (2008: 419) argues that Zimbabweans in the 'rural and urban margins' have been 'criminalised and securitised', i.e. identified as potential threats to state power and dealt with accordingly by means of 'state campaigns' making them victims of regularly recurring state violence. Looking ahead to the violent land invasions of 2000–03, we see the re-emergence of a particular kind of state-sponsored violence that is a direct legacy of practices developed during the 1970s war of national liberation (see D. Moore 2008: 16–17). As part of the violent intimidation of Zimbabweans in the run-up to the 2000 and 2002 elections, ZANU-PF activists rounded up suspected opposition supporters whom they forced to dance and chant liberation war songs at rallies known as *pungwe*. These all-night rallies constitute a form of 'political education', not to mention humiliation and brutalization, of political opponents and were widely used by ZANLA forces during the 1970s as well as during the *Gukurahundi* terror of the 1980s (Rutherford 2008: 91).

The willingness with which the government from the early days of independence resorted to violence as a response to those segments of civil society that did not fall into line, whether by deploying troops and police to crush strikes at Anglo American's coal mines and sugar estates in the very first weeks of independence in May 1980 (Bond 1998: 153), or in the following years unleashing crack troops against 'dissidents' real and imagined in the *Gukurahundi* campaign, suggests that a normal political environment in which issues of development and aspirations regarding what an independent Zimbabwe ought to look like never had a chance to develop. Given the serious nature of the intermittent violence deployed by the government throughout this early era, which is generally considered to be Zimbabwe's relatively successful period, it might well be the case that post-independence politics in Zimbabwe should be analysed and understood in the context of societal post-traumatic stress disorder that is taken to have profoundly shaped socio-political trajectories in other countries that have experienced serious trauma on a society-wide scale rather than be periodized into a 'successful' 1980s, an increasingly corrupt and confrontational 1990s and a 2000s in which the country descends into chaos and violence. In other words, the violence of the current crisis is not new, or merely the outcome of previous societal pressures left unresolved; it is indeed a *continuation* of the violence that precedes and immediately follows Zimbabwe's independence (see Ndlovu-Gatsheni 2009: 1149).

In terms of really reflecting on what post-traumatic stress in the wake of the *Gukurahundi* entails, we might consider Moyo's (2008) reminiscence about the atrocities committed during this campaign.

We quickly see pregnant women's stomachs being ripped apart with bayonets, just to make sure the unborn boys are eliminated. The reasons were that boys would grow up to become dissidents, a term that under normal circumstances would have meant anyone who had deserted the national army to take up arms against the government. However this is not what the Korean trained soldiers understood by the term. They used it loosely to mean any grown up male or anyone who was seen to be sympathetic to Joshua Nkomo's cause. We also see fathers forced to rape their daughters in front of their wives and children; we see sons coerced to have sex with their mothers. We grudgingly see families slaughtering each other. We see fathers killing their sons; sons killing their mothers and mothers pounding their babies to death. (ibid.; cf. CCJP 1999)

This is ghastly and dehumanizing violence that is comparable in its intensity if not scope to that witnessed in many other horrific bouts of societal violence of varying scale across the continent, from Idi Amin's Uganda to Rwanda during the 1994 genocide. A comprehensive and well-regarded report on the *Gukurahundi* violence in Zimbabwe suggests that the implications for society of this violence are dire indeed, as 'the multiple impact on people in physical, psychological and material terms has been enormous' and exacerbated by the fact that a deep sense of injustice, combined with fears for future violence, is bound to linger as 'no efforts have been made to alleviate their plight and those who caused the damage have not been made answerable' (CCJP 1999: 30).

Not surprisingly Zimbabwe's nominal democracy never managed to consolidate and the socialist one-party state remained a stated goal, however symbolic, supported by official rhetoric throughout the 1980s. The 1980 constitution negotiated under British supervision at Lancaster House in 1979 placed some constraints on the development of a one-party state but political opposition was clearly curtailed, as manifested by the coerced merger of ZANU and ZAPU in the late 1980s. The move in the direction of a *de jure* one-party state, which included discussion in 1990 within the twenty-six-member Politburo of precisely such a move, was however abandoned in 1991, owing partly to opposition from ZAPU members in high levels of government (Sithole 2000: 71–5). In addition, the collapse of socialism in eastern Europe and an imminent neoliberal restructuring of Zimbabwe's economy put plans for a socialist one-party state on permanent hold.

Structural adjustment, indigenization and the unravelling of patronage

Following the consolidation of ZANU dominance and an increasingly collusive corporatist pact between the state and both established (white) and emerging (black) business, Zimbabwe was by the beginning of the 1990s characterized by a fairly complicated and antagonistic, if overall stable and seemingly manageable, set of relations between the state and these market actors, even if relations between the state and civil society were more problematic. Nevertheless, as both Bayart (1993) and Sandbrook (1993) had argued in their analyses of the political economy of post-colonial Africa, the relationship between the state and market actors in Zimbabwe was one of the few which in Africa could be characterized as an 'historical bloc' (cf. Carmody and Taylor 2003). Therefore the subsequent descent into disorder following the decision in 1991 to begin a process of structural adjustment is worthy of careful attention. According to Carmody and Taylor (ibid.), 'ESAP undermined the productive base of the economy ... [thus destroying] the alliance [between state, white capital and emerging black capital] which underwrote the first ten years of independence'.

> Once ESAP came to be implemented, the more cooperative relationship between the ruling elite and the economic elites evaporated. The economic elites soon began to question the government's handling of the reform process and came to the view that the government was not wholly committed to reforms, which resulted in the perception that the government was either incapable or unwilling to implement reforms, or both. A consequence of the lack of democratic means of expression has been that the subordinate classes, the peasants, working class, and the petty-bourgeoisie outside the state, were not able to voice their interests effectively. (Dashwood 2000: 193)

The origins of ZANU as a liberation movement steeped in lengthy and brutal conflict with the Rhodesian settler regime suggest that the somewhat surprising predisposition in the early years of independence of the state to accommodate business and other capital interests was bound to unravel. This is not an argument that is generally pursued or featured prominently in accounts of Zimbabwe's turn towards increasing authoritarianism, which instead emphasize its comparatively high level of industrial development at independence, the relative ease with which the ZANU government was 'captured' by capital interests, or which understand ESAP as the watershed moment in setting the country on a path to inevitable crisis and breakdown (e.g. Bond 1998; Bond and Manyanya 2002: Darnolf and Laakso 2003). In any case, a renewed effort by the state to maintain its patronage networks while at the same time keeping popular pressures for transformation and development at bay was embarked upon before state–business relations finally collapsed at the end of the decade. While ESAP was not *the* cause of the current crisis it is not possible to properly understand the onset of this crisis without first considering Zimbabwe's experience with structural adjustment.

The road to structural adjustment So how did Zimbabwe's government move from accommodation and collusion with business interests and the new black elite tied to state patronage in the 1980 to structural reforms and an unravelling of the previous decade's corporatist arrangements in the 1990s? While ZANU-PF had by 1990 consolidated its political power (winning 117 of 120 contested seats to parliament in the 1990 elections) and domestic challenges to its power had not yet materialized as they would by the later years of the decade (Sachikonye 2002: 16), the economic situation was appreciably deteriorating. Hence the voices urging a change of direction (IFIs, multinational corporations, business interests) became increasingly powerful, among them the then World Bank chief economist and former Rhodesian resident Stanley Fisher, who devised new strategies for 'maintaining leverage' over indebted countries by increased conditionality intended to produce the policy changes deemed necessary by the Bank (Bond 1998: 353).

IFIs – the International Monetary Fund (IMF) and the World Bank – enjoyed greater leverage in Zimbabwe than they did in neighbouring countries like Botswana and South Africa, and these institutions as well as other capital actors began increasing pressures on the government throughout the second half of the 1980s (Dashwood 2000: 71–84). The collapse of the Eastern Bloc in Europe coupled with an ideological dominance of neoliberal ideas (the so-called 'Washington Consensus') within the international policy community enabled pro-market actors in Zimbabwe to halt the state-led redistributionist drive for transformation by combining forces with the IFIs to usher in ESAP in 1991 (see Bond and Saunders 2005). Once the government's fiscal irresponsibility had resulted in rapidly dwindling opportunities for borrowing, arguments for structural adjustment suddenly became quite appealing.[9] The IMF and the World Bank worked with key economic decision-makers in government, notably then Minister of Finance Chidzero, to convince the government of the need to embark on ESAP (Bond 1998: chs 11–12). Co-optation has long been an effective strategy for IFIs trying to garner support for structural adjustments from influential politicians in developing countries and following generous appointments, such as chairmanship of the twenty-two-member IMF–World Bank Development Committee at the 1986 annual meetings and chairmanship at the UN Conference on Trade and Development (UNCTAD) in 1987, Chidzero soon came around to the IFIs' point of view.

Urging government in the direction of neoliberal reform dovetailed nicely with the vested interests of externally oriented businesses in Zimbabwe, i.e. commercial farmers and the mining industry, eager to diminish state involvement in the economy and increasing capital mobility to thereby strengthen their own bargaining power vis-à-vis government. 'There [was] a lot of pressure internally from the business sector, usually oligopolistic capital, whether of a foreign multinational nature or of a domestic nature', applied to convince key government officials to move towards restructuring and liberalization of the economy (Mhone 2001). Whereas some industrialists who had benefited from protectionism did not support liberalization (Robinson 2002: 43), Jenkins (2002: 40) identifies the CZI, the ZNCC, the CFU and the Employers' Federation of Zimbabwe (EMCOZ) as particularly 'strong, white-dominated' organizations. These groups were all particularly well positioned to apply pressure on the government as they represented powerful economic interests and had a lobbying expertise built up under the previous government. The post-independence brain drain from the public to the private sector further enhanced their power and influence.

In the end, the fundamental changes in government thinking on macro-economic policy took place in the years 1987–91. At that time a consensus slowly emerged among key state officials that challenged belief in the ability of state-interventionist policies to deliver, either on developmental promises or on political legitimacy and stability. Market reforms of some kind were instead deemed necessary for Zimbabwe to attain sufficient economic growth (Dashwood 2000: 115). The inability of a stagnant economy to create jobs for the increasing number of well-educated Zimbabweans (a result of the initial improvements in access to education) created a sense that economic change was necessary. As noted by Minister of Finance Chidzero in 1987, 'the fact that increasing numbers of young graduates and school leavers walk our streets with the intellectual equipment but without jobs and unable to find a role to play in the economy, strikes at the very heart of society' (Chidzero, quoted in ibid.: 116).

This new thinking on how to achieve growth in Zimbabwe resulted in the July 1990 *Economic Policy Statement*, released along with the 1990 budget and the more detailed *Zimbabwe: A Framework for Economic Reform (1991–95)* released in 1991. *The Second Five Year National Development Plan* released in December 1991 was based on these two documents (ibid.: 114). The 1991 framework for economic reform, supposedly home-grown but 'tellingly, written in American English as are all World Bank documents' (Bond 1998: 380), would improve the Zimbabwean economy by, among other things, cutting the civil service by 25 per cent by the year 1995 and phase out 'all labor restrictions, price controls, exchange controls, interest rate controls, investment regulations, import restrictions, and government subsidies' (ibid.: 372). Zimbabwe would forgo privatization of its many parastatals only in this first phase of structural adjustment.

ESAP The optimistic predictions of ESAP were never to materialize. Instead of annual 5 per cent economic growth rates, economic growth averaged just above 1 per cent from 1991 to 1995. Only in 1994 did economic growth exceed 5 per cent. Inflation, instead of being reduced to 10 per cent, averaged 30 per cent during the ESAP years (as inflation is now counted in the many millions of per cent, it has simply become a statistical abstraction lending a sense of unreality to commentaries on the depth of Zimbabwe's current economic meltdown). Rather than a projected 5 per cent of GDP, the budget deficit rose above 10 per cent in the same time period. The trade deficit exploded during the early 1990s and the real contribution to GDP of manufacturing fell 18 per cent from 1991 to 1995.[10] On the social front, advances made in education and health provision during the 1980s were reversed during the 1990s when real per capita spending on healthcare fell by 20 per cent from 1990 to 1995 just as the HIV/AIDS pandemic hit the country (Bond and Manyanya 2002: 32–7).

Despite these many disappointments with the results of structural adjustment the World Bank's (1995b: 23) *Project Completion Report* for ESAP concluded by awarding the best possible grade, 'highly satisfactory', for the first stage of the programme.

> Trade liberalization proceeded without delays ... [and] the foreign exchange control system has been largely dismantled. All current account transactions have been freed from exchange controls and import licensing and the exchange rate is now market-determined. (World Bank 1995a: 7)

> Erich Bloch, a leading business commentator in Zimbabwe, proclaimed that

the extent that inflation has declined, the significant reductions in direct taxation, the liberalisation of trade and virtual elimination of import controls with a consequential elimination of most shortages, the immense relaxations of exchange controls, a somewhat more stable currency exchange environment, and the extent of new investment in the last two years are but a few indicators of the achievements of *Esap* to date. (*Financial Gazette*, 5 January 1995, cited in Bond and Manyanya 2002: 28–9)

Later yet, on the very eve of the government's ominous policy reversal, *The Economist* proclaimed that

Africa is a bit short of economic stars, so countries that do well tend to get noticed. Hence the enthusiasm for Zimbabwe. It has been free of full-scale civil war for nearly 20 years, earning a reputation as a stable, peaceful, and relatively organised place to do business. (*Economist*, 2 October 1997)[11]

Zimbabwe had, according to *The Economist*, reached this point by launching an economically invigorating privatization programme and by seeming 'committed to further liberalisation'. Although ESAP may not in the end have been properly or consistently implemented, poor governance and implementation of policy cannot have been the only reasons for the escalating crisis of the 1990s. The end of ESAP in 1997 and the collapse of relations between state, market and societal actors prompted the last stage in Zimbabwe's descent. Neither neoliberal policies nor the subsequent violent policy reversal have managed to alleviate the deepening crisis.

Most notably, the shift from the 1980s emphasis on developmental policies to an emphasis on attaining macroeconomic stability in the 1990s retained the nationalist character of Zimbabwe's original development strategy while significantly weakening the previous commitment to social welfare (Dashwood 2000: 114). The most significant results of the rapid liberalization of finance and trade in the 1990s were, in the end, increasing volatility and vulnerability of markets, deindustrialization and worsening problems with poverty and marginalization. Liberalization of the economy provided opportunities as well as (apparently many more) costs, with large-scale business wishing to avoid limitations posed by inherent limits on domestic demand and many manufacturers less than able to compete in international markets (Mhone and Bond 2001: 12). In addition, Zimbabwe's participation in the war to secure control of the Democratic Republic of Congo (DRC) in the wake of Mobutu's

133

demise and the looting of the DRC's natural resources exemplify the corrupt practices designed to keep Zimbabwe's patronage system alive (Maclean 2002).[12]

These are typical examples of how key state officials attempted to resolve societal pressures by pursuing short-term private gains, i.e. by making side payments to pressure groups like the war veterans and corrupt businessmen that together with government elites comprise Zimbabwe's contemporary ruling coalition. When government officials in the end became convinced that liberalization – an attempt to maintain money flows to government elites to continue funding the collusive relations with crony capital actors on which the government's power depended – would not reinvigorate the Zimbabwean economy,

> the government's response was, tragically, a self-destructive return to dirigisme plus corruption/malgovernance, without the structural transformations required to correct earlier problems of economic dis-articulation (Mhone and Bond 2001: 12–13) ... [B]y the time that political opposition consolidated in 1998–99, leading to a new, labour-led political party that nearly won the 2000 parliamentary elections [the MDC], leading ZANU ministers had come to the conclusion that ESAP was their most important policy error. (ibid.: 19)

Indigenization and exclusion Wishing to liberalize the economy was not necessarily indicative of a commitment by government to bringing about genuine socio-economic transformation, but rather as a new strategy for staying in power. A renewed push for indigenization was prompted by the fact that, by the late 1980s

> the state had no policy for the indigenisation of the private sector. Sometimes speeches were made with veiled threats about forcing affirmative action, but no directives were given and whites learned that there would be little interference, regardless of what blacks said. Blacks were promoted into management positions, and some black businesses were created, but progress on this latter course was slow during the 1980s. It has been argued that the government's attitude towards black entrepreneurs was ambivalent: a government claiming to be Marxist-Leninist was irresolute about capital accumulation, and a growing economic base for blacks could reduce their dependence on the state, and hence the government's control. (Jenkins 2002: 40)

Not so much a case of an honest conversion to economic sensibility (as defined by the then prevailing consensus), then, as a sign of shifting relations at the commanding heights of the economy.

Indigenization of Zimbabwe's economy reflects the ebb and flow of relations between the state and both established (white) and emerging (black) business and their respective lobbying groups. The pace of indigenization of the Zimbabwean economy was tempered during most of the 1980s and 1990s owing to the government's unwillingness to promote autonomous bases of power in society such as an emerging black business class independent of state patronage (Raftopoulos 1996). Where indigenization occurred, it generally involved high-level government officials acquiring commercial farms and entering into commercial ventures. A proliferation of parastatals in the 1980s created a 'state dependent petty-bourgeoisie' and the lack of structural transformation during that same period prompted increasing demands for greater involvement by black Zimbabweans in the formal economy (Bond and Manyanya 2002: 23–7). An Indigenous Business Development Centre (IBDC) was formed in 1990 to promote black entrepreneurship by allocating state assets to black Zimbabweans on preferential terms. A Select Committee on the Indigenization of the National Economy was established in 1991. A more stridently nationalist lobbying group for emerging black business interests, the Affirmative Action Group (AAG), was established in 1994 to press harder for transformation of the economy where it felt the IBDC and other groups promoting indigenization had failed (Raftopoulos 1996; cf. D. Moore 2003). To the degree that new economic groups with some significant level of independence from the state have emerged following independence, they have not enjoyed the same prolific rise to positions of influence, nor have they been as smoothly integrated with the old establishment as has the post-apartheid 'black bourgeoisie' in South Africa, and Zimbabwe therefore lacks a new generation of black businessmen who are accepted as bona fide businessmen in international financial circles, as are many of their South African counterparts.

The evolution of indigenization policies in Zimbabwe provides a stark illustration of the dangers of essentializing the notion of indigeneity. Basing indigenization policies on a narrow and arguably arbitrary notion of who is indigenous produces an exclusivist debate and politics which ends up perpetuating the marginalization of minorities. James Muzondidya (2007) provides a vivid account of the exclusivist and with time overtly racist deployment by government of indigenization policies as a means to affect socio-economic transformation for the benefit of Zimbabwe's 'native' majorities (i.e. the Shona and the Ndebele). This is a process of indigenization, first of the civil service and then of land and other spheres of economic activity, in which the various minority peoples of Zimbabwe, notably coloureds, Indians and immigrant labourers from neighbouring countries like Malawi and Mozambique (and of course the white 'settlers'), remain marginalized by the fact that they are not included in various black empowerment programmes, most importantly land reform. Given the close connection between notions of belonging and indigeneity, indigenization in Zimbabwe is to benefit the 'native African' or *vana vedhu/abantwana bomhlabathi* ('sons of the soil' in chiShona and isiNdebele respectively)[13] in whom are vested 'pre-eminent rights over the country's land and other resources', and not the rural immigrant labourers (*vabvakure/amadingandawo*) seen to lack ancestral homes in Zimbabwe or the urban minorities (primarily coloureds and Indians) with no connection to ancestral homelands in the rural areas (*kumusha*) (ibid.: 325–9).

The importance of being able to demonstrate a connection to the soil, i.e. a genuine belonging, becomes particularly important in a major controversy around which post-independence politics revolves – the issue of land ownership.

> In a country such as Zimbabwe, where the economy is primarily agro-based and access to land is an important factor determining not only livelihood but also one's sense of belonging, the continuing exclusion of subject minorities from land in the non-commercial, rural sphere meant serious marginalisation from both the economy and the nation. (ibid.: 333)

Not only does this exclusivist usage of the notion of being indigenous result in the continued marginalization of minority peoples in the post-colonial era, it also provides an instructive example of how indigenization policies based on such an understanding of indigeneity can in a volatile sociocultural context quickly be transformed from being 'merely' a policy that neglects minorities into one that *actively targets* those minorities for punitive sanctions.

> [A] common characteristic of such state-driven campaigns of exclusion and displacement has been the practice of identifying a *dangerous other* (represented in the broader sense as a threat of impurity to the body politic of the nation), and then cleansing (by fire demolition or removal), containing (by imprisonment or encampment), or excising (by torture or even death) the contaminating danger. Such dehumanising actions not only

dislodge people from place but from the rights and entitlements of citizenship, and from belonging to the nation as a whole. (Hammar 2008: 420)

Muzondidya (2007) explains how the emphasis on 'race and nativism' during and following the violent land invasions of 2000–03 originates in an already narrow understanding among the ruling elites of indigeneity, which in turn originates in a failure at the time of independence to break with the colonial/Rhodesian era's divisive categorization of the country's many peoples.[14]

[T]he Zimbabwean government has abandoned both its political conciliatory approach and the inclusive nationalism of the early period and instead adopted a radical, exclusive nationalist stance. One of the central features of this new order ... 'has been the emergence of a revived nationalism delivered in a particularly virulent form, with race as a key trope within the discourse, and a selective rendition of the liberation history deployed as an ideological policing agent in the public debate'. [Raftopoulos 2004: 160] (Muzondidya 2007: 333)[15]

With the violent land reforms that began in 2000 and with the simultaneous ushering in of a new era of 'militarization' of Zimbabwean society (Bond and Saunders 2005; Bratton and Masunungure 2008), or what Scarnecchia (2006) terms a 'fascist cycle', the official rhetoric surrounding the concept of indigeneity and the justifications for why and how indigenization ought to be carried out are ratcheted up, taking on a malicious and racist tone (cf. Rutherford 2008: 86). Increasingly, indigenization becomes a policy of reserving Zimbabwe 'for black people only', where all whites become 'foreigners or usurpers' and other minority peoples, such as the African immigrants often employed by these whites on their farms, and the coloureds and Indians who often do business in the urban areas, become a fifth column within Zimbabwean society to at best be suspected or at worst actively persecuted (Muzondidya 2007: 334). Urged on by powerful indigenous groups like the AAG and the war veterans, who have been most blatant in their 'racial attacks', 'invective and discrimination against subject races' have generally increased (ibid.: 338). And where the public discourse turns exclusivist and violent the outbreak of violence is often not far away.

The employment of a historical narrative of violent victimisation is often utilised to legitimate the use of violence ... remember the observations of Franz Fanon [1963] and his advocacy of violence to cleanse and restore the psyche of the colonial victim ... With the redeployment of revolutionary anti-imperial narratives built upon historical memories of violent victimisation comes an often explicit legitimisation of violence against the 'aliens' and the 'invaders' [as with Zimbabwe's 'Third *Chimurenga*']. (Dunn 2009: 124)

The exclusivist and increasingly racist rhetoric surrounding indigenization in Zimbabwe has not only been driven by the political calculations of government officials and lobbying groups like the AAG and the war veterans. Zimbabwe's post-colonial intellectuals have also played a role, if not always a conscious one in what has turned out to be a particularly malign 'indigenous turn' in Zimbabwean politics and society. Among this post-colonial intellectual class,

> the primary affiliations were to the 'legacy' of the liberation struggle, a strong commitment to a statist developmental project, and an anti-imperialist stance. It is fair to say that this 'Left nationalism' was the dominant ideological framework for many intellectuals in the 1980s. A great deal of the intellectual support for the ruling party in the political crisis that emerged from the late 1990s emerged from this background, stressing, in particular, a loyalty to selective 'ideals' of the liberation struggle [and] support for an 'indigenous' national economic project ... (Raftopoulos 2006: 206)[16]

We see in the example of Zimbabwe's highly exclusivist and ultimately very violent form of indigenization, which has concentrated on transformation of politics and the economy (specifically land ownership) to thereby perpetuate the government's rule by patronage and weaken its opposition, an example of how indigenization can in such circumstances amount to little more than elite enrichment at the expense of those in whose name indigenization is pursued and a catastrophe for those who become actively targeted by the government as obstacles to its policies of indigenization. In this way Zimbabwe's predatory indigenization project has played a central part in producing the country's current crisis, from which a different type of polity will eventually emerge, but where the legacy of indigenization will remain a complicating factor to be engaged with by any future government genuinely interested in braving the enormous challenge of setting Zimbabwe on a path towards healing and a sustainable future.

An unresolved crisis What is perhaps most notable regarding the ever-complicated and never quite cooperative nature of Zimbabwe's state–

business relations is how serious conflict regarding the direction of the national economy was never resolved at any level. The state has not managed to resolve its own internal conflicts regarding the proper course for national policy-making on economic matters and severe fluctuations, uncertainty and distrust characterize the entirety of the ESAP era and its aftermath.

> [S]tate policy is subject to dramatic shifts in policy depending on whether external constraints or the potential loss of power resulting from internal socio-economic conditions are more pressing. The state can implement transformative projects, such as ESAP (externally driven) or land invasions (internally driven). (Carmody and Taylor 2003)

What we see unfolding during the increasingly volatile 1990s is how the government becomes increasingly unable to contain pressures from civil society and the emerging political opposition (which coalesces into the MDC), among whom are those Zimbabweans increasingly frustrated by rapidly falling living standards and an increasingly authoritarian government (Bond 1999). With increasing turmoil throughout the decade and a growing realization on the part of both Zimbabweans and their government that ESAP would deepen the economic crisis rather than resolve it, state–business relations became increasingly unmanageable. Mhone and Bond (2001: 11) characterize this unravelling as a movement 'from dirigisme to structural adjustment and back'. The high cost of Zimbabwe's momentous involvement in the war in the DRC also served to counteract any positive effects on the macroeconomic balance sheet of ESAP-related austerity measures (see Maclean 2002: 522–4). The end result, what Bratton and Masunungure (2008: 42) identify as five 'key elements' of the ZANU-PF 'heritage', is: 1) an ideological belief in its right to rule in perpetuity; 2) a party machinery that penetrates the organs of the state; 3) a corrupted economy vested in the hands of party loyalists; 4) an institutionalized role in policy-making for military commanders; 5) and a heavy reliance on violence, increasingly outsourced to auxiliary forces.

So in the absence of viable forces geared towards broad-based development, mounting domestic pressures for a reversal of the country's wholesale economic decline and the disillusionment among state officials about the possibility for development via the neoliberal/ESAP route, the government turned against the political opposition, including farmers and other (primarily white and foreign) business interests, in a ruthless and coordinated attempt to shore up domestic political power and legitimacy and to perhaps find an independent course of action in the interests of safeguarding the political hegemony of ZANU-PF. An integral part of this strategy was to insist that this new phase in the government's attempt to reclaim a rapidly eroding legitimacy constituted a key component in the wider 'anti-imperialist' project, whereby, as evident in public speeches by President Mugabe and other government officials, Zimbabwe would be rid of foreign exploiters and local collaborators once and for all (cf. Phimister and Raftopoulos 2004; Bratton and Masunungure 2008). The combination of a sharply divisive and violent past and the lack of democratic consolidation created unmanageable problems that became exacerbated throughout the post-independence period, to finally unravel in the complete breakdown of legitimate rule in the 2000s.

The perfect storm: land invasions and Zimbabwe's final descent into violence

The notion of cleansing the soil from an oppressive or exploitative presence in the form of a 'settler' people has echoes in other post-colonial African contexts where scapegoating of minority peoples has had dire consequences. Mahmood Mamdani (2008), himself a Ugandan of Indian origin and part of the Asian community expelled from Uganda by Idi Amin in 1972, notes that the land reforms in Zimbabwe have garnered some public support (as they have in South Africa) because of the deeply felt sense that Africans having been deprived of ancestral lands constitutes one of the foremost crimes perpetuated against them during the colonial era. Mugabe has in this case ruled 'not only by coercion, but by consent', and this is where the comparison with Uganda under Amin becomes clear. Mamdani writes:

> My abiding recollection of my [return to Uganda in 1979] is that no one I met opposed Amin's expulsion of the 'Asians'. Most merely said: 'It was bad the way he did it'. The same is likely to be said of the land transfers in Zimbabwe ... [W]hatever they made of Amin's brutality, the Ugandan people experienced the Asian expulsion of 1972 – and not the formal handover in 1962 – as the dawn of true independence. The people of Zimbabwe are likely to remember 2000–3 as the end of the settler colonial era. *Any assessment of contemporary Zimbabwe needs to begin with this sobering fact.* (ibid.; emphasis added)

By the early months of 2000 Zimbabwe's social, economic and political contradictions had come to a head and the country stood poised to take its final 'plunge' (see Bond and Manyanya 2002) into the chaos from which MDC and ZANU-PF leaderships along with external power brokers (primarily South Africa, the EU and the USA) are now attempting to extricate the country while securing whatever political and economic outcomes are favoured by each. Zimbabwe had now entered

> a zone of *indistinction* ... where the frontiers between the rule of law and chaos disappear, decisions about life and death become entirely arbitrary, and everything becomes possible – marked by an unprecedented degree of torture, mutilation, and mass killing. (Mbembe 2002: 267, quoted in Ndlovu-Gatsheni 2009: 1149)

With the convenience of hindsight it seems clear that the land invasions which followed the rejection by Zimbabwe's electorate of the February 2000 constitutional referendum – holding the referendum was a government reaction to popular pressure exerted by the National Constitutional Assembly (NCA) and other actors – which aimed to entrench the power of the presidency and to pave the way for sweeping land redistribution without paying compensation to landowners, constitute a final attempt on the part of the government to disentangle itself from a by then unmanageable set of pressures and demands on its patronage networks stemming from the failed structural adjustment policies of the 1990s, the looming threat of the war veterans and the challenge of an increasingly powerful political opposition led by the MDC (Sithole 2001; Dorman 2003).

In addition, and this is important for considering the implications for future discourses on development that may emerge in the wake of the current crisis, the land invasions and subsequent stand-off between the Zimbabwean government and the MDC opposition and international detractors of Mugabe's regime (Western governments, IFIs and so on) became, as was indeed the Zimbabwean government's intention, part and parcel of a greater 'anti-imperialist' and 'pan-African' problematic. 'The land question in particular has been located within a discourse of legitimate redress for colonial injustice, language which has resonated on the African continent, and within the Third World more generally' (Phimister and Raftopoulos 2004: 385; cf. Raftopoulos 2006: 212). In this sense, the political context in which the current crisis plays out, and out of which durable solutions will have to emerge, relates the immediate questions about what to do with the collapsed economy and about power-sharing between ZANU-PF and the MDC and the future role of international actors (IFIs, development agencies, businesses, etc.) in the country not only to the theories of political transitions and development but to a wider set of post-colonial issues to do with justice, emancipation and the possibility of new conceptualizations of what development entails and what an appropriate balance between the needs of community versus individuals, and of society versus markets, ought to be. These issues will be difficult to resolve no matter what the ultimate outcome in Zimbabwe.

Land reform as a last desperate strategy The issue of land reform and of returning the land to its 'rightful owners' (an idea that has been abused for political gain throughout the post-independence era)[17] has always been central to politics in Zimbabwe as well as an issue capable of mobilizing popular actions and sentiments (Rutherford 2008: 84; cf. Worby 2001; J. Alexander 2006). Thus it is not surprising that the government in the end decided on a more drastic course of action to resolve the land issue. At the same time the government's conduct during these land invasions was also symptomatic of a perhaps greater than expected willingness on the part of the ruling elite to pursue short-term interests (as a means to remain in power) at any cost while at the same time ignoring the importance of long-term state–business cooperation for the government's ability to continue dispensing patronage. While any final decision to foment invasions of commercial farms and to fully back the landless peasants and war veterans doing so may have been made rashly in a moment of crisis (D. Moore 2008: 30–1), earlier legal decisions paved the way for a seemingly inevitable confrontation between landowners and various state-supported popular movements. Revisions in 1992 of the 1985 Land Acquisitions Act, a Land Tenure Commission report in 1994, an Agricultural Framework Document in 1996 and the designation of 1,471 large-scale commercial farms for confiscation by the state in 1997 all pointed the way to the violent process of land invasion and redistribution that has been at the core of Zimbabwe's deepening crisis ever since (Dashwood 2000: 180–1).

While land redistribution has served to enhance agricultural productivity and form the basis for broad-based development elsewhere (e.g. Taiwan and South Korea), the lack of basic accountability on the part of the government and the subsequent use of land redistribution as a government tool in a short-sighted battle against domestic political opposition became a recipe for further disaster.[18] Instead of utilizing land redistribution as a tool for genuine economic empowerment of Zimbabwe's poor peasants and implementing the policy with care to minimize negative effects on commercial farmers, the government has used land redistribution to reward political cronies, i.e. placating the war veterans and other assorted interest groups that by the late 1990s were actively threatening the government's legitimacy and power. The government has also used its land policies and attendant widespread intimidation and violence to destroy the (white) commercial farmers as an economic (and political) force in the country, thereby attempting to also hobble the political opposition that these farmers have generally supported (although many farmers have claimed to be apolitical in a bid to escape persecution by the government).

Thus the 'fast-track' land redistribution scheme became an effective tool for mobilizing war veterans and other government supporters against the government's main political rivals, in particular the MDC and its supporters among poor (urban) Zimbabweans (initially concentrated among the Ndebele minority), the country's commercial farmers and white businessmen as well as international organizations and governments (see Rutherford 2008). The MDC, which originated in Zimbabwe's labour movement and is led by former ZCTU head Morgan Tsvangirai, has garnered substantial support from white capital. Indicative of this link was the appointment of Eddie Cross, a leading CZI official who was at the time a believer in the need for further ESAP-style 'shock therapy', as economic secretary of the MDC in 2000 (Bond and Manyanya 2002: 93). Consequently the Zimbabwean government and state media have aimed consistently to highlight the connections between the MDC and white capital as represented by organizations like the CFU and CZI to thereby taint the MDC as an 'imperialist stooge' (e.g. *The Herald*, 12 June and 9 October 2002; cf. Mashingaidze 2006; Tendi 2008).

As current reports from aid organizations and other observers highlight the catastrophic humanitarian situation in Zimbabwe and the increasing toll of widespread starvation, it is worth recalling that already a couple of years into the land invasions the World Food Programme reported that as much as half the Zimbabwean population was facing 'severe malnutrition and death caused by hunger', while at the same time the government decided to put a final nail into the coffin of agricultural productivity.[19] While President Mugabe heralded the land redistribution programme as 'a firm launching pad for our fight against poverty and food insecurity', the result was in fact a catastrophic fall in agricultural output. In a further attempt at using land redistribution to silence domestic opposition the government reportedly began starving peasants who supported Tsvangirai and the MDC in the 2002 presidential election by denying them access to food aid brought in by primarily Western governments and NGOs (*Economist*, 27 June 2002).

The use of land reform as a cynical and disastrous attempt at countering increasing domestic opposition to ZANU-PF rule has generated threats by government and the war veterans against not only farmers but businesses in other sectors of the economy as well. By the time the land invasions were in full force, President Mugabe was declaring that the government was ready to seize assets of firms that did not cooperate with the state.[20] President Mugabe accused minority-owned companies of using their economic clout to foment unrest and turning 'people on the streets against our government' (*BBC News*, 1 July 2002). Threats against foreign or minority-controlled businesses operating in Zimbabwe have been articulated by government on a regular basis ever since, ensuring a steadily deteriorating business environment. By 2007, in a 'new campaign of control and punishment [opening] … one of the few remaining spaces for rentseeking', a wave of primarily urban violence targeted owners of supermarkets and shops, who were accused of 'sabotaging' the economy by means of 'over-pricing', resulting in more than a thousand businessmen being arrested (Hammar 2008: 428). In the run-up to the March 2008 elections, in which the opposition MDC won a slim parliamentary majority and the MDC presidential candidate Tsvangirai won a plurality of votes (with most observers suggesting Tsvangirai had won an outright majority if not for government manipulation of the returns) to thereby force President Mugabe to contest a run-off, which Tsvangirai then declined to participate in owing to the escalating state violence against the opposition, the government signed into law the Indigenization and Empowerment Act, allowing it to seize a controlling stake in foreign, white- and Asian-owned businesses (Africa Research Bulletin 2008: 17739). The move on this indigenization legislation, which had already been tabled by parliament in September 2007, was clearly aimed at boosting the government's populist credentials before an election that it seemed destined to lose despite a ready willingness to deploy violence as an ultimate campaign tool.

Indicative of the continuity of violence throughout the post-independence era (Bratton and Masunungure 2008: 50–2), this volatile posturing by the government followed similar behaviour during and after the 1998 'food riots' (the first in the country's history), which the government blamed on the ZCTU and Tsvangirai. Feeling threatened by the assertive and menacing tactics of the ascendant war veterans' movement, senior government officials became the movement's de facto hostages, and so placating the war veterans came to take precedence over salvaging state–business relations and the general welfare of Zimbabweans (Sithole

2000: 85). As the IMF ended technical assistance to Zimbabwe owing to loan defaults and as companies began closing down at an alarming rate, the government continued adrift without any ability to define and pursue long-term developmental policies. By 2002 the IMF's resident representative in Zimbabwe and top expert on the country, Gerry Johnson, declared disaster imminent, with the IMF predicting inflation soaring to 522 per cent in 2003 and bringing with it total economic collapse, noting furthermore that 'once you get to that point, it can go very fast' (*Daily News*, 4 November 2002). With the benefit of hindsight it is clear that Johnson might, if anything, have underestimated the coming crisis.

Origins of the crisis To really appreciate the implications of this current stage in the country's descent for any future development project in Zimbabwe it is important to be clear about the degree to which an accumulation of historical events and crises has contributed to the ferocity with which this recent episode in the country's unfortunate post-independence era has unfolded. In a recent article Bond (2007a) asks, 'when did this crisis begin?' He notes a variety of possible origins for the current crisis in the voluminous scholarly literature: with the land invasions in 2000; with 'Black Friday' in late 1997, when the Zimbabwean dollar depreciated by 74 per cent in a few hours; or earlier that year, when Mugabe decided to unilaterally grant pensions to the war veterans that the government could not afford to pay and then sent troops to the DRC to prop up the Kabila regime and 'secure investment sites'; with the adoption of ESAP in 1991; or with the accommodationist policies (vis-à-vis white domestic and international capital) of the early 1980s. In the end Bond argues for a longer view on the crisis, which locates its origins in the over-accumulation of capital and the decline in per capita GDP from the mid-1970s onwards.[21]

Bond's long view is useful as it makes it possible to properly take into account the steady accumulation of difficulties beleaguering an increasingly desperate (if steadily determined) government. Without this context it is very difficult to explain or provide a rational account for the government's unleashing of the land invasions and the subsequent violence against its own people, especially given the inevitably high costs to all involved. While there is the precedent of the *Gukurahundi* violence, it was different in that it did not threaten the national economy and the government's patronage networks in the same way as has the current crisis. In order to fully understand this chain of events, the political-economic account is not in itself sufficient. This account must be contextualized in a sociocultural environment of violence and authoritarianism that has shaped events since at least the war of national liberation, while at the same time often being underemphasized, or even ignored, in accounts of Zimbabwe's politics that employ the standard periodization of events that suggests a relatively 'successful' or 'developmental' 1980s, a failed 1990s (structural adjustment and 'neoliberalism') and a chaotic, even irrational, 2000s. While a similar periodization of events is followed in this chapter, each period is characterized somewhat differently than is the case in these standard accounts. Here, the cultural dysfunctionality fostered by a perpetual tendency to state violence, which is according to both Scarnecchia (2006) and Sylvester (2006) comparable to fascism[22] – i.e. 'postcolonial transitions in Africa, where some states inflict pernicious injury, suffering, death, and even genocide on portions of their own citizenry in the name of development' (ibid.: 66–7) – runs like a red thread through these post-independence periods and is thus accorded an important if not solely determining explanatory value in a way that is not the case in other accounts of the crisis.

Bracking's (2005: 343) analysis of how Zimbabwe's 'exclusionary mode of political rule' is developed is by contrast a useful example of how an excessive focus on political-economic determinants of Zimbabwe's crisis as it unfolds following the land invasions fails to consider the longer-term view of the importance of state violence; she argues that authoritarianism in contemporary Zimbabwe 'can be traced from the social transformation catalysed by the ... [ESAP] of 1991–1995' and the subsequent economic crisis of the latter half of the decade.

> In a general sense, authoritarian social formations are a consequence of failed markets ... just as European fascism was born in the 1930s Great Depression, elements of fascist state practices can be traced to the failure of the first generation of structural adjustment in sub-Saharan Africa, and the continued failures of the second generation [Poverty Reduction Strategy Papers] mechanisms. (ibid.: 343)

Bracking, like Sylvester (2006), makes a comparison between some forms of authoritarianism in Africa and European fascism, but in the case of Zimbabwe this link seems to be only an economic one. In neither the case of Zimbabwe nor, apparently, the case of European fascism does Bracking recognize that the economic hardships prompting an unleashing of large-scale violence by the state against its citizens, and in particular those minorities deemed to be the proverbial 'traitors in their midst', have been preceded by the commission of significant and coordinated acts of violence and murder by these ruling elites before they took power (ZANU during the war of national liberation) and in the early stages of consolidating that power (Zimbabwe's *Gukurahundi*). In Bracking's account, which is in many ways the conventional 'left' account of the origins of Zimbabwe's current crisis (e.g. Bond 1998; Bond and Manyanya 2002; D. Moore 2003), it is failed economic policies (ESAP, broadly speaking) which trigger large-scale violence. While it is entirely correct to suggest that the failures of ESAP were an important contributing factor, it is also the case that the way in which Zimbabwe's government and Mugabe himself have responded to a political challenge is not a novel phenomenon in Zimbabwean politics but is reminiscent of violent responses that predate the 1990s and ESAP (see Moyo 2008). Scarnecchia's (2006: 222) analysis of fascism in Zimbabwe recognizes 'continuity in youth league and paramilitary violence in every election since 1979', although to this recognition of continuity in violence he adds the caveat that the crisis facing the government following the 2000 referendum and elections is 'unlike any other'. In the end it is perhaps in the very uniqueness of the current crisis, in terms of its severity and comprehensiveness, that any solutions will have to be devised, as opposed to being imposed from without.

Prospects for a new beginning in Zimbabwe

Because it is difficult to analyse Zimbabwe's trajectory without becoming overwhelmed by all the things that have gone wrong, commentaries on the contemporary crisis have a difficult task in terms of articulating ways in which the country could potentially overcome its debilitating legacy and catastrophic present to instead embark on a new era of politics geared towards well-being rather than the retention of political power at any cost.[23] The sense of desperation when considering the immense suffering and traumatization of Zimbabwean people, the lasting damage done to the national economy (most obviously to agriculture and to business more generally, where hyperinflation has rendered normal economic activity impossible) and the deep divisions and mistrusts, even hatreds, created by decades of misrule has meant that most analyses of politics and development in contemporary Zimbabwe have concentrated on how to end the crisis, halt the destruction and somehow get the country back 'on track'. What is generally envisioned is a situation where state violence is stopped, economic activity can begin to recover, however modestly, economic and other aid can resume and opposing political parties (ZANU-PF and the MDC) can begin to interact within the normal bounds of democratic politics.

Zimbabwe

On 15 September 2008, the day Zimbabwe's power-sharing agreement between ZANU-PF and the MDC was announced, Dominique Strauss-Kahn, managing director of the IMF, released the following generic statement, illustrative of the general Western response – emphasizing the need to 'address the crisis' but saying little, if anything, about how to do so:

> Today's power-sharing deal in Zimbabwe paves the way for a new government that can begin to address the economic crisis. We stand ready to discuss with the new authorities their policies to stabilize the economy, improve social conditions, and reduce poverty. I encourage the government to take steps to show clear commitment to a new policy direction and to seek the support of the international community. (Strauss-Kahn 2008)

A 2008 discussion document entitled *Comprehensive Economic Recovery in Zimbabwe*, commissioned by the UNDP and produced by economists, planners and consultants in Zimbabwe, focuses on how to achieve sustainable economic growth and effectively manage economic aid as a means to recover from the current crisis.

> One common thread which runs throughout the document is that of the imperative of restoring macroeconomic stability as a pre-condition for recovery. Specific measures that flow from this include profound changes to current patterns of both monetary and fiscal policy management in order to correct widespread distortions which have acted as impediments to savings, investment and production. (UNDP 2008: viii)

Statements like these by IFIs and Western governments alike are indicative of a traditional form of problem-solving (policy) process at work which does not explicitly address many underlying (and, in the strict sense, non-economic) problems relating to Zimbabwe's disintegration, ranging from the ethno-cultural roots of patronage politics to the ongoing exercise of state violence and indeed the very historical and sociocultural roots of the Zimbabwean state itself (see Maundeni 2001), as well as the inability of major parties in this conflict to address concerns beyond those relating to the immediate distribution of political power.

If the Western reaction might seem bland, the African reaction seems hurried indeed. The seeming eagerness with which other African leaders wish to 'conclude' the current crisis and 'move on', with Mugabe left in a position of considerable power despite the crisis that his government has created, suggests that what is primarily sought here is an end to the regional volatility, inter-African acrimony and bad international press created by the Zimbabwean crisis rather than a genuine alleviation of the Zimbabwean people's plight and a reinstitution of proper accountability in Zimbabwean government – the latter arguably being impossible to achieve within the context of the ZANU–MDC power-sharing deal as currently envisioned. In a rather remarkable rush to put the Zimbabwean atrocities behind them, African leaders quickly called for sanctions against President Mugabe and leading ZANU-PF officials to be lifted. South Africa's then minister of foreign affairs, Nkosazana Dlamini-Zuma (2009), notably joined in this demand while addressing a Southern African Development Community (SADC) Council of Ministers meeting in Cape Town on 26 February 2009, stating that 'it is our view that the formation of an Inclusive Government has indeed paved the way for the people of Zimbabwe to begin the process of national reconciliation, economic recovery and reconstruction and development'. The conclusion of the power-sharing deal to form a unity government that was agreed on by the Zimbabwean government and the MDC opposition in September 2008 saw Morgan Tsvangirai sworn in as prime minister on 11 February 2009 with Mugabe remaining president and with ZANU retaining a slim majority of cabinet posts (including, crucially, defence, justice and land portfolios, with home affairs shared by ZANU-PF and the MDC) despite failing to secure a majority of votes in the 2008 parliamentary elections (Raath 2009).

These are of course necessary steps to any kind of recovery and easing of suffering, which would include the lifting of sanctions at an appropriate time. But it is also worthwhile to consider what happens after the crisis. Is it really feasible to think that a return to party politics as usual, even if that can be accomplished, will resolve the enormous economic and social problems the country is currently facing (see Bracking and Cliffe 2009)? The problem here is that there is no real era of normality to which Zimbabweans and their leaders can look back. The 1990s were beset with fundamental problems of corruption and mismanagement in an environment of one-party domination. The 1980s were, despite some success with development, a violent and increasingly oppressive decade, moving the country towards an ever harsher domination by the ruling party. It remains to be seen what lessons can be relearned from the Rhodesian UDI era, but a time when the large majority of Zimbabweans lacked democratic rights can hardly be the source from which ideas about how to begin anew can be drawn.[24]

The crisis as incubator of new solutions If solutions are to be found it is perhaps to Zimbabwe's by regional standards unique collapse that one must look. Considering again the notion of cathartic violence, it is in this facet of Zimbabwe's crisis that an opening up of new space for articulating political solutions and approaches to development that depart from orthodox solutions might emerge. If the currently envisioned power-sharing model is likely to entrench forces of oppression and perpetuate a sense of injustice as those presiding over the past brutalization of Zimbabweans remain in government, and if a standard package of economic aid combined with some market-oriented economic reform might do little for those struggling to cope with immediate everyday needs such as escaping AIDS, surviving cholera and overcoming starvation, then there might in this context of crisis and despair be found an appetite among those self-styled progressive forces in the country, whether in civil society, the academy or political leadership, to consider localized, bottom-up and genuinely inclusive approaches to meeting urgent needs. This would constitute a genuinely indigenous path towards healing and development (however defined) as opposed to the exclusivist policies of indigenization pursued so far by ZANU-PF. Such an approach could be facilitated by reorienting national politics and economics away from servicing government and its cronies by means of predatory policies and instead towards policies aiming at societal cohesion and thus an easing of the violent fragmentation of social, political and economic life that has rendered development impossible. In this way, more people would be able to cope in a situation where a substantial alleviation of poverty is realistically a long time off. The current crisis might, in other words, focus minds in a way so that the thinking 'beyond development' as envisioned by post-development theory seems less implausible, less utopian.

The difficulty, as is recognized with all interesting and innovative post-development ideas more or less irrespective of their particular merit, is how to translate such thinking beyond development into action and policy, or simply into changed (societal) behaviour where government policy is not the main focus and perhaps not directly relevant, in terms of what forces will eventually drive these changes. While it is true that a resilient civil society, which is the most likely catalyst for any radical rethinking of development, survives in Zimbabwe despite government efforts to eradicate it – and with the exception of violent social formations such as the 'Green Bombers', enforcing discipline and adherence to government policy in rural areas, which have been encouraged to aid government in its suppression of opposition (D. Moore 2008) – there is clearly a very real possibility that the enormity of the current crisis makes those looking for a new/different way out become risk-averse rather than bold. If that is the case, they will therefore concentrate on how to get back to 'normality' with the help of orthodox solutions rather than embrace new and likely unproven ideas. As with so many issues that need resolving in Zimbabwe today it is much too soon to tell, in the middle of such a volatile situation, just how the attitudes to change and a future Zimbabwe will align in an immediate post-crisis environment.

In the end, however, the point at which Zimbabwe has arrived suggests that transformation would have to be bottom-up; there has been too much damage done by the state for it to remain a viable driver of any move beyond the contemporary development orthodoxy. It will therefore rest on Zimbabwe's civil society to act as catalyst, perhaps in coopera-tion with international actors such as regional governments, NGOs and other civil society bodies and, at a later stage, perhaps also in cautious coordination with a future ruling MDC, if progressive forces within that party emerge dominant and ZANU-PF loses its current ability within the confines of the power-sharing deal to stall meaningful reform. Larmer et al. (2009: 48) note that the social movements which during the late 1990s put pressure on ZANU-PF and resulted in the creation of the MDC were eventually discouraged by the MDC's subsequent adoption of 'neoliberal policies' which consequently saw the party's urban support base partly 'demobilized', and ZANU-PF has in recent years also been effective in turning its own version of social movements against the opposition, as witnessed by its politicizing of the rural poor and radicalizing of war veterans. Whatever shape such alliances take, they would have to be innovative in a societal vacuum of sorts that the enormity of the current crisis has brought about; there would be no easy way for those working for change to rely on appeals to popular tradition in the same way as in Botswana. The rupture caused by the current crisis and the steady corrosion of society produced by three decades of ZANU-PF misrule have rendered such foundations for change all too thin. While this suggests that prospects for change are bleak, it is nevertheless in the emerging post-crisis interregnum that any change of course will be possible.

Now is the time for change In a recent study of civil society and its trans-formation in Zimbabwe, D. Moore (2008) identifies the interregnum, a period 'between reigns', as the crucial moment and space where a concrete change in social and political direction can emerge. Moore examines two interregna and the role of civil society in each, the first being the late 1970s as Zimbabwean independence draws near and the latter emerging with the current crisis, where ZANU-PF's traditional form

of governance seems exhausted (which is further indicated by the formation of a power-sharing government including the MDC and Tsvangirai
as prime minister) but where it is also the case that a new socio-political
order has not yet been established. It is this current interregnum which is
crucial for understanding why a change in direction along the lines hinted
at in this chapter might be possible, despite the seemingly entrenched
positions of both opposing parties.

Zimbabwe's current stand-off between ZANU-PF and the MDC, which
continues seemingly unabated into the nascent power-sharing era, is
mirrored in civil society more broadly by the continued conflict between
the generally reactionary force of 'agrarian patriots' supporting ZANU-
PF's draconian redistribution policies and violent oppression of political
dissent and the generally progressive force of 'critical cosmopolitans'
supporting the MDC and an agenda for a democratic Zimbabwe (ibid.:
7; cf. D. Moore 2004). How the power struggle between these overlapping
political and societal forces is eventually resolved will determine Zimbabwe's future in at least the medium term. The problem, however, is
not that these two socio-political groupings, or forces, represent different
visions of how to extract Zimbabwe from the current crisis and what the
aspirations for a developing Zimbabwe should be. Neither the so-called
agrarian patriots nor the critical cosmopolitans seem willing to deviate
from well-worn notions of how to reclaim and strengthen sovereignty
(most important for the former) and how to promote development (more
clearly articulated by the latter).

Agrarian patriots seem intent on regaining a domestic consensus
for a politics of redistribution, 'anti-imperial' posturing and political
centralization once the MDC opposition has been neutralized by being
brought into government yet left without the ability to act decisively
on its own agenda. Thus they represent a return to politics as usual
that is not in any sense emancipatory, developmental or democratic.
Critical cosmopolitans wish to re-engage with the global economy, to
promote good governance and thereby restore economic productivity so
that standard development policies, including aid and domestic reforms
aiming to improve capacity across sectors and activities, can be effectively
implemented. They recognize that Zimbabwe's deep crisis requires drastic
action and even difficult compromises with those responsible for past
misdeeds. But their aim is essentially an embrace of 'normalcy' which,
if successful, might enable Zimbabwe to join the club of other relatively
stable and nominally democratic developing nations, but which will not
improve the likelihood that Zimbabwe will escape underdevelopment

and marginalization any more than has been the case for other African countries that have achieved success in that regard. At some point, both of these tendencies must be tempered and an effective way of bridging this urban–rural 'divide' must be found as a rural–urban civil society alliance of some kind would be best positioned to sustain pressure for transformation.

If these are Zimbabwe's only options, then the notion of moving beyond development to chart a truly novel path towards a sustainable future seems far-fetched indeed. The existence of the current interregnum, however, holds at least the possibility of a departure from both of these two scenarios. In the end it is in this moment of fluidity, this transitional moment where civil society most obviously 'relates to – and often "becomes" – "political society"' (D. Moore 2008: 35), which those who reject a return to business as usual and an embrace of a development orthodoxy that has so far produced very little of the sort can find an opportunity to build public support for new ideas and to channel these ideas into decision-making power. A transition from authoritarianism is not in itself a guarantee of improvements in life chances for those previously oppressed. A political and economic transition must be accompanied by a realignment of social forces to support a paradigm shift in the thinking about development, together with concrete changes in policy, if emancipatory goals are to be attained. Where such a paradigm shift seems elusive the future of development remains uncertain, as in the case of South Africa, to which this study now turns.

6 | South Africa: normalization of uneven development

This is one country where it would be possible to create a capitalist black society, if whites were intelligent, if the nationalists were intelligent. And that capitalist black society, black middle class, would be very effective ... South Africa could succeed in putting across to the world a pretty convincing, integrated picture, with still 70 percent of the population being underdogs. – Steve Biko[1]

South Africa exhibits that most bitter of social outcomes: destitution amid plenty. – Willie Madisha[2]

Miracle, tragedy or just ordinary?

On 22 April 2009 the ANC was returned to power in the country's fourth national elections, albeit with less than the two-thirds majority it received in the previous election and with a strengthening of the Democratic Alliance (DA) and the new Congress of the People (COPE). The result paved the way for Jacob Zuma being inaugurated as post-apartheid South Africa's fourth president on 9 May 2009, the third man to win that office by contesting a free and fair election in which all South Africans were able to vote (his predecessor, Kgalema Motlanthe, having been elected by parliament following the ANC's National Executive Committee [NEC] 'recall' of President Mbeki). Moreover, Zuma's election as president of the ANC at the party's December 2007 conference in Polokwane was the first competitive contest for leadership of the party since 1949, when the Youth League 'radicals', notable among them Walter Sisulu, Oliver Tambo and Nelson Mandela, led the way in replacing the older moderate leadership in the wake of the NP's 1948 election victory, which ushered in the era of apartheid (Feit 1972). The 2009 national elections are a sign of how far South Africa has come in terms of consolidating the political gains of the transition from apartheid, but they also contain a premonition of the dangers faced by all new democracies struggling with unresolved societal divisions, intolerable inequality and pressing societal needs. Whereas the election in 1994 of Nelson Mandela was universally heralded as an unqualified victory for democracy over the forces of (racial) oppression and the election in 1999 of Thabo Mbeki was a sign of South Africa's rapidly maturing democracy whereby a popular leader willingly confined himself to one term in office, Jacob Zuma's election took place under a cloud of suspicion and in the context of widely expressed concerns about the degree to which South Africa's ruling elites and South African society more generally are committed to liberal democracy (Gumede 2008; Mangcu 2008). South Africa's honeymoon as the darling of freedom fighters and democrats alike across the world has long since passed, and today South African politics are scrutinized with a much greater degree of scepticism (and not necessarily a simplistic 'Afro-pessimism') than was the case in the early years of the post-apartheid era.

The worldwide optimism generated by South Africa's transition was widely commented on and contributed to by scholars and journalists alike, with Patti Waldmeir's (1997) *Anatomy of a Miracle* epitomizing the triumphant interpretation of this transition and the articulation of the so-called 'miracle thesis'. According to the general line of this argument South Africa exemplified by its successful and relatively peaceful transition the possibility for societies torn apart by long histories of brutal oppression, grave injustices and deep-seated prejudices to transcend severe societal trauma by means of accepting a democratic order in which the future place and belonging of all segments of society are acknowledged.[3] South Africa's transition became understood as a refutation of the notion that heterogeneous and in particular multi-ethnic societies with long histories of division and violence were doomed to protracted strife among their conflicting segments and thus unable to consolidate democracy.

Optimistic accounts of the post-apartheid order were contested and arguably eclipsed by much more sober and/or pessimistic reassessments of South Africa's transition and the lingering problems (social, political and economic) of the post-apartheid dispensation, including the ANC's style of governing. Challenges to the miracle thesis range from those focusing on the way in which South Africa's liberators were co-opted by existing interests in the established order (Bond 2000), the variety of global and local constraints on the post-apartheid economy and political landscape that prevented the ANC from pursuing a radical transformation of society (Marais 2001), and an eroding commitment within the ANC to democratic governance, the rule of law and inter-ethnic tolerance (A. Feinstein 2007; Mangcu 2008). A variation on these sobering themes was provided by Neville Alexander's (2003) *An Ordinary Country*. According to Alexander's bleak prognosis of the transition South Africa should not, *pace* the miracle thesis, be considered an exceptional case but rather an 'ordinary country' among others in the developing world (cf. Habib and Kotzé 2004).[4]

Being ordinary in this regard does not suggest great hope for the future as

> the nature of the negotiated settlement precludes the realisation of most of the reconstruction and development electoral promises made by the parties that fought for freedom from racial oppression ... this is a fact that has to be stated up front ... so that the 'ordinary' men and women of South Africa can begin to prepare themselves for the bleak years – perhaps decades – ahead. (D. Alexander 2003: 3)

Increasing levels of violence associated with protests against the lack of delivery of basic services in South Africa's impoverished townships and the recent spate of xenophobic and murderous violence against immigrants and refugees from Zimbabwe, Mozambique and other African countries suggest that this is not a future that South Africans already brought to the brink of desperation will easily accept or cope with (Gibson 2006; Booysen 2007; Neocosmos 2008).

By comparison with transitions to independence in the neighbouring countries examined in this study, the South African transition stands out for several reasons. South African democracy has been consolidated to some significant degree, as is the case with democracy in Botswana. Both South Africa and Botswana continue to face serious developmental challenges relating to the regional HIV/AIDS pandemic and, interrelatedly, very high levels of socio-economic inequality manifested in high levels of unemployment and poverty. South Africa, however, is also characterized by much higher levels of violence and societal fragmentation posing a greater threat to the democratic order itself (Hough 2008; S. Pillay 2008) than is Botswana. At the same time, a more active civil society – including labour, media, citizens' organizations, and so on – could safeguard democracy in South Africa in ways that Botswana's by comparison passive civil society might not. Compared to Zimbabwe, the neighbouring country to which those fearful about South Africa's future most often compare and contrast it, South Africa has clearly been successful in terms of consolidating democracy, safeguarding the rule of law and containing the intra-societal conflict resulting from a shared history of settler colonialism in the context of a regional apartheid system. The controversy over how to deal with land reform in South Africa is not likely to trigger the same kind of political and social explosion it did in Zimbabwe (Goedel 2005) and the ANC's politics of indigenization, part of the tendency towards what Ndlovu-Gatsheni (2007) and Mangcu (2008) term 'nativism', has not become as radically exclusivist and xenophobic as have those of the ZANU-PF.

Looking back at the post-apartheid era, the nature of South Africa's contemporary development can usefully be conceived of as shaped by three crucial shifts in politics that each relate to some significant reconfiguration of power relations within the ANC.[5] The first shift, which also involves shifting relations between the ANC and key global and local market actors, was the move from the more explicitly redistributionist and developmental RDP to the neo-liberal GEAR programme under the stewardship of then Deputy President Thabo Mbeki. Whether this shift was as significant as its detractors would have it, it produced the socio-political context in which debates on development in South Africa have taken place ever since by its coming to symbolize a strong commitment by the ANC leadership to market reform and full integration into the global economy, which would prove increasingly controversial over time, especially in terms of that leadership's relations with its Tripartite Alliance partners in the South African Communist Party (SACP) and COSATU. The second shift was the emergence of a clear programme for effecting a racial or ethnic transformation of the South African economy, as exemplified by BEE and a concomitant 'nativist turn' intended to provide the sociocultural underpinnings of that transition. This shift was somewhat ironically or even paradoxically initiated by President Mbeki, who, owing to his perceived closeness to Western (liberal) economic thinking and an attendant aloofness from ordinary people, is himself also seen as a representative of the very Westernization that many South Africans found increasingly unacceptable. The third shift is the currently unfolding move away from a relatively unified and hegemonic ANC rule and vision for the future development of South Africa towards an increasingly uncertain future. This shift results from the ouster of Mbeki as president of the ANC and of his close associates from the party's NEC at the Polokwane conference in December 2007, the subsequent removal of Mbeki as president of South Africa in September 2008 just months short of him completing a final term as president, Jacob Zuma's ascendancy within the ANC and, finally, the open challenge to the ANC mounted by the newly created COPE from significant defectors from within the ANC's own ranks.

In examining the important achievements in the transition from apartheid coupled with the controversial compromises of that transition and the diminution of the NDR that those compromises entailed (Andreasson 2003; Southall 2004)[6] the chapter proceeds as follows. In providing the

157

general political economic context in which contemporary developments unfold, the chapter first charts the move from the RDP to GEAR and beyond. This trajectory constitutes the move towards normalization, i.e. economic liberalization embedded in procedural democracy, in an unevenly developed post-colonial society. Second, the attempt to indigenize South Africa's socio-economic transformation by promoting BEE and by anchoring transformation in a cultural reorientation towards 'African values' as symbolized by Mbeki's notion of an 'African Renaissance' (Vale and Maseko 1998; Bongma 2004) is outlined and evaluated in the light of contemporary developments, such as the debate about *ubuntu* as a cultural guiding principle and the transition from a 'neoliberal'-cum-'nativist' leadership under Mbeki (Ndlovu-Gatsheni 2007) to what might become a conspicuously populist and more distinctly 'traditionalist' leadership under Jacob Zuma. Third, the implications of the 'phenomenon' of Zuma's rise to power for moving beyond development to thereby redirect the post-apartheid trajectory away from the current process of normalization and the betrayal of hopes for 'a better life for all' that the miracle transition was intended to accomplish are considered in the context of South Africa's by regional standards quite active and diversified civil society and scholarly tradition, in which heterodox approaches to development are more likely to find a positive reception than elsewhere in the region. While South Africa might in a negative sense represent the normalization to which its neighbours could aspire (or at least be destined to move towards) it might also be the crucible in which the right mix of indigeneity and modernity, of tradition and progressivity, of scholarly and societal diversity, is most likely to produce new solutions to the developmental dilemma. Drawing on Steve Biko's intellectual contributions to the anti-apartheid movement and the greater quest for post-colonial emancipation, the chapter concludes by considering that a reassertion of the 'syncretic' tradition out of which the ANC emerged dominant (ibid.; Mangcu 2008) could turn out to be the wellspring from which new ideas about a better future can be drawn.

From exceptional case to ordinary country

The arrival in 1652 of European settlers at what is now Cape Town and the creation of the Cape Colony by Jan van Riebeeck as the local governor for the Dutch East India Company mark the beginning of a fundamental transformation of southern Africa, and modern South Africa is essentially a product of the industrialization that commenced at a rapid pace in the decades following discovery in 1871 of diamonds in the Orange Free State and gold on the Witwatersrand in 1886 (de Kiewiet 1941; Stadler 1987; C. H. Feinstein 2005). The expansion of European influence with the eventual establishment of colonial rule of one form or another in what became known as Southern Rhodesia, Bechuanaland and territories beyond produced the settler colonialism that dominated economic and political developments in the region until the transitions in recent decades. South Africa emerged into the post-Second World War era as a semi-peripheral industrialized nation (Andreasson 2001) with an institutionalized dual economy channelling the nation's wealth towards the white minority by means of often violent exploitation and the systematic economic and political marginalization of the country's black majority (see Bond 2007c).

Given South Africa's status as Africa's most advanced and diversified economy, the transition to democracy took place in the context of well-established capitalist class relations and of an established parliamentary order, albeit one racially circumscribed and increasingly under pressure from the South African security establishment's efforts to root out opposition. The ANC, like the ZANU-PF in Zimbabwe, inherited an industrialized economy and a sharply racially delineated class structure, while a more developed economy in South Africa entailed a more complex set of class relations than in Botswana. Moreover, not all sectors of South Africa's business community had identical relations with the government nor the same preferences vis-à-vis the policy of apartheid. In fact they displayed markedly different preferences about what future direction the economy ought to take based on whether they stood to gain or lose from the dismantling of the increasingly introverted apartheid economy and its particular features in terms of social and economic regulation (Lipton 1986).

In terms of political contestation the predominantly black opposition to apartheid contained both militant and accommodationist factions, those who sought nothing less than a comprehensive defeat of white power and those focusing on removal of apartheid restrictions that prevented black South Africans from participating fully in the democratic process and in society. And whereas reactionary white South Africans supported P. W. Botha's hard-line response (the policy of *kragdadigheit*) to the liberation struggle, others would provide F. W. de Klerk with a mandate to negotiate a transition to democracy and the *de jure* end to white rule, with these divisions among white South Africans roughly mirroring the split within the NP between the hard-line *verkrampte* and the accommodationist *verligte* (Lipton 2007: 69–71; cf. O'Meara 1996).

Complicating this divide was the fact that de Klerk himself, an NP leader from the conservative Transvaal, had cultivated a conventionally conservative, indeed *verkrampte*, image (Waldmeir 1997: 111–12). As with the logic that only Nixon possessed the required anti-communist credentials to go to China and negotiate US recognition of the communist regime in Beijing, so only a *verkrampte* Afrikaner could lead white South Africa to democracy (see Schrire 1991: 125–31).

The need for a negotiated transition to a non-racial democracy became obvious by the 1980s owing to increasing societal violence, economic stagnation and international isolation. According to Price (1991) the structural incompatibilities inherent in apartheid gave rise to a 'trialectical process' whereby the 'security contradiction' facing the South African government became overwhelmingly costly, thus forcing the government into its first serious negotiations with the anti-apartheid forces. Talks between exiled ANC leaders and representatives of progressive forces in South Africa were an important step in moving towards transition. South African businessmen led by Gavin Relly, Harry Oppenheimer's successor as head of the Anglo American Corporation, met with ANC president Oliver Tambo in Lusaka in September 1985. In 1986 Pieter de Lange, chairman of the Afrikaner Broederbond, met with Thabo Mbeki, then the ANC information director, in New York at a dinner hosted by the Ford Foundation.[7] In August 1987 a contingent of white, mainly Afrikaner, South Africans led by Frederik Van Zyl Slabbert, founder of the Institute for a Democratic Alternative in South Africa (IDASA) and a former Progressive Federal Party leader, met with ANC members in Dakar (L. Thompson 2001: 244; cf. Waldmeir 1997). Following the release of Nelson Mandela and the unbanning of the ANC, the SACP and other anti-apartheid organizations, these informal talks shifted to formal negotiations between the NP and the ANC on the transition to multiracial democracy.

Frequent rounds of negotiation produced a series of documents and settlements on the road towards transition (Grundy 2000: 34–9). By the time Nelson Mandela was sworn in as president on 10 May 1994 a clear precedent had been set by the ANC indicating a willingness to negotiate with both an opposing political (and military) force and with key market actors, global and domestic (Allen 2006). Not surprisingly the results of these negotiations have been characterized both as a masterful outmanoeuvring of the NP by the ANC (Waldmeir 1997) and conversely as a co-optation of the ANC leadership by the NP and corporate elites (McKinley 1997; Bond 2000). Gumede (2007: 79) provides a more nuanced picture by suggesting that the NP was 'masterfully trounced' in terms of the political settlement, whereas the ANC was 'outfoxed' in terms of the economic settlement.

Despite nervousness in the white establishment about the ANC's intentions, the period of talks and rapprochement before 1994 increased the understanding between the ANC and its adversaries, some of whom eventually became its partners, about what their respective concerns and needs were (S. D. Taylor 2007). South African and international business emphasized 'economic realities' and the notion that policy-making would have to operate within a fairly narrow set of constraints dictated by domestic and international economic imperatives.

> Recognition of ... fiscal realities was facilitated by the involvement of the ANC in discussions with the National Party government, white-led business interests, the IMF and other economic bodies during the transition period. One analyst observed astutely: 'The ANC is probably the only liberation movement in history to speak of financial discipline before it assumes power.' (Ward 1998: 41)

The ANC also emphasized the need for the private sector to play a significant part in the economic transformation of South Africa for broad-based development to be possible and societal stability ensured. This political push for business to shoulder an increased responsibility for transformation and development resulted in proactive if controversial (in terms of intentions and effectiveness) moves by big business to take a lead in promoting inclusive corporate governance and increasing accountability in CSR (Andreasson forthcoming). Early in the transition, however, the ANC was also committed to some degree of state-led transformation of the economy, including increased attention to redistributive needs. Manifested by the nominally social democratic RDP, such a policy trajectory would nevertheless be based on market principles (Lodge 1999: 10–11). It marked at minimum a sharp rhetorical shift from Mandela's stated position upon his release from prison in 1990 that 'the nationalization of the mines, banks, and monopoly industry is the policy of the ANC and a change or modification of our views in this regard is inconceivable' (*The Sowetan*, 5 March 1990).

The 'neoliberal turn' The 1990s saw the abandonment of the ANC's ostensibly socialist stance and its gradual embrace of neoliberal free market principles.

As the ANC assumed power, its key economic policy advocates such as

Alec Erwin and Trevor Manuel, despite their labor background, became converts to market liberalism as the optimal way to alleviate South Africa's poverty and development problems. Unlike Zimbabwe, however, this view quickly gained consensus in the highest circles of the ANC government, including President Mandela and Deputy President Mbeki, though the RDP initially served as a means of reserving the credibility of the ANC's expressed commitment to fundamental socioeconomic restructuring. (S. D. Taylor 2007: 166)

There is an ongoing debate about whether the ANC was ever committed to socialism, something which the former Communist Party member Mbeki was later to deny when, by the late 1970s, he had a falling-out with Joe Slovo and Chris Hani over suggestions that the ANC should become a 'Marxist-Leninist liberation movement', arguing instead that it was the SACP which properly represented the socialist strand of the struggle against apartheid (Gumede 2007: 67). So while Mbeki was still a banned 'communist' in exile he proclaimed that 'the ANC is not a socialist party' and it would not become one for 'the purpose of pleasing its "left" critics' (Mbeki 1984: 609). In any case, the early 1990s rhetorical shift and the reorientation in thinking that it presumably indicated was translated into an actual change of policy with the phasing out of the RDP in the first few years of the ANC administration and its replacement by the explicitly neoliberal GEAR in 1996.

This neoliberal turn was prompted by the policy of privatization of state assets begun by the NP in 1989 (Hentz 2000) and was also indicative of a greater global shift in economic thinking towards what later became known as the 'Washington Consensus' on neoliberal orthodoxy.[8] Privatization ensued in part because of the NP's desire to

remove state-owned assets beyond the control not of the state as such, but of those interests that were about to adopt state power. In this case, then, withdrawal of the state from ownership was designed to perpetuate the economic power of large-scale capital. (Fine and Rustomjee 1996: 53)

Similarly, Vieira and Wallerstein (1992: 368) note that

the privatization policy under way during apartheid's final phase could be a significant limitation on the capacity of a democratic South Africa to carry out an affirmative policy establishing ethnic and social balances. It could also come to restrict the availability of state resources for promoting an economic policy of regional cooperation.

The ANC thus came to power in a situation where momentum already existed in the direction of increasing privatization, liberalization and a rolling back of the role of the state in the economy. In addition, the incoming ANC government inherited an economy in serious trouble owing to the fiscal and monetary deterioration during latter-day apartheid. This situation made it imperative for the incoming ANC government to work effectively with market actors who had gained increasing economic leverage from the privatization process and the opening up of South Africa's economy in a way that significantly strengthened business's 'exit' option (Bond 2000; Allen 2006; cf. Hirschman 1970).

The ANC thus pursued a market-friendly policy to attract FDI, achieve economic growth and create jobs, and overall policy aims of the state converged with preferences of key market actors, although businesses became increasingly concerned about government programmes aiming at the racial transformation of South Africa's economy. Acting on neoliberal preferences regardless of an at least rhetorical commitment by the ANC to lead on major socio-economic transformation meant that plans for redistribution and structural transformation of society had to be deferred, thereby preserving a most unequal status quo for at least the medium term. From this perspective, and following the logic of Margaret Thatcher's famous dictum that 'there is no alternative', the ANC government saw few options but to accommodate market demands (see Allen 2006).

From RDP to GEAR and beyond The ANC came to power promising a comprehensive programme of development aimed at raising living standards for the majority black population. More equitable spending in areas such as education, healthcare and social infrastructure would help alleviate immediate poverty as well as make possible the integration of black South Africans into the economic mainstream. The rhetorically ambitious ANC platform centred on the RDP, due in large part to an initiative by COSATU and conceived through extensive consultation and discussion within the ANC and the anti-apartheid movement (Bond 2000: 89) as well as between the ANC and corporate South Africa, came to accommodate a wide range of 'contesting social and economic forces' (Marais 2001: 237). More than a development programme, the RDP aimed to fundamentally reorder South African society by departing from the confining strictures of the inherited apartheid economy and the political and social priorities on which it was based (Rapoo 1996). Thus the RDP would improve life in South Africa by breaking the vicious cycle of uneven development and underdevelopment perpetuated by past policies.

The RDP was, according to Bond (2000: 89–121), never earnestly pursued, although the ANC has continually insisted that GEAR is merely a tactical supplement to the RDP strategy and not a departure from the latter – 'an elaboration of principles and perspectives set out in the RDP' (Marais 2001: 187). Echoing Bond's scepticism about the ANC's intentions, Everatt (2008) argues that the ANC government rather quickly came to view South Africa's poor as 'morally lacking', dependent on 'handouts' and therefore 'undeserving' rather than a genuinely victimized constituency central to the project of transformation, as they had been during the anti-apartheid struggle. Because the RDP was weakly and intermittently implemented in the first two years of ANC government, it is difficult to speculate on what its actual effects could have been. The GEAR macroeconomic policy framework was presented in June 1996 as 'non-negotiable' by Minister of Finance Manuel, with then Vice-President Mbeki speaking of it in similar terms of 'non-negotiability'. The reorientation from RDP to GEAR resulted from the fact that the business response to the RDP had been mixed at best and in the end the government felt it needed to move beyond it to improve its partnership with business and the global economy into which South Africa was reintegrating (Hanson and Hentz 1999: 499).[9]

Where the RDP focused on broad developmental objectives GEAR entailed an orthodox emphasis on a conservative monetary and fiscal macroeconomic stance where improving conditions for private enterprise would stimulate economic growth. Economic growth would alleviate unemployment and eventually enable government to undertake significant developmental projects together with the private sector. GEAR stated that the strongest form of redistribution was formal sector job creation and the shift from the RDP to GEAR was generally in line with conventional Washington Consensus thinking on how to best foster economic growth and development. This would best be done by scaling back the role of the state in the economy and focusing on creating macroeconomic stability. Investor confidence, investment inflows, jobs and economic growth would then follow.

As GEAR failed to deliver on its projections in all areas except lowered inflation, budget deficit reduction and export targets (Bond 2000: 78–82; P. Pillay 2000: 4–5) the ANC's Alliance partners aligned with leftist forces in society to lobby harder for a relaxed fiscal stance and to move beyond GEAR to deal with the continued inability of the South African economy to generate sufficient growth for tackling the country's severe problems with underdevelopment and poverty. Others joined in the call for moving on, with Mohammed Jahed, then of the National Business Initiative, expressing the need to transform GEAR into a truly collaborative framework taking the interests of all societal stakeholders into account.

> Here I am going to express my personal opinion and what I have seen amongst my friends in government and in politics. I think that there is a need now for a GEAR II to be developed. If you look at the background on how GEAR I was developed ... you had the Tripartite Alliance, you had business, and you had members of civil society, all forming their own kind of economic strategy. So COSATU had its own, government had its own, the ANC had its own, and business had its own ... The point here is that [GEAR] actually developed in isolation of different parties. And hence you find ... criticism against GEAR by COSATU, SACP, [by] elements within the ANC and so forth. I think the new process we need to focus on now is that the new policy or macroeconomic framework must be developed by everyone, together ... And that is going to be the new challenge for South Africa. (Jahed 2001)

The ANC's left wing hailed an April 2002 Alliance Summit as a victory because government was understood to have made an important concession on economic policy, shifting its emphasis from foreign to 'inward' investment, as was initially emphasized by the RDP (*Mail and Guardian*, 15 April 2002). Prior to this summit economist Rian le Roux suggested that South Africa was, following several years of monetary and fiscal restraint, now able to increase spending on developmental projects. The financial turnaround since the mid-1990s was, according to le Roux, 'nothing short of a fiscal miracle' and evidence of South Africa having moved 'from a vicious circle to a virtuous circle' (*Independent Online*, 19 February 2002). A growing sense that the bitter pill of restructuring the stagnant apartheid economy into a liberalized and market-oriented emerging-market economy able to generate relatively high levels of economic growth had now been digested prompted calls for a post-GEAR policy, where an expansionary fiscal stance could properly address the need for improvements in state capacity, infrastructure and the like, thus helping to produce the much-vaunted South African 'developmental state' (Southall 2006b; Andreasson 2007b; Fine 2008).

ASGISA symbolizes the latest instalment in the ANC's post-transition transformation of the South African economy and the role of the government in promoting markets and development. Essentially, ASGISA has been promoted as a strategy to overcome what Mbeki understands as South Africa's debilitating legacy of 'two economies' in one country:[10]

The 'third world economy' exists side by side with the modern 'first world economy' ... [but is] structurally disconnected from [it].... [To] end the 'third world economy's' underdevelopment and marginalisation ... will require sustained government intervention [and] resource transfers ... includ[ing] education and training, capital for business development and ... social and economic infrastructure, marketing information and appropriate technology. (Mbeki 2003, quoted in Gelb 2006: 24)

To overcome this gap between developed and Third World economies in one country, ASGISA prescribes a major expansion of infrastructure and skills and the boosting of job creation by prioritizing labour-intensive export sectors such as tourism and business process outsourcing (ibid.: 25).

ASGISA is in a sense the final step towards South Africa's normalization as an emerging market of note, supposedly able to compete in the global economy while also addressing the huge developmental backlog at home. By aiming to 'eliminate the second economy', i.e. bringing the majority of South Africa's poor into the developed economy, the ANC imagines that a successful implementation of ASGISA will make it possible to 'more than meet the Millennium Development Goals' so that the 'second decade of freedom will be the decade in which we radically reduce inequality and virtually eliminate poverty' (Mlambo-Ngcuka 2006a). ASGISA thus represents an alignment of economic policy with the increasingly prominent discourse on the developmental state.

In the end, whether the ANC's economic policies are deemed to be successful or a failure will significantly affect the nature and direction of debates and the political contestation over transformation as envisioned in the ANC's pursuit of the NDR. Cultural and developmental (in the broadest sense of the term) aspects and consequences of South Africa's post-apartheid trajectory are furthermore an integral part of the broader project of transformation. Without resolving the lingering question about the importance of indigenization and a revival of African values, South Africa will not be able to move on to further consolidate the political and economic gains already made.

African Renaissance or nativist cul-de-sac?

A common feature of politics in post-colonial countries profoundly shaped by historical legacies of settler colonialism is the need for some form of indigenization to accompany developmental policies. In practical terms this has generally meant shifting participation in politics and in the formal economy away from historically dominant white minorities for whose needs these political systems and economies were previously geared towards an increasing rate of participation by 'indigenous' peoples. In southern Africa this refers principally to black Africans.[11] Indigenization has increasingly also come to refer to a broader process of cultural transformation, and this 'culture politics' has often been as contentious as debates on economic transformation via affirmative action policies like BEE. Indeed, '"Rainbowism" as the official imagination of the South African nation soon found itself in tension with resurgent forms of nativism and populism' (Ndlovu-Gatsheni 2008: 68).

In a controversial debate article in the *Mail and Guardian*, entitled 'Wrath of dethroned white males', University of KwaZulu-Natal vice-chancellor Malegapuru Makgoba argued stridently for the need to comprehensively reorientate South African society away from the Western values on which colonial domination was based towards African ones representing the cultures of South Africa's black majority.

> Africans will not transform this country through previously dominant foreign rules, values or cultures. No dominant group ever transforms society through subservience and alien values ... now that Africans are dominant we must Africanise and not apologise for our Africanness ... When we say '*Mayibuye iAfrika*' [let Africa return] we mean it and mean business. (Makgoba 2005)

The debate ignited by Makgoba's rather confrontational arguments is part and parcel of the greater debate about the need for an African Renaissance in South Africa as a means for formerly colonized black South Africans to reclaim not only political and economic power, but cultural self-determination as well. If *ubuntu* has generally been the philosophical and cultural language in which this kind of cultural indigenization has been couched (see Chapter 3), the African Renaissance constitutes the tangible goal towards which South African society ought to aspire. In more concrete terms, whereas *ubuntu* is the spirit of this broader transformation of society, BEE has been the primary tool wielded to bring about transformation, although it is fairly obvious that BEE has not been directly concerned with the cultural aspects of that transformation. And just as there is a danger that BEE becomes merely an elite enrichment scheme which does little to broaden access to jobs and improved living standards for poor South Africans, there is also a danger that the cultural aspirations grounded in *ubuntu* and reflected in the notion of an African Renaissance spill over into a nativism or chauvinistic nationalism that

167

places the notion of a pluralist democracy in which all belong, the so-called 'Rainbow Nation', in danger, as has been argued by both Ndlovu-Gatsheni (2008) and Mangcu (2008). In such a case *ubuntu* becomes little more than the rhetoric in which politics as usual is couched.

South Africa's syncretic heritage Before BEE and the more general (some would argue superficial) articulation of a cultural reorientation based on the concept of *ubuntu* can be considered, these developments must first be related to the syncretic tradition of politics and societal values more broadly out of which the ANC has emerged as South Africa's political hegemon. Because the ANC is Africa's oldest nationalist party, and because South Africans have arguably fought Africa's longest liberation struggle, Ndlovu-Gatsheni (2007: 25–6) argues that 'there is no liberation struggle that was so cosmopolitan in ideological terms as the South African one'. This 'cosmopolitanism' is not synonymous with the notion of syncretism as it is used here, i.e. the combination of a variety of ideological beliefs and practices that have together shaped ANC politics and South African society more generally, but it is indicative of a struggle that has throughout its existence drawn on a diverse array of ideas and approaches to the traditional and the modern in its articulation of alternatives to settler colonial domination (see Ferguson 2006, on Africa's hybrid or 'alternate' modernity). This embrace of diversity was always controversial, as indicated by the protestations of Africanists like Anton Lembede, who opposed the '*bambazonke*', or catch-all, 'ideological disposition' of the ANC (ibid.: 30–1) and who as a result of this opposition also agitated, along with Oliver Tambo and Walter Sisulu, in the immediate post-Second World War era for the expulsion of communists from the Transvaal Congress on account of the supposed incompatibility of communist and Africanist ideologies. The ideational lineage of this syncretic tradition is crucial for understanding how shifts in ANC thinking have produced important shifts in policy. Moreover, a rediscovery of the ANC's and the nation's syncretic heritage might temper more exclusivist (or indeed xenophobic and racist) forms of nativism, thus making politics more accepting of new ways of thinking about South Africa's future and what development for all really ought to entail for the large majority of South Africans still left on the margins of the wealth creation that has continued apace since the end of apartheid.

In a recent study of the 'historical roots of the post-apartheid citizenship problems', Ndlovu-Gatsheni (ibid.: 27–31) outlines 'four strands' of the ANC's syncretic ideational lineage. These are: 1) an 'African bourgeois ideology of legitimation', basically a moderate and elitist ideology seeking inclusion of Africans in existing political and social institutions and an acceptance of Western liberal ideals (cf. Ekeh 1975); 2) an exclusivist form of black liberation, originating in an 'Ethiopianist outlook' and closely related to the pan-Africanism and a nativism where the struggle against apartheid was primarily interpreted in race terms, and which argues that 'citizenship in post-apartheid South Africa should be rooted in African communal identities, values, and virtues', with the Pan-Africanist Congress (PAC) under the leadership of Robert Sobukwe and the BCM led by Steve Biko its concrete political manifestations (cf. Gerhart 1978; Halisi 1997);[12] 3) a traditionalist form of thought originating in ethnic nationalism, exemplified by the Inkatha Freedom Party (IFP), its Chief Gatsha Mangosuthu Buthelezi advocating liberation along ethnic-national lines (an approach often criticized by the left for essentially complying with the apartheid regime's notion of 'separate development', culminating in its Bantustan – ethnically defined 'homelands' – policy); and 4) 'Afro-Marxism', emphasizing the class struggle over that of race and exemplified by the SACP (although it is difficult to determine the degree to which a more traditionally Western form of Marxism, as opposed to Afro-Marxism, influenced the SACP).

An understanding of the ANC's syncretic heritage as resulting from an intermixing of these four strands of thinking about liberation and about what kinds of values should underpin the post-apartheid order finds popular expression in a common understanding of the ANC as a 'broad church', encompassing a range of South Africans opposed to apartheid but whose different ethnic, class, religious and ideological backgrounds have sometimes caused difficulties given the divisive national culture in which their movement exists. While the Afro-Marxist and ethnic nationalist ideologies (ethnic nationalist here meaning the 'separatist' line initially advocated by the IFP and later also by various Afrikaner organizations) have receded in terms of their influence on national politics, the main ideological contestation over what direction politics will take in a post-Mbeki era may well depend on the outcome of a struggle for influence between a liberal or 'African bourgeois' tradition, perhaps best represented by COPE's recent challenge to ANC dominance, and the sort of African 'nativism' that many fear is ascendant within the ANC today. Whereas current ANC leaders like ANC president Jacob Zuma and, especially, ANC Youth League (ANCYL) leader Julius Malema are understood to represent the nativist and populist faction, the role of former president Mbeki in this battle of ideas is somewhat unclear, as

169

is his role in relation to COPE. Mbeki has on one hand been demonized by the left for his 'neoliberal' credentials and aloof demeanour (Mbembe 2006) but has also been considered responsible for an increasing racialization, indeed a nativist turn, of South African politics during his presidency in the light of major controversies ranging from HIV/AIDS to crime and Zimbabwe (Mangcu 2008).

In the most vociferous criticism of the Mbeki legacy, the former president becomes the embodiment of a toxic combination of all that is worst in both the African bourgeois and nativist traditions.

> Although of a secular nature, this new millenarianism and nativist revivalism is using the eschatological language of the 'revolution second coming' in order to paint as the epitome of the Antichrist one of the most worldly, cosmopolitan and urbane political leaders modern Africa has ever known [Mbeki]. Even though the followers of the maprofeti [Zuma] do not believe in the morality of the Christian church – especially in matters of adultery – they are threatening President Thabo Mbeki with God's wrath. They want to exact vengeance, to humiliate him and to punish him for his alleged political sins – a neo-liberal, aloof, secretive and paranoid intellectual who is bent on centralising power and on driving South Africa towards a Zimbabwe-style dictatorship. (Mbembe 2006, quoted in Ndlovu-Gatsheni 2007: 44)

It is in the context of this syncretic, fractious and sometimes volatile cultural and intellectual climate that a more specific cultural politics has been articulated and pursued.

Ubuntu and the African Renaissance Because *ubuntu* emphasizes a communal humanity, this traditional African philosophy is well suited as a cultural/philosophical anchor of any politics aiming to heal rifts in a divided society like South Africa's and to promote a collective (in terms of the country's diverse population) challenge to the legacy of underdevelopment, antagonism and mistrust bequeathed by the colonial and apartheid eras. The communal notion of care for others and the notion of self-reliance (Mbigi and Maree 1995; van Binsbergen 2001), not merely in the individual sense but also in the deeper sense of what African traditions can offer people in Africa when it comes to devising new solutions to contemporary developmental problems, that *ubuntu* entails is also useful as a grounding for the more explicitly political project of an African Renaissance. Whatever the merits of aspiring to a society and politics guided by the spirit of *ubuntu*, and however steep the challenges of meaningfully translating such potentially ephemeral concepts into a concrete basis for a new kind of politics, *ubuntu* and its reflections in the language of the African Renaissance have become an integral part of the public discourse on indigenization and of addressing the 'third pillar' of the NDR. The key question is whether *ubuntu* can indeed become the conceptual vehicle through which the ANC and South Africa as a whole can transcend past divisions and the ideological restrictions on its ability to think anew about how to best forge a genuinely sustainable path to greater well-being. If this is possible, this cultural (and spiritual) regeneration would indeed fulfil Mbeki's dream rooted in his 'I am an African' speech (Bongma 2004: 291)[13] of an African Renaissance led by South Africa and inspiring an entire continent to greater achievements, thereby reclaiming Africa's dignity on the global stage.

The aspirations embodied in this call for a renaissance are ambitious indeed:

> The African Renaissance vision is an all-embracing concept that draws its inspiration from the rich and diverse history and cultures of Africa. It acknowledges Africa as the cradle of humanity, whilst providing a framework for the modern Africa to re-emerge as a significant partner in the New World Order. This framework touches all areas of human endeavour; political, economic, social, technological, environmental and cultural. (Jana 2001: 38, quoted in Bongma 2004: 292)

Mbeki made this renaissance an integral part of his speeches to international audiences, laying out his ambitions for South Africa and the continent throughout the 1990s and into the present decade. In the context of these speeches the renaissance focused primarily on the need to reject tyranny and corruption in Africa and to instead embrace a fairly liberal notion of good governance and prudent policy-making so that African nations would be able to claim their place at the global table of genuine democracies (Bongma 2004: 292). Only when this new cultural politics was directed at a domestic audience did the tone become more nativist in nature. The problem, according to van Kessel (2001: 43), is that one could never be certain whether Mbeki's renaissance was primarily promoting modernization (as in the rhetoric about good governance), neo-traditionalism or Africanization. That ambivalence about the meaning of and intentions behind the renaissance remains, and it constitutes the main line of demarcation between those who see it as a positive project and those who fear its divisive and anti-democratic potential.

In addition to the exhortations to *ubuntu* and an African Renaissance

171

emanating from leading politicians, others have also taken up the challenge to promote 'African values' in South Africa's public life. Titus Mafolo, founder of South Africa's controversial Native Club, a 'think tank' aspiring to 'explore and promote African identity' (Carroll 2006), notes that despite political transformation and an ongoing if less rapid and comprehensive economic transformation, there is still resistance to the notion of cultural transformation (cf. Ndlovu-Gatsheni 2008).

> Many South Africans would readily seek to locate our transition somewhere between the existing dominant global ideologies ... and adopt a negative stance towards anyone suggesting the indigenisation of our revolution. In part, this is because both in apartheid-colonial education and propaganda as well as in the general teachings of the liberation movement there was, at worst, the denigration and, at best, the marginalisation of indigenous knowledge systems. Accordingly, the body of knowledge as represented by Ubuntu would generally be regarded as part of nativist thought that can only drag our country backwards. Those who attempt to articulate Ubuntu are dismissed as anachronistic idealists ... Even comrades that are agnostics and materialists respectfully acknowledge Christianity, Islam and Judaism as religions, but African belief systems as superstitions. Accordingly, we should look no further for colonised minds that need, as Ngugi Wa Thiongo' says, decolonisation. (Mafolo 2006)

Initiatives like Mafolo's Native Club, of which President Mbeki's office was a sponsor (Gumede 2007: 165), have been criticized for their potential to divide and for amounting to little more than a nativist reaction to liberal democracy and an economic order hopelessly compromised by its origins in and associations with Western colonialism and ideology. Indeed, its allegedly racially exclusivist membership suggests the initiative might amount to little more than 'racial nationalism' that 'smacks of a deep inferiority complex', thus endangering rather than promoting democratic dialogue (Kadalie and Bertelsmann 2006). On the other hand, Ndlovu-Gatsheni (2008: 54) argues that dismissing initiatives like the Native Club, and indeed nativism in a very general sense, as nothing more than 'fake philosophy and anti-racist racism is too simplistic and runs roughshod over the key contours of this phenomenon'. This interpretation stands in contrast to that of Mangcu (2008), who portrays nativism as a clearly negative challenge to South Africa's syncretic heritage. What these kinds of criticism presumably ignore are the positive aspirations of nativism understood as a benevolent form of African empowerment.

We seek to build a climate congenial to continued reflection and self-examination by the native intelligentsia, asserting itself in the realm of arts and culture, socio-economy and politics. The SA intelligentsia faces a cardinal responsibility *to mobilise the weakest and most vulnerable sections of the society to find their voices, to live up to its historical obligation of developing and sustaining critical consciousness among the people.* We see the scientific, literary and artistic members of our society playing a central role in the regeneration of our young people, in the form of creative writing, poetry, participating in debates and generally contesting ideas. (Titus Mafolo writing in the *Financial Mail*, 19 May 2006, quoted in Ndlovu-Gatsheni 2008: 71–2; emphasis added)

This argument about duties on the part of the intelligentsia towards the masses may seem all too replete with the trappings of an old-fashioned elitist and top-down notion of vanguardism to which some parts of the liberation movement (including the Mbeki camp accused of 'Zanufication' of the ANC's internal structures) have for too long been wedded. While the notion of finding and listening to the voices of the marginalized and promoting critical consciousness certainly fits well with the way in which post-development understands how new thinking on development might emerge, i.e. the milieu in which such thinking can be sustained and thrive, elitism and top-down processes do not. This tension between positive and negative aspects of nativism and of the promotion of African values in public life remains a point of social and political contestation, not just between black and white but within the ANC and the Tripartite Alliance as well. And considering the relatively short period in which a variety of actors in South African society have sought to counter the ideological legacy of colonialism and apartheid with aspirations towards an African Renaissance, it is too early to tell what the eventual outcome of this kind of cultural politics will be.

Whether a new African politics anchored in the concept of *ubuntu* can move beyond the rhetoric of an Africanist intelligentsia and the politicians who, like Mbeki, argue that an African Renaissance is the only durable sociocultural foundation on which a prosperous South Africa (and African continent) can be built remains to be seen. Translating such ideas into politics requires finding an instrument with which to transform society in a more 'African' direction. So far the most concrete instrument for doing so has been the policies relating to BEE, although the degree to which the aims and outcomes of BEE can really contribute to genuine socio-economic transformation, let alone the kind of broader emancipation envisioned by the proponents of the African Renaissance anchored in *ubuntu*, remains highly controversial.

Black Economic Empowerment If *ubuntu* is the philosophy and general set of values in which an indigenous (i.e. African) politics can be located, then BEE can be conceived of as indigenization incarnate, the embodiment in policy of the general pursuit of indigenization. On a positive reading BEE becomes a vehicle through which not only the South African economy but the country's knowledge production and values can become transformed in an African image, thus helping the majority of South Africans to better connect with and buy into the contemporary democratic dispensation. Understanding the emerging BEE elite as an African 'vanguard' seizing hold of the commanding heights of the economy as well as exerting increasing influence within the nation's intelligentsia by means of forums such as the Native Club (Ndlovu-Gatsheni 2008) suggests that South Africa is moving closer to achieving the comprehensive goals of the NDR. On a negative reading BEE becomes a sordid affair where entrenched elites co-opt the new African bourgeoisie – an elite enrichment scheme leaving the poor neglected and which, by perpetuating South Africa's inequalities and indignities, will lead to a dangerous populist backlash. More fundamentally, from this critical point of view, there exists a fundamental tension, indeed contradiction, between the goals of BEE and the broader goals of the NDR (Southall 2008: 284).

BEE has under Mbeki's direction actively promoted the rise of party-connected individuals into elite circles of South African corporate life. Illustrious ANC cadres, such as Saki Macozoma, Popo Molefe, Jayendra Naidoo, Cyril Ramaphosa and Tokyo Sexwale, were early examples of key political players who transitioned from 'struggle' politics into powerful corporate positions. As a result BEE has since its inception been dogged by accusations of elitism and outright corruption (ibid.), but even notable scholarly critics of BEE as it has become practised have also recognized that the ANC had in 1994, owing to the extreme inequalities bequeathed to it from the apartheid era, 'no option … but to use state power to promote greater black ownership and control of the economy' (Southall 2006a: 69). In any case, the fact that relatively few individuals became the main beneficiaries of major BEE deals was eventually acknowledged by the ANC leadership and has resulted in the enactment in 2003 of the Broad-Based Black Economic Empowerment Act, designed to disperse the benefits of BEE among a wider segment of society, as opposed to the relatively narrow elite who have in the past been the main beneficiaries of such policies. According to President Kgalema Motlanthe (then general secretary of the ANC), BEE often entailed 'transfer rather than transformation' and has accordingly failed to create 'new markets and new drivers of domestic demand in the economy' (quoted in *Business Day*, 1 October 2004).

BEE constitutes a key government strategy for indigenization, and long-term socio-economic transformation, of South Africa's economy by promoting a black capitalist class in all spheres of the national economy. Chabane et al. (2007: 562) trace the origins of BEE to the spirit of the 1955 Freedom Charter (the symbolism of which is now being claimed by COPE, the breakaway faction from and new opposition to the ANC) and, more specifically, to the 1994 RDP, which prescribed 'legislative and other means' to 'protect or advance' previously 'disadvantaged' individuals or groups. Overlapping interests between black political and business actors, the origins of which lie in the emergence of an embryonic black business class during the apartheid era,[14] have ensured an active pursuit of this form of indigenization, which has recently been formalized in charters setting out sweeping targets for (ownership) transformation of core industries such as mining and financial services (ibid.). To comply with BEE legislation South African companies must promote appropriate levels of black ownership and black representation at all levels of operation, from entry-level employees to highest-level executives (Lewis et al. 2004; Southall 2004). Controversies about whether BEE is for 'blacks only' or whether it properly benefits other minorities (and white women) as well are ongoing and remain unresolved.[15] Such questions are, in terms of both public perceptions and political rhetoric surrounding this concept of empowerment, directly tied to deeper understandings of indigeneity and belonging.

There is of course no guarantee that the black capitalist class which BEE seeks to promote will be any more likely to base their operations on concerns for the poor than do white capitalists. There is, according to Friedman and Chipkin (2001: 26), 'a deep gulf between the policy preoccupations of the elite, regardless of ideological stripe, and the poor'. Mzi Khumalo, a former political prisoner who became chairman of the mining holding company JCI, is but one example of the controversies that the new BEE elites have generated. On the issue of corporate responsibility he argued that 'we are here to run a business. I am not for any of this brotherhood stuff.' Khumalo subsequently authorized the retrenchment of thousands of mineworkers from JCI before the company folded, and he was forced to quit following allegations of serious mismanagement

(*Sunday Times*, 21 March 1999). With this in mind it should perhaps not be entirely surprising that Mbeki once upon a time argued that

> black capitalism, rather than being the antithesis [to white capitalism exploiting black South Africans], is rather confirmation of parasitism, with no redeeming features whatsoever, without any extenuating circumstances to excuse its existence. (Mbeki 1985)

While the emerging black business elite have supported BEE, established white businesses (local and multinational) have, not surprisingly, taken a more cautious approach. As a rule, big businesses are more receptive to the arguments for BEE than are small ones, the latter being more concerned about short-term costs of compliance with BEE legislation. It has not been considered politically expedient for any businesses, especially domestic ones, to come out very strongly against the fundamental idea underlying BEE, which is that both private and public sectors have a responsibility to ensure that 'previously disadvantaged' South Africans are integrated at all levels of the economy and that such integration is in the long-term interest of all parties involved. In fact, business opposition to what is after all a fairly radical and highly interventionist government programme of race-based redistribution has been surprisingly muted (Iheduru 2008). According to Colin Reddy of BusinessMap, which monitors BEE compliance by companies in South Africa, 'business people are talking largely about the details of implementation [of BEE policies], rather than expressing total opposition to the very notion [of BEE]' (quoted in *Business Day*, 1 April 2005).[16]

There have, however, been tensions between the state and business throughout the BEE era as South Africa's political economy continues to revolve around 'an odd combination of new (political) power without money and old money without power' (*Financial Mail*, 15 December 2006, quoted in Southall 2008: 297). The Sectoral Charters focusing on transformation of key sectors of the economy have in particular been controversial. For example, the 2002 Minerals and Petroleum Resources Development Bill transferred sovereign rights to all mineral resources in South Africa to the state, which now grants corporations the right to exploit these resources provided that they promote BEE and contribute to the socio-economic development of areas where they operate. The bill has been criticized on four main points: 1) it compromises security of tenure by not allowing for automatic transfers of old to new company mining rights; 2) the renewal of mining rights is not automatically renewable beyond the initial thirty-year period; 3) the bill allows for administrative discretion not subject to appeal in granting mining rights; and 4) several ministries have an input into decisions regarding where minerals may be beneficiated, thus complicating the entire process (*Business Day*, 11 June 2002).

The Johannesburg Securities Exchange (JSE) Gold Index fell 11.8 per cent on the day the proposed minerals bill was leaked to media. Further losses by Anglo American and BHP Billiton on the London stock market followed the initial 'shock' on the JSE (*Mail and Guardian*, 8 August 2002). Local South African and international media were quick to pounce on the South African government's 'intentions' and the 'dangers of nationalization'. 'Pretoria aims to undermine white-owned mineral rights', 'Anglo Platinum reviews expansion plans' and 'Mining giants tackle empowerment charter' were some immediate headline responses in Africa's leading business daily to the minerals bill (*Business Day*, 14 August 2002). The initial danger alert was followed by government assertions that there are 'no plans to nationalise mining industry', and Steven Friedman, a well-known policy analyst and director of the Centre for Policy Studies in Johannesburg, noted in an opinion piece entitled 'There is scope to avert a business nightmare' that state–business collaboration would not be impossible (*Business Day*, 15 August 2002). Following the initial outrage, government felt pressured to respond.

> Shaken by the 'savagery' of market reaction to a leaked black empowerment charter, the government has elevated the issue of empowerment in mining beyond the exclusive remit of Minister of Minerals and Energy Phumzile Mlambo-Ngcuka. 'They now realise the charter has implications for the entire economy,' said an analyst who asked not to be named. Mlambo-Ngcuka will be accompanied by Minister of Finance Trevor Manuel, Minister of Trade and Industry Alec Erwin and Minister of Labour Membathisi Mdladlana at a top-level powwow with Anglo American and De Beers next Wednesday. (*Mail and Guardian*, 8 August 2002)

While acknowledging support for the basic principles of the minerals bill, De Beers director Jonathan Oppenheimer noted upon its announcement that it might threaten the company's planned expansion projects in South Africa, at that time totalling a projected 8 billion rand over a five-year period. According to Oppenheimer, 'the company needs a 20- to 30-year planning horizon and the Bill, in its current draft form, does not give sufficient clarity to enable us to confidently commit to that level of investment' (*Business Day*, 10 June 2002). South Africa's largest

South Africa

petrochemical company, Sasol, would later engender controversy when reporting to the New York Stock Exchange (Sasol is listed on both the JSE and the NYSE) that BEE constituted a 'business risk', as did Anglo American's then chairman Tony Trahar when suggesting that doing business in South Africa was still 'politically risky' (Gumede 2007: 286). These are clear examples of big business using its clout to influence government policy-making by threatening an 'investment strike' – a threat that was at the time harshly denounced by President Mbeki.

The results of BEE since 1994 have been 'uneven and difficult to quantify'; an initial drive to transfer (primarily financial) assets into black ownership by means of controversial Special Purpose Vehicles seemed to have failed by the end of the 1990s when black ownership of the Johannesburg Stock Exchange fell to below 4 per cent from a peak of about 10 per cent in the mid-1990s (Southall 2004: 318). As a result

[t]he private sector remains overwhelmingly in white hands: 98% of executive director positions of JSE-listed companies in 2002 were white … by far the most important point is that blacks have made extremely limited inroads into the ownership, control and senior management of the private corporate sector. (ibid.: 318–19)

The problem of declining black ownership during the late 1990s relates to a more fundamental problem inherent in the BEE process. As the NDR 'charged the ANC with using state power to deracialise the economy', the ANC came to 'regard the parastatals as "sites of transformation"', whereas the private sector property is protected by the constitution and 'the close scrutiny of the government's policies by global markets' (Southall 2008: 291). So when it comes to empowerment in the private sector, the fact that ANC 'cadres' lacked both business skills and capital of their own meant that the ANC had to pursue an empowerment policy whereby they have attempted to create 'capitalists without capital' (Southall 2004). The potential problems of such a precarious basis for empowering black capitalists have manifested themselves during the current global financial crisis.

Stephan van der Walt, head of corporate finance at Bravura Equity Services, says: 'A basic financial principle, which is so often ignored on a large scale on BEE transactions … is that shares cannot be funded by debt, as the ability to repay a fixed debt obligation is dependent on a volatile share price … [T]he common Special Purpose Vehicle (SPV) BEE funding structure is problematic in that the value of liabilities often exceeds the value of assets when the purchased shares do not perform to expectations. (Milazi 2008)

By this arguably crude measure of indigenization of South Africa's economy, acquiring the political kingdom has not delivered the economic one. Moreover, this particular form of indigenization leaves itself open to the critics who argue that indigenization exacerbates societal divisions owing to a sense of resentment felt by those who feel excluded by BEE and may therefore worsen an already volatile situation when desperately poor South Africans come to view BEE as merely an enrichment vehicle for a few well-connected elites.

New directions with Zuma?

So where do these developments leave South Africa in the wake of the country's fourth democratic elections? What future for the ANC-led project of transformation and the ideals of the NDR? Now that the ANC has been returned with yet another overwhelming majority at the polls, despite challenges from the breakaway faction COPE and a strengthened DA, is it really feasible to expect its hegemony to erode in the foreseeable future? Whatever the future for the ANC as ruling party, social movements seem to be re-emerging as agents of some significant strength by putting pressure on government and articulating new visions for a politics of prioritizing the needs of the poor (e.g. Gibson 2006). A deep unhappiness with the 'ordinary country' that South Africa has become remains a powerful sentiment among not only the ANC's political opponents but among its grassroots supporters as well, as they have now handed the ANC yet another chance to deliver.

What will Jacob Zuma, as a political 'phenomenon' quite unlike those ANC leaders who have until now shaped the post-apartheid era, mean for South African democracy? Will Zuma's government usher in a period of increasing populism and nativism as its detractors worry, and would there in such an environment be any room for a national debate on genuine alternatives to development? Will South Africa, as the most complex and cosmopolitan national culture on the African continent, reflected in Zuma's first cabinet being the most racially diverse in South African history, ultimately prove to be the crucible in which some genuinely novel solutions to Africa's development impasse will emerge? Can South Africa produce a second miracle, one that proves more lasting in nature and more beneficial to all its inhabitants than did the first one?

All of these questions are giving rise to a crescendo of voices across society, from discontented liberals to the restless poor, asking what will be done and indeed what can be done to move South Africa beyond the current impasse. When Zuma is heralded as 'the Messiah' by some of his most ardent supporters he is saddled with very high expectations indeed. In this sense, Zuma's leadership of South Africa may well be the pivotal moment determining South Africa's long-term trajectory of democratic governance and development.

False prophet or champion of the masses?

> In a certain kind of way Zuma will be our first African president ... Nelson Mandela transcended everything and was a world figure. Thabo Mbeki spent a lot of time in England wearing pinstripe suits and smoking a pipe. Zuma is a real African. (Zuma biographer Jeremy Gordin, quoted in the *Guardian*, 20 April 2009)

The stakes are inevitably high in South Africa's current power shift, which, following the brief interregnum presided over by President Motlanthe, has replaced Mbeki's strange mix of Anglophilia and intellectual nativism with Zuma's supposedly traditionalist populism. Mbembe's (2006) analysis of the current situation exemplifies that of the strong sceptics, whereby even a socio-political apocalypse, what commentators would describe as 'the Zimbabwe scenario', is a possible outcome of the current nativist turn. In his article on the dangers of 'false prophets' (i.e. Jacob Zuma) Mbembe suggests that recent developments in South African politics and within the ANC constitute a 'Nongqawuse syndrome'. Nongqawuse was the nineteenth-century Xhosa prophetess whose prophecies created a millenarist movement culminating in the Xhosa cattle killings in 1856/57 and produced a humanitarian crisis and socio-political collapse of the Xhosa nation.[17] For Mbembe, the current trend towards nativism in South Africa contains aspects of millenarianism and thus the danger that it will lead to self-destruction and despair, as did the prophecies of Nongqawuse.

This criticism of Zuma as false prophet rests on three 'patterns' that constitute the 'Nongqawuse syndrome' (ibid.). First is the appearance of the false prophet (*maprofeti*), 'usually of very humble origins', who claims that a great resurrection is about to take place, claims that are backed by 'a certain level of mass hysteria' and the authority of the prophet himself, which rests on vague notions of his ancestry, tradition and culture. Second, the prophet's 'exuberant' behaviour is combined with a silence in the face of emergent 'mob rule' which the prophet generally condones and which may well become the catalyst for the promised resurrection. Third, established elites display 'cowardice' when challenged by this nativist and populist resurgence. As the prophet's message gains a foothold among an impoverished populace desperate for any hopeful message promising radical change, the prophet is 'ridiculed' by his more sophisticated opponents, who fail to see the seriousness of the situation. This argument about a new millenarianism in South Africa is of course the tale of Zuma's rise from humble origins to leader of the ANC and now also of Africa's most powerful nation. This is a rise that has been characterized and indeed made possible by Zuma's populist and traditionalist stance. It has allowed him to dismiss challenges to his moral authority, from the rape trial to the corruption charges, by referring to them as elite conspiracies hatched by his political opponents (within the ANC and supported by reactionary elements in society). Zuma has also been aided by the support provided him by the Tripartite Alliance and by South Africa's poor, who are desperate to line up behind a political force promising to wage battle against entrenched privilege and the 'neoliberal' ideology held responsible for the country's lack of comprehensive transformation. In other words, only Zuma can take the NDR forward by addressing all three of its pillars – the political, economic and cultural.

Contra Mbembe's argument about Zuma being a false prophet or representing a millenarian yearning for a new politics in which the people are empowered and reclaim control over government, Mangcu (2008: 166) suggests that there is 'something much more sophisticated at work' in the politics that have produced Zuma's ascendancy. Refuting the notion of Zuma the phenomenon as representative of an irrationalist and millenarian turn, Mangcu (ibid.: 169) argues that what is emerging is a 'well-organised movement' akin to Laclau's (2005) notion of a 'populist frontier'. According to this argument the politics of this populist movement, which is challenging the elitist and 'neoliberal' politics of the Mbeki administration, unfolds as follows. The challenge to state-centric and elitist politics begins with a variety of new social movements, such as the Treatment Action Campaign (TAC), which agitates for improved access to antiretroviral drugs to combat South Africa's AIDS epidemic (Friedman and Mottiar 2005; Mbali 2006), anti-privatization movements (McDonald and Ruiters 2005), landless people's movements (Mngxitama 2006) and other groups fighting their respective battles with the state without much interaction with each other.

It is when various actors in these movements begin to interact with each other in a substantial manner to collectively articulate critiques of the politics they challenge and make common cause in their respective struggles that the populist front emerges and where 'someone like Jacob Zuma emerges to hold [the] non-ideological frontier together' (Mangcu 2008: 169). This frontier is non-ideological because it represents a variety of movements that all challenge the status quo but not necessarily from the same ideological standpoint. According to Laclau (2005: 123, quoted in Mangcu 2008: 169): '[s]ince any kind of institutional system is inevitably at least partially limiting and frustrating, there is something appealing about any figure who challenges it, whatever the reasons and form of the challenge'. This notion of Zuma saying the right things at the right time fits well with the notion that his politics are vaguely defined, with both the left (including the ANC's Alliance partners, the SACP and COSATU) and cultural traditionalists finding his message appealing. Hence those who have pledged their support to this new movement within the ANC have done so 'to Zuma rather than to specific policies' (Gumede 2008: 267). As Mangcu (2008: 169) aptly put it, '[n]o populist leader in his or her right mind would risk dividing their frontier by proclaiming on ideology'.

In the final stage, where this populist movement attains power, the 'frontier' that brought it to power will begin to 'dissemble', mainly because 'positions must now be taken' (ibid.: 169). Just as the ANC had to take controversial decisions on the direction of South Africa's economic trajectory (e.g. with the move from RDP to GEAR), which had a detrimental effect on the relations among the diverse elements of the 'broad church' of support that brought the ANC to power, so will a future Zuma government have to make difficult choices among its various and not always commensurate priorities. In such an environment, which a future Zuma government will surely face, there are few reasons to expect that even the most adept political leadership will be able to govern inclusively when its support base contains everything from a self-styled progressive left, unions and social movements to cultural traditionalists and even ethnic/ nationalist chauvinists, as well as political insiders (like Zuma himself)[18] and those on the margins.

> Zuma built an odd left-populist coalition of disgruntled grassroots activists, trade unionists, socialists, unemployed youth, veteran guerrilla fighters, women's lobbies, supporters of causes ranging from the death penalty to virginity testing, black business tycoons, evangelicals, and 'the walking wounded' [those within the ANC who had been marginalized or ostracised by the Mbeki administration]. (Gumede 2008: 265)

So can Zuma's 'frontier' bring about a move beyond the current orthodoxy? While Zuma's ultimate 'insider' status in conventional ANC politics may suggest that this is not likely, it is also the case that social movements in South Africa are stronger in terms of capacity and more diverse in terms of ideology (and therefore capacity for innovation?) than elsewhere in the region. And because of the Tripartite Alliance these social forces are also better represented in government and other official circles than they would otherwise have been, and certainly more so than are their civil society counterparts in Botswana and Zimbabwe. This is a key advantage in terms of promoting transformation as the diversity of the 'populist frontier' implies an open-endedness in terms of goals and therefore also suggests a greater chance that a genuine break with development orthodoxy can take place. There is no other major movement with the same ability to contest governing power as ideologically and politically inclusive anywhere else in the region as the social forces behind Zuma's ascent to power. Nevertheless, the question remains open as to whether he and the forces that have supported his ascent can deliver on bold promises against the backdrop of increasingly violent protests and strikes in the context of a globally linked economic recession, and whether such delivery will really challenge the status quo in terms of the orthodox thinking on development which has so far guided South African policy-making.

It is the difficulty in forecasting what direction Zuma's government will take which frightens liberals and the left alike, albeit for different reasons. There is a fear among the former of left-wing populism and a fear of reactionary social politics combined with a continued accommodationist stance vis-à-vis big business among the latter. Although Zuma's rise to power is generally understood as having been made possible by the ANC's left wing he does not, in his own words, 'owe anyone anything' (*Mail and Guardian*, 24 April 2009). No camp within the ANC can take Zuma for granted and both his supporters and detractors (within and outside the ANC) may well be mischaracterizing his intentions. While the possibilities for a reorientation of politics and debates on development under Zuma's presidency cannot be determined with any degree of confidence at this early stage, it is nevertheless possible to suggest other areas where South Africa's project of transformation can obtain new stimulus. One debate that is highly relevant to the ongoing project of transformation is the rediscovery and reassessment of the social and political philosophy of Steve Biko.

Biko and Black Consciousness Stephen Biko had emerged on the national stage by the late 1960s as a formidable and intellectual student activist – a powerful critic of apartheid and of the greater historical moment of African colonization (Mngxitama 2006). The challenge of Biko, a young man in his twenties, to the apartheid mindset as it had taken root and festered in white and black South African minds alike blossomed at a time when the government, in the wake of the Sharpeville massacre in 1960 and the subsequent banning and harsh persecution of both the ANC and the PAC, had driven active opposition to apartheid underground or into exile. During a 1976 trial, Biko summarized the essence of the struggle prompted by Black Consciousness (BC) as 'the liberation of the black man first from psychological oppression by themselves through inferiority complex and secondly from the physical [oppression] accruing out of living in a white racist society' (Biko 1978: 100). Thus what was to become known as the BCM came to articulate a new and radical form of resistance at a time when the temporary beating into submission of the major liberation organizations left a vacuum to be filled.

> [Black Consciousness] entered a context where the most radical critique of the apartheid system had come in the form of the ANC's 1955 Freedom Charter, which would later be adopted as the platform of the Congress Movement. Broadly social democratic, the Charter's interpretation of the settler colony paradoxically denied the basis of a revolutionary challenge to the apartheid state. (Mngxitama et al. 2008: 4; cf. McKinley 1997: 22)

In the context of this post-Sharpeville and pre-Soweto uprising 'lull', BC emerged as an in many ways deeper and more fundamental challenge to the apartheid system than either the challenge posed by the ideologically 'broad church' of the ANC (including those who would later advocate elite integration via BEE as a means to 'transform' South Africa) or the nationalism of the PAC. At the same time, BC is of course in many ways intertwined in terms of bidirectional ideological influences with both the ANC and the PAC. The history of cross-pollination between the BCM and the major liberation organizations is a fact of liberation struggle history, even if the BCM would, following the death of Biko, be dismissed by Mandela as lacking in novelty and philosophical depth, being 'in essence a rehash of Garveyism' (Mandela 1978: 40, quoted in Mngxitama et al. 2008: 13). More disturbingly the BCM's Azanian People's Organization (AZAPO) would later come under violent attack by the ANC when BC was perceived as challenging the ANC's central role in the liberation struggle and the role of the United Democratic Front (UDF), which ANC exiles had sanctioned until they dismantled it upon returning home (Mngxitama 2006: 7). For Gibson (2006: 14–15), who contrasts the 'new' type of social movement represented by the BCM with 'old' ones like the ANC, it is what Biko called a 'quest for a true humanity', for Gibson a 'universal quest for agency and self-determination', which can provide intellectual space for a genuine democratic politics in the post-apartheid era.

The potential for anchoring a new post-apartheid politics in Biko's thought, which is not merely an expression of political activism but which constitutes a contribution to liberation philosophy proper (M. P. Moore 2008), rests on the claim that BC is inherently radical rather than simply nativist in the traditional-cum-reactionary sense in which it has been misunderstood in less nuanced accounts that dismiss it (and the BCM) as 'anti-white' or racialist in nature (Mangcu 2008: 3–4). When stating that 'being black is not a matter of pigmentation – [it is] a reflection of a mental attitude', Biko (1978: 48, quoted in Mangcu 2008: 3) articulates a vision for South Africa that sits quite uneasily with the reality of BEE policies and the nativist thrust of politics under Mbeki's leadership as characterized by Mangcu (2008). Moreover, Gibson (2006: 17–18) argues that the designation of all those peoples dismissed as 'non-whites' by the apartheid regime as 'Black' (Africans, coloureds, Indians) opened up a new space for radical politics because of the utter rejection of the divide-and-rule tactics inherent in the regime's policy of separate develop-ment underpinning the creation of the Bantustans that this notion of 'Blackness' entailed.

In this sense BEE would have been considered 'anathema' to the BCM (Mngxitama et al. 2008: 10) as it promoted

a completely non-racial society. We don't believe, for instance, in the so-called guarantees for minority rights, because guaranteeing minority rights [as advocated by the NP and IFP during the transition to demo-cracy] implies the recognition of portions of the community on a race basis. We believe that in our country there shall be no minority, there shall be no majority, just the people. And those people will have the same status before the law. So in a sense it will be a completely non-racial egalitarian society. (Biko, quoted in Mangcu 2008: 3–4)[19]

Because of its explicit recognition of South Africa's syncretic heritage in both politics and culture, BC represents a very different critique of white colonialism to that more crude and vindictive kind which has become the basis for indigenization by the ZANU-PF in Zimbabwe (see Scarnecchia 2006). BC also distinguishes itself in comparison with a more traditional and inherently conservative thrust of indigenization as envisioned by the BDP and Tswana chiefs in Botswana (see Maundeni 2004). This understanding of BC fits well with Ndlovu-Gatsheni's (2007: 25–6) characterization of the very cosmopolitan nature of the South African liberation struggle when compared with liberation movements elsewhere in Africa. At the same time the radical nature of BC and the emphasis it places on the emancipation of black people and on the importance of recognizing the inherent value of African thought irrespective of any 'validation' and 'legitimization' by a Western, colonial intellectual paradigm means that new ideas about development and emancipation based on BC will inevitably come up against and clash with the reality of modern-day South Africa. While home to a diverse cultural heritage, South Africa is also the most Westernized society in Africa and the most thoroughly integrated into the global economy. In that sense the radicalization of thought posed by BC will continue to be perceived as a threat to the post-apartheid settlement, what Saul (2001) calls the 'post-apartheid denouement', and to the procedural democracy and elite economic integration on which that settlement uneasily rests.

The challenge posed by Biko's BC to what is a settlement forged by outgoing and incoming representatives of state power (the NP and the ANC, the latter increasingly insulated from the broader social movements from which it had drawn support) holds promise precisely because, as Gibson (2006: 24–5) argues, if social movements are to be effective they must 'aid the mental liberation needed to see past the fetish of the state form' with all its inherent limitations on what is deemed possible. Here the bold aims of BC echo a long tradition of thinking about African and colonial emancipation that hearkens back to the importance placed by Fanon on mental emancipation of colonized peoples. And it relates also to a vision of emancipation, however unfulfilled, articulated in Mbeki's notion of an African Renaissance (Vale and Maseko 1998) and to the more constructive aspects of new phenomena such as the Native Club seeking to promote African intellectual independence and integrity among South Africa's intellectuals and policy-makers (Ndlovu-Gatsheni 2008). This understanding of liberation fits well with Gibson's reading of Fanon, suggesting that

> Fanon's brilliance was not a product of 'ontological pessimism' [about the inevitable degeneration of social movements when taken over by 'ultra-vanguardist militarists'], but a product of his ability to *practice dialectics* [cf. Mngxitama et al. 2008 on Biko] and undertake a critical

analysis of the contradictions in the national liberation movements with which he had been deeply involved. He argued that if national consciousness was not deepened into an awareness of social needs (i.e. into a humanism) it would inevitably retrogress. This practice of Fanon's humanism is akin to Michael Neocosmos' [2006a] notion ... of an 'authentic democracy' which emanates from mass movements in society. (Gibson 2006: 34)

And if national consciousness does not become enlightened by *ubuntu* it degenerates into a racial and ethnic chauvinism – Fanon's 'total brutality' (ibid.: 35).

So BC is important to considerations of a different post-apartheid trajectory, indeed to any notion of thinking beyond development.

By borrowing from the resistance that came before it – the anticolonial struggles on the African continent, philosophers and thinkers, and the Black Power movement in the United States – Black Consciousness made resistance not only imaginable but possible. (Mngxitama et al. 2008: 1)

In this sense BC is the philosophical-cum-political thrust necessary to move beyond mere talk of reforming the current system by means of tinkering with macroeconomic policies like the RDP, GEAR and ASGISA – shifting the gravity leftwards or rightwards but not producing a qualitative shift in the ultimate aims of government policy. It was the 'genius' of the BCM that it recognized the strength of political consciousness and mobilization, ultimately the strength of *adaptation*, that South Africa's syncretic tradition entailed – a recognition which constituted the BCM's core contribution to '"culture making" and political mobilization' (Mangcu 2008: 121). This political thrust is the kind of force which, if reignited and re-engaged with, may finally usher in a new moment where the 'third pillar' of transformation, i.e. cultural emancipation, emerges and is taken seriously as a means and justification by which priorities might be re-oriented so that the values represented by *ubuntu* can become concretized in developmental policy-making. With such a process unfolding it then becomes possible to actually think beyond development.

But what does this thinking beyond development really mean in the contemporary South African context? It means thinking about more than reforming the status quo, instead considering larger issues about how to *heal* a society that is dangerously fragmenting under the pressures exerted by modernity and globalization. It means thinking about how Africans as peoples with their own histories and values can not only become integrated, thus being made to fit into an existing order not really of their own making, but how instead they can actually *shape* and indeed create new priorities for the future – the 'universal quest for agency and self-determination' (Gibson 2006: 14). This is a necessary step for any claim to implementing a new politics that can finally and decisively turn the page on the old colonial order.

It is in this way that BC, injected into the spirit of today's new social movements and eventually into values underpinning government, could contribute to a more hopeful trajectory. It is furthermore Biko's explicit recognition of South Africa's 'joint culture' which can provide post-development thinking (as outlined in Chapter 3) with an anchoring in the South African cultural context, thus making any new vision beyond development as currently constituted better able to deal with the reality of a multicultural South Africa in which several strands of ideology and political thinking compete for primacy. This recognition of a joint culture forged by black and white, what Mangcu (2008) identifies as South Africa's 'syncretic heritage', also enables those wishing to articulate an alternative future to do so in a more constructive and self-confident way than has been the case with those who during Mbeki's very divisive presidency came to promote increasingly abrasive nativist accounts of what South African culture is (ibid.; cf. Ndlovu-Gatsheni 2007). In this sense BC does not simply advocate or entail the reversal of discrimination but would in fact reflect the noble sentiment in Mandela's famous 'I am prepared to die' speech, rejecting domination of any group of South Africans by any other group.[20] This constructive understanding of the joint legacy of African and European in South Africa is also recognized in Mbeki's poignant 'I am an African' speech, delivered at his inauguration as President of the Republic in 1999, even if that sentiment did not on the whole shape politics during his years leading the nation.

If in the end the modernist and nativist strands of conceptualizing politics, development and transformation in South Africa are fraught with serious dangers, then it might be Biko's notion of a joint culture which remains standing as the best guardian of South Africa's syncretic heritage and thus the sort of environment in which post-development thinking can flourish. It could then be the case that South Africans faced with a contemporary developmental impasse find that the thinking originally championed by a young man whose own part in the greater liberation struggle came to an early end as he lay naked and dying in a police Land Rover, en route to a faraway hospital following what was in apartheid South Africa an all too common round of police interrogation and beating, provides the means to conceiving of solutions that so far have seemed so elusive.

Strength in diversity?

Considering politics in contemporary South Africa as profoundly shaped by the ANC and its syncretic ideational heritage, what becomes immediately obvious is how the heterogeneity of the ANC's tradition distinguishes it from much more homogeneous ideational heritages in Zimbabwe under ZANU-PF dominance and, especially, in Botswana led by the BDP. It is this heterogeneity in thinking about what a post-colonial order should look like which makes the South African case more difficult to analyse on account of its inherent complexity, but also very intriguing because of the promises for innovation that this heterogeneity entails. South Africa is in this sense poised at yet another crossroads as a new era following the dominance of a 'neoliberal' ANC under the leadership of Thabo Mbeki is replaced by the leadership of Jacob Zuma and an ANC dominated by more explicitly populist, and in some cases also nativist, politicians, and the return of those, like Winnie Madikizela-Mandela, who were marginalized during the previous era. This new crossroads may have as profound an impact on South Africa's future direction as did the nature of the transition in 1994 from apartheid to multiracial democracy.

There is in all likelihood more scope for constructive interaction between 'top' (state) and 'bottom' (civil society) in South Africa in terms of formulating a vision for transformation than is the case in either Botswana or Zimbabwe, where change is less likely to be driven by a well-balanced interaction between state and societal actors. If social movements are able to break the 'state form' fetish (Gibson 2006) and harness *ubuntu* to inspire a reconnection with traditional views on governance in the spirit of South Africa's syncretic tradition and hybrid modernity, then the 'third pillar' of (cultural) transformation may be able to catapult public debate and eventually also public policy beyond the orthodox left–right impasse. For this to happen, the Tripartite Alliance must continue to function as a genuinely diverse and broad church in which a wide range of ideological streamings continue to interact, cross-pollinate and enjoy access to the actual levers of power, and the transition from Mbeki to Zuma should at least be a step in that direction as opposed to a retreat from it.

What is perhaps most disconcerting about the South African trajectory is that, when compared with the challenges posed by post-independence developments in Botswana and Zimbabwe, it might just be an example of the kind of dysfunctional normalization towards which other countries in the region might move (if not necessarily aspire). A post-diamond-boom Botswana that manages to facilitate some degree of economic diversification and generate a more active civil society might not look very different from South African society today. Likewise a post-Mugabe Zimbabwe that manages to get its economy back on to a modest growth trajectory, restore the rule of law and achieve a transition to at least nominal democratic rule would also resemble contemporary South Africa to a much greater degree than is the case today. In both cases these developments – economic diversification, democratization and so on – would be considered genuine achievements indeed. If this is what Alexander's 'ordinary' future looks like, then prospects for genuine development and increased well-being are modest indeed, and a genuine move beyond development as per the hopes of post-development thinkers not very likely at all.

Whether South Africa will constitute an exemplary case or one of warning remains to be seen. The country will in any case continue influencing politics in the southern African region and beyond, thus shaping global perceptions of Africa and Africans in ways that will inevitably have a direct impact on the developmental prospects of all Africans. In this sense the South African case remains pivotal among the ones considered in this study, the conclusion of which is now at hand.

Conclusion: comparative lessons from southern Africa

In *The Anti-Politics Machine*, James Ferguson argues that:

> It seems to us today almost non-sensical to deny there is such a thing
> as 'development,' or to dismiss it as a meaningless concept, just as it
> must have been virtually impossible to reject the concept 'civilization'
> in the nineteenth century, or the concept 'God' in the twelfth. (Ferguson
> 1994: xiii)

In examining the ways in which southern African countries have pursued development, the intention here is not to employ the critique of
mainstream blueprints for development and a sympathetic engagement
with post-development theory which casts into doubt various shibboleths
of modernism to thereby reject completely the notion of development in
the way that some post-development thinkers have previously done (e.g.
Esteva 1985; Rahnema 1997b). Instead the intention has been to use the
insights of post-development theory, combined with an analysis of how
socially and culturally driven shifts in the region's political economy
have reconfigured states and their priorities, to rethink the 'development project' – its means, aims and goals – and to determine whether
there exist in southern Africa today identifiable social foundations in
which a thinking beyond development can be anchored. This has been
done with an aim to understand the possibilities for envisioning and
pursuing a better future than that which is deemed possible within the
contemporary paradigm of a quasi-liberal, procedural democracy and a
culturally and economically globalized world order (however piecemeal
and fraught that order may currently seem). This examination is intended
to encourage questions about alternative trajectories, including those
which reject the epistemological and ontological foundations on which
orthodox development thinking rests.

It is important to ask whether there really is something beyond the
current development paradigm, tangible goals that can be identified and
towards which Africans can aspire – new ways of understanding how
well-being could be secured in the greater context of a human existence
fully cognizant of the cultural, social, spiritual and natural dimensions of
that existence. Such an effort acknowledges the importance, as outlined

in the Introduction, of a communal effort at reinventing development and the need to overcome the alienation that modernity has produced. In concrete terms, is it possible for communities and nations to build a better future for all its members based on principles other than those deriving from the dynamics of the global economy as currently constituted and the perceived need to enhance local/national/regional competitiveness in a global marketplace at whatever cost (since marginalization in our increasingly interconnected and volatile global society supposedly cannot produce anything but misery and hardship)? In other words, what options are left for those who have already experienced failures of both state-led and liberal development blueprints to deliver broad-based development that can become sustainable in the cultural, social, political, economic, environmental and spiritual senses of that term? What role can be found for traditional forms of rule, indigenous notions of community, human relations and spirituality – in this case a holistic view of what it means to be fully human as embodied in *ubuntu* – in a contemporary age where theories about international convergence and exhortations to international best practice (in terms of governing both states and markets) seem to suggest few possibilities for seeking out alternative paths? These interconnected questions form the basis for some final reflections on Africa's developmental dilemma, the variety of post-transition trajectories in southern Africa and what lessons can be learned from the region's experiences with the end of settler colonial rule and its first steps towards a post-colonial age in which the fates of countries and peoples will be directed primarily by indigenous political dynamics, traditions of governance and sets of cultural values, rather than by exogenous systems and values transmitted, in however indirect or diluted fashion, from the former colonial homelands of the Europeans who played such a crucial role in shaping modern-day southern Africa.

It is by rethinking southern Africa's trajectories, and the political economy of transformation constituting the intellectual context in which these trajectories unfold, that we can begin to understand whether the questions we ask are feasible to begin with – such as why the dream of liberation has for too many been deferred, or even abandoned, and how a different future can be not only envisioned, but practically pursued. If the questions about Africa's future deriving from orthodox understandings of development are insufficient and misleading, *and whether this is the case is the key issue on which the arguments developed in this book depend*, then what different questions need to be asked about Africa's developmental dilemma and the way beyond? If existing visions for development lead to the cul-de-sac of 'normalization' that is contemporary southern Africa, with its persistently high levels of socio-economic inequality and suffering, is it possible to identify societal foundations capable of supporting thinking beyond development in any of these countries? Can these countries really accommodate and sustain a post-development thinking that would push statesmen and civil society alike beyond the current impasse in ways that have been hinted at in this study? Can bold new thinking percolate into the public sphere and eventually into politics and decision-making, thus reorienting the region towards a different and more hopeful future? It is on the answers we provide to these questions that the possibility of transcending Africa's developmental dilemma ultimately depends.

In attempting to answer these questions, three main considerations – about post-development theory, southern Africa's historical trajectories and what the future for the region may hold – have guided the material presented throughout the preceding chapters. These main considerations are as follows:

1 how post-development theory can be re-engaged with and reassessed to provide a concrete guide to a new politics of development for southern Africa;

2 what can be retrieved from existing (institutional) relations between states, markets and societies within the confines of which these actors have attempted to forge a durable 'nexus' capable of delivering broad-based development; and

3 the potentialities inherent in the unfolding 'indigenous turn' in southern African politics and whether it is in this politics that a new thinking about development anchored in a socially legitimate and therefore sustainable context can be found.

A brief summary of findings and conclusions By briefly reviewing the three case studies presented in this book we can arrive at some conclusions regarding the main considerations noted above. A solid cultural basis for a durable social compact exists in Botswana on account of its notable continuity between pre- and post-colonial rule and the way in which its transition to independence and subsequent trajectory have been less marred by volatility than has been the case in neighbouring countries. Because this is a compact that is shaped mainly at an elite level, however, it also poses a challenge for any successful reorientation of priorities to help the country embark on a more equitable future. Those who wish to steer Botswana in the direction of an economically diversified and democratically consolidated future must take great care to balance the importance of nurturing a traditional inheritance that has provided societal stability and the state with an ability to act in a capable, and where necessary also autonomous, manner with the steadily rising expectations and aspirations of a populace who may now increasingly come to feel that their commitment to the state and to the traditions on which it has been securely based has in some ways also hampered the determination with which development has been pursued. Good (2008: 144) argues that the 'debilitating effects' of Botswana's widespread poverty and elitist culture 'are scorched into Botswana society', and that while this does not suggest the impossibility of a better future, '[c]hange is destined to be slow'. It may of course be the case that Botswana's conservative approach to change instead provides it with the stable trajectory and preserved cultural legitimacy so often lacking in Africa, which in the end makes a fundamental, almost subterranean, shift in development thinking more likely to emerge and be considered legitimate there than elsewhere in the region.

The current crisis in Zimbabwe might well prevent any serious thinking about new ways to pursue development. The new government, in whatever form it evolves and consolidates beyond the currently fragile pact between Mugabe's ZANU-PF and Tsvangirai's MDC, will likely be reluctant to embrace fundamental change. Civil society might feel pressured by the current crisis into going along with anything promising a break with the status quo, even if that anything is in the end premised on the same old understandings of and plans for development. What room for bold thinking and visions when there is an immediate need for basic crisis management and alleviation of most urgent suffering? If, on the other hand, the current crisis ends up constituting a genuine interregnum, a window of opportunity may have opened for those wishing to propose a different way ahead. Hyperinflation and societal collapse can set a country on course towards a fate worse than authoritarianism, as we know from the demise of Weimar Germany. But desperate times can also produce innovative measures, some of which may already be emerging. As argued by Bracking and Cliffe (2009: 112), '[o]utside observers need to familiarise themselves with thinking that [is occurring] in Zimbabwe', including 'approaches to recovery that adopt different social change paradigms, incorporating equity and social justice' and where ultimately the 'coalition of social forces demanding change in Zimbabwe surely requires a different operating paradigm'. The case of Zimbabwe and its future development remains the most volatile of the three in this study, but how Zimbabwe arrived at its current crisis and the way in which it must now extricate itself from it offer us an important lesson about the high costs incurred by any post-colonial society in which the state is unable to anchor its developmental projects in widely legitimate societal values and where an increasingly desperate quest for such legitimization is overcome by short-term and predatory policy-making.

In South Africa, a more diverse civil society underpinned by that syncretism praised by Mangcu (2008) as constituting a comparative advantage in terms of devising a functioning post-colonial politics for a deeply divided society could be the terrain in which new ideas emerge and gain a hearing – first in civil society and among scholars where such debates are already well under way, and ultimately also within the governing class. If current challenges to the ANC's hegemony have a practical effect in this regard it might be that any successful post-Mbeki leadership must listen more carefully to its diverse range of 'stakeholders', from its grass roots to the private sector, the intelligentsia and so on. Attention to a wider range of voices does not simply suggest a 'left turn' away from Mbeki's 'neoliberal' stance, as per popularized political analysis of left and right power shifts within the ANC and the Alliance. Rather it suggests that a pragmatic willingness to consider new ways to pursue development could emerge, receptive to arguments pointing to an entirely different set of priorities and goals than those currently animating politicians and guiding policy. There are, as Gunner (2009: 48) argues in her essay on the symbolism of Zuma's revival of the struggle song '*Umshini Wami*' ('My Machine Gun'), 'troubled waters under the new era'. But it is nevertheless an era pregnant with possibilities as perhaps no other has been since the terminal decline of apartheid and the transition to democracy. South Africa's leaders, social activists and peoples have one of Africa's richest and most diverse sociocultural legacies to draw on in their renewed struggle to overcome the legacy of apartheid and the emerging pessimism about the potential of their once so proudly proclaimed Rainbow Nation.

While accepting the overall contours of Saul's (2001) description of a (regionally applicable) post-apartheid denouement, i.e. southern Africa's disappointing developmental trajectory as illustrated by all three case studies, which formed the empirical point of departure of this study, it is, based on these findings, also possible to identify some points of modest optimism. Botswana's relative stability and higher levels of legitimate rule, South Africa's syncretic heritage and adaptability and even Zimbabwe's (final?) crisis as the potential catharsis of a long history of steadily increasing oppression and violence stretching back to the 1970s war of

195

liberation are all aspects of these countries' post-transition trajectories out of which alternative approaches to development may emerge.

To summarize the potential for transformation from a comparative perspective: any move beyond development in Botswana is likely to be conservative in nature and driven by a state-led and generally top-down process where a direct appeal to national tradition and the populace as a whole, rather than to organized civil society, will underpin and legitimize a new course. Prospects for a new vision in Zimbabwe are very difficult to predict given the volatility of the current situation, but if such a vision can materialize and help to guide a new post-crisis politics of development then it is likely to emerge and perhaps become radicalized in its nature via a bottom-up process where civil society leads in the absence of a (for the foreseeable future) discredited state. The South African scenario is perhaps the most complex to analyse and, like that of Zimbabwe but for different reasons, contains a great degree of uncertainty on account of the current transition within the ANC leadership and the new challenges to the ANC's hegemonic role. At the same time, South Africa probably holds the greatest promise for a genuine break with development orthodoxy because of its greater scope for state–society interactions on somewhat equal terms, which is a consequence of its rich variety and vitality of civil society, embracing a multitude of modern, traditional and hybrid post-colonial politics.

Having thus summarized and drawn some conclusions from these three case studies, we can now restate in slightly modified form the tentative conclusions hinted at in the Introduction. First, trajectories in southern Africa demonstrate that conventional development strategies based on accumulation and growth are insufficient and cannot provide a better future for all its inhabitants, as evidenced by the failure of both statist and neoliberal development schemes. Second, countries in southern Africa can learn important lessons from their divergent trajectories, as well as the general and worrying trend towards consolidation of structural inequalities across the region. It is, however, worrying that all three countries in this case study have been unable to overcome very high levels of inequality, despite great variations among them in terms of state legitimacy, democratic consolidation, government capacity and societal cohesion. Third, the difficulty in pursuing development in southern Africa suggests that high levels of inequality, societal divisions and contested historical and cultural legacies provide post-colonial governments with particularly vexing problems, as the case of Zimbabwe in particular illustrates. A lasting failure to deal with such problems carries a real risk of state failure and societal collapse. Fourth, hopes for a sustainable future in southern Africa, and the global South more generally, will be extinguished if the insights of post-development theory in terms of thinking differently about development are not heeded and ways of transcending traditional development strategies not found. The convergence of these trajectories, all leading to developmental failure of some kind, makes the case for concluding the 'Era of Development' and beginning anew. Finally, and as implied by the previous point, a sustainable future will be impossible to achieve if pursued simply along the lines of past successes with industrialization and modernization and without regard for the alienation and social fragmentation to which the settler colonial experiences have given rise. In that context, pursuing the (East Asian) developmental state model will therefore not on its own solve the region's developmental problems and may instead exacerbate these problems by ignoring alternative ways to proceed.

A historical moment? The many questions posed in this conclusion and which are implicit throughout this study ultimately relate to the greater issue of whether or not those who come to govern throughout southern Africa, and the people who vote them into power or otherwise support them where free elections do not constitute the primary determinant of selecting rulers, will remain wedded to a modernist paradigm of governance and development along the lines prescribed by a broadly market-based and quasi-liberal orthodoxy, or whether they will respond to the variety of pressures stemming from the region's impasse by seeking out new solutions – choosing to radically depart from conventional notions of development as they have come to dominate the post-Second World War Era of Development. Any such change would entail a major shift in thinking on the part of those in government, civil society and elsewhere, as opposed to a mere tinkering with existing plans. Considering the current impasse in a greater historical perspective, could today's aspiring Renaissance men and women of Africa, like the European Renaissance men before them, embrace as their own the motto *plus ultra* – yet farther! – thereby rejecting the notion of inherent limitations to ideas and possibilities. Could they boldly venture beyond what are considered appropriately bounded debates on development, and in doing so come to emulate the spirit of discovery, such as that which is depicted in the atlas of Marco Coronelli's *The Argonauts* and in Francis Bacon's *Instauratio Magna*, where the proverbial ship of human discovery breaks free of the boundaries of ordinary knowledge and sails through the Pillars of Hercules (with their warning of 'nothing farther beyond') – that ancient demarcation line between the known world and the unknown, traditionally understood as the very limits of human exploration and knowledge? Or is there really nothing new under the sun in terms of what could possibly be realistic expectations regarding Africa's future?

Pliny the Elder's oft-cited adage, *Ex Africa semper aliquid novi* ('out of Africa, always something new'), might well be the grand expectation against which Africa's success or failure in the twenty-first century ought to be measured. Africa will be judged, most importantly by Africans them-selves, of course, on the basis of whether its leaders and peoples can to-gether provide new solutions to long-standing problems of development, and in doing so inaugurate a genuinely post-colonial African order. Or is the continent bound, as per Afro-pessimist prognostications, to recede into the oblivion of that pre-modern and supposedly hopeless Hobbesian state of nature from which its detractors have argued it never properly emerged into actual history in the first place? This is what ultimately is at stake in the debate about Africa's development, and our understand-ing of the momentous events currently unfolding will inevitably play a significant role in shaping that future.

The fate of southern Africa, and the possibility for 'progress' in Africa and the developing world more generally, thus depends on the ability of its peoples, the erstwhile 'targets' of development, to reclaim agency in their own right and to forcefully articulate and substantiate normative arguments about why a different world is both possible and necessary where current economic and political arrangements are hopelessly in-adequate. The philosopher Peter Singer provides in his ambitious *One World* (2002) an ultimately mistaken but nevertheless useful illustra-tion of what really is at stake at this moment in history, i.e. what kind of qualitative transformation of societies and their politics, of *how we see and understand the world in which we live*, is necessary for mankind to improve on and transcend the contradictions and dilemmas of the present age.

The fifteenth and sixteenth centuries are celebrated for the voyages of discovery that proved the world is round. The eighteenth century saw the first proclamations of universal human rights. The twentieth century's conquest of space made it possible for a human being to look at our planet from a point not on it, and so to see it, literally, as one world. Now the twenty-first century faces the task of developing a suitable form of government for that single world. It is a daunting moral and intellectual challenge, but one we cannot refuse to take up. The future of the world depends on how well we meet it. (ibid.: 200–1)

Singer's vision of a 'one world' scenario in which historical, scientific and rational progress (underpinned by his utilitarian logic) will eventually allow us to agree on some universally acceptable form of government to tackle underdevelopment and attendant problems of injustice and environmental degradation will obviously not come into being as long as a diverse range of civilizations and cultures survive. Rather than one homogenized world, our best hope lies in finding a global modus vivendi that accepts the fact of value pluralism across cultures along with the notion that societies will always seek different solutions and formulate a diverse array of goals, as well as accept a wide range of socio-political arrangements designed to reach those goals, depending on the historical and cultural contexts in which those societies exist.[1] While this diversity is good and ought to be treasured and protected as an affirmation of our complex nature, Singer's bold vision impresses on us the significance and urgency of the historical moment in which we live – a moment where existing ideologies no longer seem to fulfil our needs but new directions nevertheless seem difficult to envision. In the end, the challenge to rethink what development can become and how transformation in Africa can be possible must be the ideational foundation from which any further inquiry into the pursuit of well-being proceeds.

Notes

Introduction

1 'Colonialism of a Special Type' remains a core element of analysis in the SACP 2007 Draft Programme, *The South African Road to Socialism* (SACP 2007: ch. 2).

2 The four 'Asian tigers' are Hong Kong, Singapore, South Korea and Taiwan. The term refers to their exceptional, state-led post-colonial development trajectories (Castells 1992).

1 Foundations for development in southern Africa

1 This pursuit of well-being is generally what is understood as development (e.g. Sen 1999) when that concept is not constrained by a narrow economistic interpretation as in Rostow's (1960) 'stages of development' and subsequent definitions of development inspired by modernization theory. This contemporary conceptualization of development nevertheless remains subject to criticisms of the 'development project' in its entirety, as articulated by various post-development scholars (e.g. Escobar 1995; Rahnema and Bawtree 1997).

2 See Patel and McMichael (2003) on 'fascist relations' in global capitalism today.

3 Find the Project for a New American Century at www.new americancentury.org/Rebuilding AmericasDefenses.pdf.

4 Holmstrom and Smith (2000) examine primitive accumulation in post-Soviet Russia (and China).

The early 1990s 'shock therapy' reforms of the Russian economy, led in part by Western technocrats and expertise, resulted not only in serious deprivation and impoverishment of the population, but also in the emergence of old and new innovative forms of accumulation and enrichment, what the authors term 'gangster capitalism'. Neither broad-based development nor democracy has resulted from these reforms.

5 Capitalist accumulation is distinct from the pre-capitalist form of accumulation called 'primitive' by Marx and 'previous' by Adam Smith. Primitive accumulation refers to the process of separating the producer from the means of production, which in turn enables a capitalist accumulation where labour is already alienated and wage labour is employed by those in control of capital (Marx 1990 [1867]: 873–6). Primitive and capitalist forms of accumulation are inextricably linked, both containing significant elements of violence, cruelty, disempowerment and dehumanization.

6 On the role of coercion in capitalist accumulation, see Perelman (2000) and Meiksins Wood (2003).

7 Recent approaches to southern Africa as a region include Bradshaw and Ndegwa (2000) on prospects for democracy; Lee (2003) on the political economy of regionalism; Love (2005) on southern Africa in world politics; Saul (2005) on post-independence liberation struggles;

S. D. Taylor (2007) on state-business relations; and Söderbaum (2008) on civil society.

8 Roux (1964: 87) outlines two distinct historical periods in South Africa, in terms of the impact of European civilization on the African peoples of the country. The first period, which originates in European settlement of the Cape in the mid-seventeenth century and ends with the Bambata rebellion in 1906, entails the systematic subjugation of African kingdoms and dispossession of lands. This is a period of various tribal wars which sees Africans engaging in active armed struggles against the European invaders and their ultimate reduction to an 'internal proletariat'. This was a process of subjugation largely characterized by African tribal divisions. The second period, from the early twentieth century onwards, is characterized by a struggle for democratic rights within the modern South African economic and political framework (following Union in 1910), a struggle that remained peaceful until the 1960s, when, following the Sharpeville massacre, the armed struggle of the ANC, the SACP and affiliated organizations began in earnest. This was a period characterized by increasing, although often problematic, unity of African peoples in opposition to European rule.

9 The relationship between white capital (long dominated by the 'English community') and white rule (from 1948 increasingly the preserve of Afrikaners) was never straightforward. At times, the racist policies of exploitation facilitated greater profit-making and competitiveness on the part of capitalists. At other times, especially with increasing economic diversification and increasing domestic and international resistance to apartheid, the capitalist class saw government policies on race (especially the colour bar in employment, which artificially increased the cost of labour) as an obstacle. See Lipton (1986) for the classical statement on this conflict in the liberal tradition. In a quite different way, and from a distinctly opposed viewpoint, Simons and Simons (1983 [1969]: 610) characterize this conflict as the result of 'the impact of an advanced industrialism on an obsolete, degenerate colonial order'.

10 Mhone (2000) distinguishes between South Africa and Zimbabwe, on one hand, as typical settler-dominated economies, and Botswana, on the other, as a peripheral or 'resource-based rentier monocultural' economy. In South Africa and Zimbabwe, settler elites created enclaves of capital accumulation and luxury consumption in the midst of pre-industrial societies that over time became institutionalized dual economies. In Botswana the national economy was characterized by dependence on the South African economy, on a single major resource (minerals, mined for export) and the emergence of economic enclaves.

11 Solomon (Sol) Tshekisho Plaatje was South Africa's first prominent black journalist and newspaper editor, born in 1876 near Boshof in the Orange Free State. His acclaimed novel *Mhudi* (1930) is generally credited with being the first novel written by a black South African. His *Native Life in South Africa* is one of the great political books of South Africa, outlining the systematic dispossession of black South Africans that began in

earnest with the 1913 Land Acts. Sol Plaatje died in 1932.

12 The Natives Land Act No. 27 1913 restricted black ownership of land to designated (ethnically defined) 'reserves', reducing land reserved for black Africans, comprising about two-thirds of South Africa's population, to a mere 7.3 per cent of the total land – an area 'totally inadequate to sustain an independent and viable peasant economy ... [thus leaving Africans] vulnerable to the growing labour demands of white farmers and the mines' (C. H. Feinstein 2005: 43–4).

13 The characterization of the region's socio-economic (and political) trajectory as one of primarily continuity is reflected in the editorial introducing a recent issue of the *Journal of Southern African Studies*, stating that '[t]he dramatic political transitions of the 1990s in some parts of the region have ushered in important changes, but have frequently also allowed for a remarkable persistence in the authority and status of elites at local level' (McGregor 2007: 465).

14 See Haggard and Kaufman (1995) and Bond (2000) for, respectively, theoretical and empirical discussions of the political and policy-related implications of conservative, or pacted, transitions where pre-transition negotiations between incumbent and incoming elites narrow possibilities for post-transition political and economic change.

15 Polanyi (1944) noted that the influence of *haute finance* on domestic politics has been momentous since at least the days of the Rothschilds. In southern Africa, Wernher and Beit and Rhodes played instrumental roles as financiers,

linked to imperial finance and the Rothschilds in Europe (Turrell 1987), during the Anglo-Boer war and the imperial struggle for the country's diamonds and gold in the early days of South Africa's industrialization.

16 See Walter (2005) and Koelble and LiPuma (2006) for the effects of financialization (and neoliberal globalization more generally) on developing countries and emerging markets like South Africa.

17 Find the Freedom Charter at www.anc.org.za/ancdocs/history/ charter.html.

18 See Bond (2004b) for the ANC government's subsequent 'accommodationist' approach towards international capital and Western neo-imperialism, characterized as 'Talk Left, Walk Right'.

19 In a speech on the eve of the ANC's 2005 National General Conference, SACP General Secretary Blade Nzimande (2005) suggested that there were 'strong continuities' between apartheid-era Black Advancement policies and BEE policies today.

20 See the International Federation of Red Cross and Red Crescent Societies report on declining human development indicators in southern Africa at www.reliefweb.int/library/ documents/2006/IFRC/ifrc-saf-1Jan.pdf.

21 See Andreasson (2007b) for a discussion of the prospects of creating 'developmental states' in southern Africa.

22 See Hirschman (1970) for the classical statement on business 'voice' (e.g. lobbying and agenda-setting) and 'exit' (except in cases of significant 'sunken costs' in a particular location) in influencing economic policy.

23 On 'social majorities' that are generally the objects (if not always passive ones) of development strategies contrived by the world's 'social minorities', see Parfitt (2002: 4).

2 The elusive developmental nexus

1 The most recent reference of note to Achebe is Bates's (2008) *When Things Fell Apart* on 'state failures' in late-twentieth-century Africa.

2 While societal organizations, grassroots movements and other popular groupings clearly also have an influence on these debates and political developments, this chapter focuses primarily on state and market actors and on the established literature on the interactions between such actors, as they tend to have a disproportionate influence on developmental trajectories in societies where cohesive societal organizations with real lobbying power are scarce and generally weak. In this regard the analysis follows Evans (1979: 13), who notes that people are absent from his analysis of development in Brazil 'because they are absent from the decision making that is being described'.

3 The concept of a regional apartheid system refers to the settler-based society and political economy of southern Africa shaped from the seventeenth century onwards by European settlement in South Africa and nearby territories, expanding noticeably with the discovery of gold and diamonds in the latter half of the nineteenth century, the establishment of corporation rule by the British South Africa Company north of the Limpopo river in Rhodesia and the onset of industrialization in the region by the early twentieth century.

4 Evans (1989) defines states along a continuum based on how they affect development. At one end of the developmental spectrum is the predatory state that extracts very large amounts of investable surpluses and provides so few collective goods in return that economic transformation is prevented. The predatory state acts in a hostile manner vis-à-vis market actors and society in order to increase immediate revenues aimed at enriching state officials. Revenues from capital ventures and taxes are often channelled through unproductive public enterprises designed to keep bloated bureaucracies afloat. Levels of trust and credibility of the state are low and this neo-patrimonial system of governance leads to declining economic performance. Public unrest is likely to increase and be dealt with by coercion and violence. On the other hand, developmental states manage to 'foster long-term entrepreneurial perspectives among private elites by increasing incentives to engage in transformative investments and lowering the risks involved in such investments' (ibid.: 562–3). While developmental states might engage in some rent-seeking and redistribution of resources to buttress political alliances, they generally promote development. The intermediary state falls in between the predatory and the developmental state and contains significant elements of both (see Martinussen 1997: 238–9).

5 The Rostowian notion of 'stages of development', which lay at the heart of the modernization thesis so influential in earlier post-war studies of Third World development, remains essentially intact, if reformulated to de-emphasize linearity

and to temper the overtly ideological language of Rostow's (1960) 'Non-Communist Manifesto'.

6 Frank's notion of the development of underdevelopment is well represented in Marxist and other 'critical' work on the political economy of Africa, from Rodney's *How Europe Underdeveloped Africa* (1982) to Bond's *Looting Africa* (2006).

7 The role of the state versus that of market forces in fostering economic growth and development is central to the history of political economy. Political economists and others interested in historical processes of development, from List (1966 [1885]) to Weber (1968 [1922]) and Gerschenkron (1962), have all recognized the role of the state in facilitating industrialization and development (see Evans 1989: 566–9). These arguments recognizing the central role of the state have co-existed more or less antagonistically with the classical liberal and, especially, neoliberal schools of thought reliant on market-based policies to achieve growth and development which have been intermittently predominant in economic discourse since Smith's (1937 [1776]) invocation of the 'invisible hand'.

8 On corporate governance and CSR in South Africa see, for instance, Rossouw et al. (2002), Fig (2005),Rossouw (2005) and West (2006).

9 See Bassett (2008: 198–9) on the increasingly urgent need to 'broaden the number of beneficiaries' of South Africa's neoliberal post-apartheid macroeconomic strategy, which has resulted in a move towards increasing public spending and direct transfer redistribution as evident in the new, 'pro-poor' macroeconomic framework Accelerated and Shared Growth for South Africa (ASGISA) introduced in 2006.

10 Analysing business influence on economic policy-making in South Africa – capital's 'formative action' – Bassett (2008: 186) relies on Gramsci's understanding of (a liberal) hegemony, whereby 'the rule of capital [is] consolidated through the state and society in a network of institutions and cultural practices that shape "common sense" in such a way that most dissent can be incorporated ... while those which cannot be accommodated become marginalised as unfeasible'.

11 On late and 'late late' development, see Gerschenkron (1962) and Kohli (2004).

12 For a recent review of the reformist nature of the post-war developmental state and its relation to neoliberalism, see Radice (2008).

13 State corporatism generally refers to arrangements where a more authoritarian state directs and controls economic activity, as for example in the East Asian Newly Industrialized Countries (NICs) during their post-Second World War stage of rapid socio-economic development. Social corporatism entails a greater role for non-governmental entities (i.e. corporations, labour and civil society) in defining and participating in corporatist arguments and is therefore more amenable to democratic politics, as in the classical western European post-war examples of corporatism in Austria and Sweden. Social corporatism is also referred to as liberal or neo-corporatism (Grant 1985: 1). See R. Wade (1990: 377) on differences between state and social corporatism and Lehmbruch and Schmitter (1982) on strong and weak neo-corporatism.

14 Schmitter (1974: 93–4) defines corporatism as 'a system of interest representation in which the constituent units are organized into a limited number of singular, compulsory, noncompetitive, hierarchically ordered and functionally differentiated categories, recognized or licensed (if not created) by the state and granted a deliberate representational monopoly within their respective categories in exchange for observing certain controls on their selection of leaders and articulation of demands and supports'.

15 The importance of an ability of public officials to withstand predatory urges stands in sharp contrast to the kind of extreme neo-patrimonialism embodied in the African saying that 'it is our time to chop [eat]', meaning that any ruling elite, whether in power thanks to democratic elections or sheer force, is expected to use its political power to maintain neo-patrimonial networks by which it rewards its own support base at the expense of everyone else (Lindberg 2003).

16 For a historical overview of the concept of neo-patrimonialism in Africa and more generally, see Erdmann and Engel (2006).

17 See Berger (1981), Diamant (1981) and Swenson (1991) on corporatism in Europe.

18 See Handley (2005) and Bassett (2008: 190–3) for overviews of how South African business, multinational corporations and international financial institutions actively engaged with the ANC in the years leading up to the 1994 democratic transition and in subsequent years when the ANC government steadily liberalized South Africa's economic policy environment.

19 See O'Donnell (1998) on horizontal accountability and Andreasson (2003) on virtual democracy in southern Africa.

20 While Underhill and Zhang (2005: 4) are critical of 'the developmental state model' and its tendency to dichotomize state and market actors, it is in the southern African context nevertheless useful to locate the discussion of state–market relations and the notion of a 'developmental nexus' within broader political and societal debates on how southern African states can become developmental, which in the regional context generally means an approximation of the East Asian model, irrespective of whether this is a realistic aspiration or not. Simply put, the East Asian model is still perceived as the most obvious existing alternative to a Western, market-driven form of modernization and development which politicians and other actors on the left tend to be deeply suspicious of.

21 See the World Bank (1992) for its definition of good governance, including its four core components: sound public sector management; accountability of public officials; establishment of legal frameworks; and transparency.

22 See Blyth (2002) for a seminal study of how economic ideas have played a crucial role in great institutional transformations (in this case, of embedded liberalism in the USA and Sweden).

23 Echoing Weber, Geertz (1973: 5) argues that 'man is an animal suspended in webs of significance he himself has spun [i.e. culture]'. Here culture becomes an integral part of a particular context in which people operate and political phenomena

take place. Analysis of political phenomena becomes superficial when this cultural context within which they exist is not taken into account. While people are certainly not slaves to 'behavioural straitjackets' – cf. Rubinstein and Crocker's (1994) critique of Huntington's (1996) clash-of-civilizations theory – that determine their every choice and action, culture does supply frameworks within which cognitive processes and judgements about pertinent behaviours take place. In this sense, (political) culture is an explanatory variable that cannot be ignored in the pursuit of properly explaining political behaviour and phenomena.

24 It was Edmund Burke, that arch-defender of particularity and tradition, who argued that 'the circumstances and habits of every country ... are to decide upon the form of government', who Ali Mazrui (1963) considered to be articulating views most compatible with those of traditional African thinking on rule and legitimacy. When Burke (1986 [1790]) suggests in his *Reflections on the Revolution in France* that 'people will not look forward to posterity who never look backward to their ancestors' he is according to Mazrui (1963: 132) 'at his most African – not the African who has just graduated from a university ... but the African who is still steeped in ancestral ways'.

25 Collier's (2007) acclaimed analysis of global poverty is more optimistic than that of the critical development scholars, but he does recognize that a large portion of humanity, the sixth that constitute his 'bottom billion', have been bypassed utterly by the market forces that in recent decades have produced

at times remarkable rates of global growth. Moreover, his preferred solution to global poverty, which relies on the force (including military intervention where necessary) of wealthy nations (the G8) to devise radically new ways of ensuring that market-driven globalization will work in the interests of the poor, is perhaps a sign of desperation in the face of neoliberalism's failure to deliver a global economy where 'rising tides lift all boats' as much as it is a genuinely 'new' solution.

3 Beyond development

1 On *ubuntu* from a range of disciplinary viewpoints, see Mbigi and Maree (1995), E. D. Prinsloo (1998), Louw (2001), van Binsbergen (2001) and Venter (2004).

2 That factors beyond mere poverty and associated indicators of underdevelopment play a significant role in the aggressive onset of the HIV/AIDS epidemic in southern Africa is evident from the fact that countries in the region have HIV prevalence rates that are eighteen times higher than in countries elsewhere with similar levels of poverty and inequality (Marks 2007: 863).

3 This Era of Development is generally understood to originate with 'Point Four' of US president Harry Truman's inaugural speech on 20 January 1949. In addition to points articulating US backing of the United Nations, support of the Marshall Plan, and the creation of NATO, a fourth point was adopted regarding the need for the USA to extend technical assistance to parts of Latin America and poor countries elsewhere, since 'for the first time in history, humanity possess the knowledge and skill to relieve the suffering

of these people' (Truman, cited in Rist 2002: 71).

4 A recent study of levels of happiness in China refutes the notion that income growth in poorer societies leads to increases in happiness. This lack of correlation between growth and happiness is explained by the emergence of 'frustrated achievers' and the increasingly unequal distribution of the growth that is occurring (Brockmann et al. 2009).

5 Post-development as a 'total rejection of development' coalesced around the journal *Development: Seeds for Change* in the 1980s and has been most prominently represented by scholars in Latin America and India; in Europe it is primarily a small group of French, Swiss, German and English scholars who have promoted post-development theory (Pieterse 1998: 361).

6 According to Seers's (1963) thesis, the *general* case is the one of underdevelopment in the Third World, while the *special* case is that of development and prosperity in the West. The problem with the modern development paradigm is that the historical context and socio-political dynamics which produced the special case of development are used as the model in attempts to understand the general case as well.

7 The acquisitive and self-interested nature of a Promethean *Homo oeconomicus*, or 'economic man', is understood in wholly positive terms in liberal economic accounts from Adam Smith onwards. The post-Second World War development paradigm entails a more nuanced view on the individual pursuit of self-interest. Although the degree to which market reliance features prominently in blueprints for development

increases over time, and becomes the dominant vision in relation to Africa's development following the World Bank's (1981) *Accelerated Development in Sub-Saharan Africa: An Agenda for Action* report, there is also a recognition of the need for effective (state) institutions and resilient communities, the basis of which is not solely dependent on the classical or neoliberal economic conceptualization of the (asocial and 'ahistorical') individual. See Landes (1969) for a classic example of the Promethean allegory in accounts of development, in this case the social and technological changes giving rise to the Industrial Revolution in Britain. As for the power of ideas, Keynes argued in an oft-cited passage of *The General Theory* that the world is indeed 'governed by little else'.

8 A 'mere' shift in thinking can itself have significant political and economic consequences. A recent example would be the decline of Keynesian economic thought and the resurgence of classical liberal economics that produced the Thatcherite revolution of the 1980s (e.g. Blyth 2002; Gray 2002), the consequences of which were truly global.

9 If, however, technological innovation could *consistently* outpace the destructive consequences of growth-based development, the question of approaching what are likely definite limits to the biosphere's 'carrying capacity' would be moot. Evidence of such a consistent capacity of technology to lead and thereby resolve the current problems associated with (industrial) development does not, as far as this author is aware, exist.

10 The degree to which these middle classes in developing regions are really growing is apparently

unclear. The Asian Development Bank has released revised data, based on purchasing-power-parity (PPP) measures, which suggest that China's economy is perhaps 40 per cent smaller than previously estimated. More importantly, the data suggest that China has perhaps 300 million people living below the Bank's one-dollar-a-day poverty line, three times as many as previously estimated. The Bank also estimates that India has twice as many people living below the poverty line as previously thought, perhaps close to 800 million rather than 400 million (Kiedel 2007).

11 In terms of Africa's relations with the Western world, ideas of civilization and progress featured prominently in arguments underpinning the entire colonial endeavour. They did so in specific instances such as the General Act of the Berlin Conference, which saw Africa carved up and parcelled out to colonizing states according to European expediency, and the League of Nations Covenant. The latter followed the Kiplingesque logic of a 'white man's burden' by placing the burden of administering nations 'not yet able to stand by themselves under the strenuous conditions of the modern world' on to the already 'advanced' nations, following which earlier forms of biological racism were eventually replaced by 'an equally pernicious form of cultural racism which based its judgements of superiority and inferiority on essentially ethnocentric norms' (Tucker 1999: 5).

12 Although we do not know what, exactly, the natural limits to increasing human activity based on depletion of natural resources are, it is increasingly evident that we are pushing against those limits in the twenty-first century. This pushing against limits is taking place in a manner both quantitatively and qualitatively different from the nature of pressures produced by human activity in the nineteenth century, in which Malthus (1970 [1803]) articulated his important proto-post-development arguments.

13 On the global consequences of Western racism and cultural chauvinism more generally, see Lindqvist (1996) and Bessis (2003).

14 There are important similarities between Steve Biko's notion of modern South Africa being characterized by a 'joint culture' and what Mangcu (2008) describes as a 'syncretic tradition' (see Chapter 6) and the plural and hybrid modernities being theorized by Ferguson (2006) and others.

15 Find the UNDP's HDI website at hdr.undp.org/. Moreover, when more always means better we end up with a situation where the drive to grow and accumulate ever more cannot be interrupted without endangering the economic interests of those who benefit from it. Hence a process that becomes 'entirely focused on production of the maximum rather than the optimum' (Rist 2002: 16).

16 Given the important role accorded to education in development, Illich's (1970) criticism of schooling in poor countries is a good example of a post-development line of reasoning that becomes a prime target for the accusation of irresponsibility: 'The higher the dose of schooling an individual has received, the more depressing his experience of withdrawal ... The schools of the Third World administer their opium with much more effect than the Churches of other epochs. As the mind of a

society is progressively schooled, step by step individuals lose their sense that it might be possible to live without being inferior to others ... [The] hereditary inferiority of the peon is replaced by the inferiority of the school dropout who is held personally responsible for his failure. Schools rationalize the divine origin of social stratification with much more rigour than Churches have ever done' (quoted in Rahnema and Bawtree 1997: 98). An appropriately nuanced approach would not reject education, but rather emphasize ways in which this form of potential alienation can be coped with. For a quite different criticism of modernity in his more recent works, John Gray has been accused by fellow philosopher Kateb (2006) and others of being a nihilist.

17 On Africa's history and civilization, see Davidson (1990) and the 'Black Athena' controversy (Bernal 1987; Lefkowitz and MacLean Rogers 1996).

18 In Bhutan, King Jigme Singye Wangchuck coined the term Gross National Happiness (GNH) in 1972 in an attempt to produce a society and an economy compatible with the spiritual values of Buddhism and the particular needs and aspirations of Bhutanese people. The GNH indicates how people actually perceive their overall lot in life as opposed to measures that may indicate only what the 'average' person can consume, even though at some basic level of course there will be a correlation between ability to consume, survival and, indeed, 'happiness'. Donnelly (2004) operationalizes and measures GNH along eight 'happiness categories': 'guaranteed life security', 'healthy body and mind',

'warm families', 'strong communities', 'good environment', 'freedom', 'pride' and 'living in harmony with nature and mankind'. According to Bakshi (2004), GNH 'pertains to quality of nutrition, housing, education, health care and community life'. These components link the GNH to material, ecological and mental/spiritual components of well-being.

19 On the concept of alienation in Marxist theory, see Ollman (1971); on anomie, see Durkheim (1984 [1893]).

20 On 'Afrocentricity', see Asante (1987) and Bekerie (1994).

21 For the National Heritage Council's reporting on the *ubuntu imbizo*, see www.uhurucom.co.za/root_article.html and Mlambo-Ngcuka (2006b).

22 For the philosophical origins of the concept of an African Renaissance, see Ramose (2003a).

23 On the issue of 'culturally compatible' politics (democracy) and development in post-independence Africa, see Osabu-Kle (2000).

24 Both Ramose (1999) and, somewhat reluctantly, van Binsbergen (2001) acknowledge that the intellectual and political process of appropriating *ubuntu* for purposes of government in southern Africa could be extended to inform debates on problems associated with globalization.

25 Information on the UNIDO and South–South cooperation at www.unido.org/doc/59119/ and on the UNDP's South–South cooperation unit at tcdc1.undp.org/aboutus.aspx.

26 The Malaysian experience with sustaining economic development in a divided society has received considerable attention in South Africa (e.g. van der Westhuizen 2002).

4 Botswana: paternalism and the developmental state

1 Quoted from the president of Botswana, Festus Mogae's, last State of the Nation Address (Republic of Botswana 2007).

2 In his study of state-building and democracy in southern Africa, du Toit (1995: 8–9) emphasizes shared historical experiences of Botswana, South Africa and Zimbabwe: 'all three countries were profoundly [affected] by the *Mfecane*, a social, political and military transformation ... all three experienced colonial rule; all three came under the Metropolitan power of Britain; all three included important white minorities ... and still do. Cultural pluralism, extending well beyond the white/black distinction, is a prominent feature of each ... The forces of modernization ... are operative in each.' Picard (1985: 5) states that '[t]he people of Botswana are intimately linked with and affected by South Africa and what happens there'. Moreover, Parsons (1985: 32) casts doubt on the 'colonial benign neglect' thesis by arguing that British administrators of the Bechuanaland protectorate were involved in a project of 'deliberate underdevelopment' revolving around the maintenance of Bechuanaland as a labour reserve for South African mines and farms. Nevertheless, Botswana's history as a protectorate rather than a settler colony, as well as the country's (by comparison) peaceful and moderate transition to independence and majority rule (Picard 1985: 17–19), sets in some significant ways Botswana apart from modern trajectories in the other two cases.

3 There is an important debate in the literature on southern African transitions as to whether liberation movements that eventually became governing parties really were progressive (or at least 'radical') or whether they were instead co-opted by established economic (and political) groups that, from the very beginning, managed to 'hijack' and circumscribe these transitions in terms of their transformative potential (e.g. Bond 1998, 2000; Marais 2001; Alexander 2003; Saul 2005). Nevertheless, the transition to independence in Botswana, in terms of the moderate or indeed conservative character of its BDP leadership, stands in clear contrast to the ideological nature of post-liberation leaderships managing transitions in neighbouring countries.

4 Maundeni (2001: 107) notes that scholars such as Bayart (1993), Mamdani (1996) and Chabal and Daloz (1999) consider the continuity between pre- and post-colonial forms of rule as problematic, in that they trace Africa's current economic and political problems to this continuity.

5 Samatar's (1999) miracle account of Botswana's post-independence development trajectory is not as uncritical as some of its detractors would have it. In fact, Samatar (ibid.) recognizes already in the introduction of his book that the miracle is a qualified success, stating clearly that Botswana's high degree of socio-economic inequality is 'often ignored in conventional circles' and that at least some of the problem with inequality in Botswana could have been avoided 'had the political leaders worked from ... different ... assumptions ... emphasiz[ing] growth with equity'; indeed, 'the value of the miracle would have been greater were the social predisposition

of the leadership changed' (ibid.: 12). This seems a rather frank and unambiguous recognition of the need to qualify any discussion of Botswana's relative success in pursuing development with the recognition that serious obstacles to a more broad-based improvement of living standards remain.

6 World Bank GNI rankings at siteresources.worldbank.org/ DATASTATISTICS/Resources/GNIPC. pdf; Freedom House ratings at www.freedomhouse.org/template. cfm?page=410&year=2008; Transparency International's Corruption Perceptions Index at www.transparency. org/policy_research/surveys_indices/ cpi/2007; Heritage Foundation's Index of Economic Freedom at www. heritage.org/Index/countries.cfm; World Economic Forum's Global Competitiveness Index at www. weforum.org/pdf/gcr/2008/rankings. pdf.

7 The British High Commission in South Africa administered the Bechuanaland protectorate (now Botswana) from its establishment in 1885 to independence in 1966 (Samatar 1999: 45–57).

8 See Samatar (1999: 155–64) for an outline of the origins and operations of the BDC.

9 This joint state–De Beers mining venture was formed as the De Beers Botswana Mining Company in 1969 with the government holding a 15 per cent share in the company and De Beers the rest. By 1975 the government had increased its share to 50 per cent, and in 1991 the company changed its name to Debswana Diamond Company (Pty) Ltd (see company history at www.debswana. com/debswana.web/).

10 As the son of the paramount chief of the Ngwato, Sekgoma Khama II, Seretse Khama was heir to the chieftainship of the Ngwato, the dominant Tswana tribe. He was married to an Englishwoman and educated at Fort Hare in South Africa, Oxford and the Inns of Court, London (Parsons et al. 1995).

11 Samatar's (1999) discussion of 'class leadership' is echoed in Werbner's (2004) discussion of the role played by the Kalanga minority, constituting a particular class within a class despite a measure of 'cultural' discrimination against the Kalanga by the Tswana majority, in enhancing the administrative capacity of the state.

12 The World Bank has linked mineral-exporting economies to lower growth rates and domestic savings, a worsening of income inequalities and difficulties in achieving economic diversification (Nankani 1979). Wheeler (1984) relates the poor developmental outcomes in some African countries to the existence of substantial mining sectors in these countries. On the 'resource curse thesis' generally, see Auty (1993), Ross (1999) and Sachs and Warner (2001).

13 The *kgotla* originated as an open forum for discussion of important matters between village headmen and local people that has deep roots in Tswana tradition. The *kgotla* has survived modernization and is still an important forum where politicians today meet with local people and village representatives to discuss and explain government policy. The role of the *kgotla* has been that of a 'judicial and communications mechanism' where disputes can be resolved, grievances aired and consensus reached. 'It follows the

substance of the well-known Tswana proverb *kgosi ke kgosi ka batho*, or "The Chief is the Chief by the virtue of the people"' (Odell 1985: 61).

14 See also Maundeni's (2004: 619) argument that civil society in Botswana is not as weak as it is commonly understood to be from the perspective of (Western) state–society analyses, but has in fact 'contributed more to Botswana's development than is often acknowledged'.

15 Tsie (1996: 602) notes a divide becoming apparent in the years prior to independence between a 'modernist' faction of 'cattle accumulators' and the Tswana chiefs constituting a 'traditionalist' faction, with the former emerging dominant over the latter in post-independence politics.

16 The fact that the major international (and a few local) corporations in Botswana became established in the country after independence in 1966 may have had a positive effect in terms of stable state–business relations. Influential capital actors in South Africa and Zimbabwe that were already well established at the time of the transitions to majority rule had powerful incentives to protect established privileges, whereas in Botswana both state and capital actors have probably found it easier to establish good relations as they were less burdened by past political liabilities and antagonisms.

17 See Gaseitsiwe (2000) for an overview of the planning process in Botswana.

18 Englebert (2000) attributes the government's ability to foster a stable societal environment in which to effectively pursue developmental policies to a higher level of continu-

ity between pre- and post-colonial patterns of governance (i.e. a higher degree of state legitimacy) as compared to other African countries.

19 By suggesting that Western-style democracy that is pluralistic and confrontational (most obviously so in its 'Anglo-Saxon' form) is not the yardstick by which African democracy should be judged, or even that it is incompatible with African culture and understanding of democracy, Maundeni's (2004) defence of democracy in Botswana echoes previous debates on 'Asian values'. Because Asian cultures allegedly value communitarianism over individualism and deference over assertiveness, as do traditional African cultures, it would be a mistake to attempt grafting Western-style democracy on to Asian societies. Therefore it should rather be expected that any successful democracy in Asia (and, similarly, in Africa) would take a form that reflected appropriately its own cultural preferences and values. 'Indeed, whereas the principles of democracy are universal, their expression and practice cannot be transplanted wholesale from one community to another' (Makinda 1996: 557). For examples of these debates, see Fatton (1990), Saul (1997), Kaarsholm and James (2000), M. R. Thompson (2001), Dallmayr (2002) and Bradley (2005).

20 Writing from an anthropological perspective, Goodell et al. (1985: 252–3) argue against conflating patronage with paternalism, noting that the former implies a relationship between adults and the latter a relationship between an adult and a child. In the case of patronage, a reciprocal relationship is implied where the client can initiate services

that force the patron to respond, whereas in a paternalistic relationship the 'child' is only in a position to receive favours from the 'father'. This means that there is a form of accountability present in patron–client relationships which is lacking in paternalistic ones. From this point of view paternalism would seem even less compatible with notions of democracy and inclusivity than does the patron–client relationship. In the politics literature (on development), however, the distinction between these two forms of power relations is not as forcefully delineated. For the purposes of this discussion paternalism concerns the more general form of hierarchical relations in society between elites and the people whereas patron–client relationships refers to the more instrumental understanding of how a societal environment best described as paternalistic actually works in practice.

21 Lindberg (2003) adds a further complication to the relationship between neo-patrimonialism and democratization by pointing out that not only does neo-patrimonialism make democratic transitions more difficult, but that democratization once it has occurred can contribute to the perpetuation of neo-patrimonialism.

22 Hitchcock (1980) notes a long tradition of serfdom that, in the case of the Basarwa's subordinate social and economic status, can be argued to have survived in new forms into the modern era. It is indeed possible that such a tradition can desensitize rulers and middle classes alike to high levels of inequality in society and to the material suffering of the poor, thereby constituting a dangerous downside to paternalistic rule when it comes to acting on suffering and injustice and providing public goods in return for recognition of legitimacy and right to govern in a top-down mode of governance. While Botswana's social relations would not be considered as rigid as, for example, India's traditional caste system, it is possible to see some parallels between the relative complacency of prosperous middle classes in each of these societies towards the very poor, the lower castes in India and those arguably not considered fully equal citizens in Botswana (i.e. the Basarwa).

23 See the brief discussion on the 'art of suffering' and coping with hardships in Chapter 3.

24 Information on Abahlali baseMjondolo at www.abahlali.org/; the Anti-Privatisation Forum at apf. org.za/ (Buhlungu 2004).

25 It is of course the case that Botswana's society has already undergone major change on account of modernization. As Parsons (2006: 675) notes, '[a]fter 30 years of breakneck economic growth and external political threats, Botswana society matured and developed middle-aged spread in the regional peace of the 1990s. The country then celebrated the new millennium by a consumer boom of shopping malls and property speculation and other evidence of the rise of a local but globalised petty-bourgeoisie.' Nevertheless, politics in Botswana remains steeped in traditional references and remains to a large extent dependent upon a popular acceptance of government that is rooted in and legitimized by an understanding of politics constituting an ongoing process of upholding tradition.

5 Zimbabwe: the failing state revisited

1 Zimbabwe's President Robert Mugabe, quoted in Jongwe (2008).

2 Following the electoral victory of Mugabe's predominantly Shona-supported ZANU in 1980, the party incorporated Nkomo's predominantly Ndebele-supported ZAPU in a coalition government. Following a breakdown of this coalitional arrangement in 1982, and the subsequent massacres of (mainly Ndebele) ZAPU supporters in Matabeleland in the mid-1980s by government troops, ZANU and ZAPU formed a Unity Accord in 1987 and formally merged to form ZANU-PF in 1989 (Dashwood 2000: 21–2).

3 Worby (2003: 67) suggests that 'Western journalists, bereft of explanation … see things more simply and ahistorically … Zimbabwe is plunging into darkness – an anti-civilisational state, a perverse and amoral condition'.

4 Settler colonies represent two important exceptions to the general experience of colonialism in the 'Third World'. Settler colonies tended to produce a significant degree of independent capitalist development and more advanced class formations as a result of that capitalist development. This class formation, in turn, produced a more militant response to colonialism than was the case in indirectly governed European colonies, as evidenced by the violent struggles for independence in the settler colonies of, for example, Algeria, Kenya and Rhodesia as compared to processes of decolonization elsewhere in Africa (Good 1976).

5 In addition to the scholarly literature documenting Zimbabwe's ongoing crisis, current bestsellers on contemporary Zimbabwe in the popular press all conjure up the images of failure and descent into darkness and chaos as the central features of modern Zimbabwe, as evidenced by titles such as *Cry Zimbabwe* (Stiff 2002), *Power, Plunder and the Struggle for Zimbabwe's Future* (Meredith 2007), *Through the Darkness* (Todd 2007) and the truly bizarre *A Hitchhiker's Guide to a Failed State* (Chisvo 2007).

6 Southern Rhodesia became Rhodesia following UDI in 1965.

7 For example, during the decade 1979–89 the government achieved massive increases in school enrolments across primary, secondary and tertiary levels. In the same decade, budget account expenditure on education increased from 10.3 to 17.3 per cent and expenditure on health increased from 4.6 to 5.1 per cent while defence expenditures decreased from 23 to 12.1 per cent (Dashwood 2000: 41–3).

8 For examples of recently published research on various aspects of anti-colonial politics in southern Africa invoking the spirit of *A luta continua*, see Ishemo (2004), Martin (2004) and Saul (2007).

9 Interestingly, Zimbabwe's debt burden was not remarkable at this time as compared to that of many other African nations, a fact that seems to complicate suggestions that the debt burden was the overriding problem (although it was no doubt a serious concern). Zimbabwe's borrowing was moderate during the first decade of independence. The debt service ratio in March 1992 amounted to 22 per cent of total exports, a decrease from a peak debt service ratio of 35 per cent in 1987. At this time, total disbursed debt was

less than 170 per cent of one year's exports for Zimbabwe, as compared with a sub-Saharan average of 340 per cent in 1991 (Finance Minister Bernard Chidzero addressing parliament, cited in Schwartz 2001: 44). Clearly the ability of IFIs and capital actors to influence the thinking among key government decision-makers was as important as actual financial constraints at the time.

10 According to Zimbabwe's Central Statistical Office the ESAP period was of the four major growth plans guiding Zimbabwe in the 1980s and 1990s least able to meet planned growth rate targets (Mumbengegwi and Mabugu 2002: 7). The First Five-Year National Development Plan came the closest to meeting its growth target, followed by the Zimbabwe Programme for Economic and Social Transformation (ZIMPREST), which succeeded ESAP. The Transitional National Development Plan and ESAP were least able to meet planned growth targets (somewhat ironically, ESAP was also the plan that set the lowest target).

11 Arrighi (2002: 10) subsequently notes another sharp shift in *The Economist*'s judgement of African economic prospects. A 1997 cover story entitled 'Sub-Saharan Africa is in better shape than it has been in a generation' was followed by a 13–19 May 2000 cover story proclaiming Africa to be 'The Hopeless Continent'. *The Economist*, wondering whether Africa had an inherent character flaw keeping it backward and incapable of development, prompted South Africa's *Financial Mail* to ask whether the editors of *The Economist* had an inherent character flaw making them incapable of consistent judgement.

12 Zimbabwe's involvement in the DRC war was essentially driven by the prospect of extracting natural resources from the war-torn country's soil. In particular, the diamond trade in the eastern DRC and copper and cobalt trade in the south-eastern Katanga region were of great interest to Zimbabwe's leadership. Osleg, a company controlled by the Zimbabwean Defence Force, was pivotal in extraction of resources from the DRC. A Zimbabwean parastatal received about 1.2 million acres of DRC farmland and the Zimbabwean railway made weekly copper runs from the DRC to Zimbabwe. In short, a comprehensive government-military-business complex arose to help Zimbabwe procure its share of the DRC loot (Maclean 2002). One key player in the DRC minerals looting, notorious Zimbabwean businessman Billy Rautenbach, was appointed in 1998 by Justice Minister Mnangagwa to chair Gecamines, a major cobalt and copper operator in the DRC's Katanga province. Rautenbach's dealings in loot from the DRC (channelled to ZANU-PF and its cronies) involved top Zimbabwean government officials, the Zimbabwean military and over a hundred front companies (ibid.: 524). By 1999 the South African Office for Serious Economic Offences had raided Rautenbach's offices in Johannesburg and confiscated assets deemed to stem from illegal business practices. South African authorities confiscated some R60 million of Rautenbach's assets and he became a fugitive from South African justice. Since Rautenbach fled South Africa in 2000, he is believed to be hiding out in Zimbabwe, where he has strong ties to the ZANU-PF government, and

the South African government has consequently not been successful in having Rautenbach extradited to face several fraud charges in South Africa. Rautenbach was also implicated in improprieties with Hyundai and Volvo ventures turned sour in Botswana and South Africa (*Daily News*, 3 October 2002).

13 As with Malaysia's *Bumiputras* ('sons of the soil') it is the connection with the soil, a land in which one's ancestors have lived (for a long time), which defines who is indigenous to Zimbabwe. In the Zimbabwean case it is arguably less problematic for the Shona and Ndebele, who have been the dominant people in the region for longer than have peoples of other groups (most obviously whites, Indians and coloureds, but also African peoples with origins in lands outside what is today Zimbabwe) to claim exclusive right to being indigenous in this way than it is for, say, the Zulu, Xhosa, Tswana and others in South Africa and Botswana to claim indigeneity on such grounds as they live in lands where the Khoi and San resided long before their arrival. On the complexity of early patterns of population in South Africa, see L. Thompson (2001: ch. 1).

14 This separate treatment of Zimbabwe's minority peoples has roots in the Rhodesian era, where land policies recognized only whites and 'indigenous Africans' (i.e. Shona and Ndebele) and where a variety of other laws applied differently to peoples depending on their status as whites, 'indigenous Africans', 'colonial natives' (Africans from elsewhere), coloureds, Indians and so on (Muzondidya 2007).

15 It can of course be argued that the Zimbabwean government's approach was never very conciliatory, despite the accommodation in the early independence era of white business interests and until 1987 a reserved share of seats for whites in parliament. In fact, Muzondidya's (ibid.: 331) suggestion that there were 'new, though limited' opportunities for 'subject minorities' in the '*meritocratic society*' (emphasis added) of the post-independence era seems difficult to square with the litany of very serious and in many cases blatantly racist indignities and injustices suffered by these minority peoples ever since that the author delivers in the following pages of the same article.

16 For examples of Western intellectuals engaging with and endorsing the ideological struggle waged within ZANU-PF and the liberation movement more generally, see D. Moore (2008: 17–19).

17 For a critique of popular (moral) arguments – arguments 'flawed beyond repair' – in favour of Zimbabwe's land expropriation, see W. H. Shaw (2003).

18 In outlining the disastrous effects of South Africa's systematic destruction of black agriculture, Lipton (1986: 106) notes that efficient, small-scale and labour-intensive farming often has a competitive edge over large-scale, capital-intensive farming based on low-paid and coerced labour in developing countries. Output per acre in vegetable, root crop and possibly cereals is often higher for small family units than for large farms (Lipton 1977). 'Despite long-held beliefs to the contrary, the economies-of-scale argument that applies to industry often does not work for agricultural production (as distinct from marketing)' (Lipton

1986: 106). Small-scale farming is especially useful in countries where much of large-scale agriculture consists of raising cash crops for export. In countries like Zimbabwe, where tobacco farming has been an important export earner, much of the revenues from the tobacco export are used for luxury consumption rather than for the benefit of the poor.

19 By June 2002, about 2,900 commercial farmers (approximately 60 per cent of the total number of commercial farmers at the time) whose farms had been designated for redistribution were legally obliged to cease working their farms. They had then to leave their homes within another forty-five days. In addition, another 35 per cent received preliminary notices of confiscation of their farms. These policies were being mercilessly implemented at a time when Zimbabwe was facing its worst food shortages in sixty years. The results were predictably disastrous as the commercial farmers produced a third of the country's cereals. In addition, some two million farm workers and their dependants became destitute as a result of their employers being evicted from their farms (*Economist*, 27 June 2002).

20 Several companies (many owned by local Asian and white entrepreneurs), including Anglo American subsidiary National Foods, became identified as 'prone to economic sabotage' and were threatened with takeover by the government. A government list of forty companies, most of them involved in labour disputes or having been closed or liquidated, was initially released by government as being designated for takeover (*Mail and Guardian*, 14 May 2002).

21 For recent analyses of problems relating to the over-accumulation of capital, a concept with roots in traditional Marxist economics, see Perelman (2000) and Harvey (2003).

22 The vitriolic attacks by the Zimbabwean government on its political opponents and the country's white minority and the deeply racist rhetoric employed in these attacks are reminiscent of the Nazi regime's hate propaganda which prompted the 1938 Kristallnacht pogrom as well as Idi Amin's expulsion in 1972 of the Indians in Uganda. According to Sylvester (2006: 69), '[e]choes of an earlier development era in Europe, with its even harsher scapegoating biopolitics, are discernible in this case; but Zimbabweanists are reluctant to say so openly. We avoid giving the devil his due by continuing to refer to the government as authoritarian or neo-authoritarian (e.g. Darnolf and Laakso 2003; Raftopoulos and Campagnon 2003) or totalitarian (Chan 2005).' The overtly racist rhetoric employed by state officials against Zimbabwe's white minority community was already becoming notable during the 1996 election campaign, when Mugabe and other officials resorted to 'an increasingly virulent anti-white rhetoric … [as they] sought to shift the blame for urban decline to white farmers and industrialists' (Carmody and Taylor 2003).

23 The problem of African politics being conceived of as a zero-sum game in terms of the competition for power and resources between different (often ethnically defined) societal groups is generally defined as an underlying driver of dysfunctional politics in post-colonial Africa.

24 Bond (1998, 2007b) suggests that there are important lessons to be drawn from the UDI era in terms of how the country managed to promote domestic industry and economic growth at a time when, owing to international sanctions, it was less integrated into the global economy.

6 South Africa: normalization of uneven development

1 Biko, quoted in an interview with Gerhart (1972: 41–2).

2 Quoted from an address to the Harold Wolpe Seminar (Madisha 2005).

3 It remains controversial to assert that South Africa's transition was even relatively peaceful given that many South Africans died in the years leading up to the 1994 elections. See Sparks (1996: ch. 11) and Waldmeir (1997: ch. 11) on the escalation of mass violence during the last years of the transition, in particular the Boipatong massacre of 17 July 1992, which posed a near-fatal threat to the negotiated transition. The transition was, however, certainly peaceful in comparison with the wars of liberation in Namibia and Zimbabwe, and the even more destructive ones preceding and following liberation in Lusophone southern Africa.

4 N. Alexander's (2003) analysis, focusing on political compromise by the ANC and continuities in the structures of inequality and marginalization, echoes arguments about the South African transition by Bond (2000), Marais (2001) and Saul (2005), among others.

5 Marthinus van Schalkwyk, President F. W. de Klerk's successor and former leader of the now defunct New National Party (NNP) who then became an ANC member and currently serves as minister of environmental affairs and tourism, came to conclude that 'the real debate on the future of the country is within the ANC and not outside' (*Economist*, 14 August 2004).

6 The NDR has been a cornerstone of the anti-apartheid struggle with the ANC reaffirming its identity as a liberation movement during its second National General Council (NGC) in Tshwane in June/July 2005, in part by reference to its continued commitment to the NDR (ANC 2005).

7 The Broederbond was a secret society formed in 1918 to promote Afrikaner interests and became a very powerful force within the NP-dominated ruling class (Schoeman 1982). For its arguably secondary role to that of the Dutch Reformed Church and a 'secular intelligentsia' in shaping the 'apartheid plan', see Giliomee (2003).

8 On the origins of the Washington Consensus, see Williamson (1993).

9 Any suggestion that GEAR represented a major break in policy orientation is controversial, however. As suggested by actors involved in this policy shift in both state and private sectors (e.g. Aboobaker 2001; Gelb 2001), the transition from RDP to GEAR was arguably not the 'great shift' in the ANC's economic policy orientation that some of its opponents have suggested (e.g. Bond 2000).

10 See Everatt (2008) on parallels between Mbeki's conceptualization of 'two nations' (or economies) in South Africa and British prime minister Benjamin Disraeli's description of his contemporary nineteenth-century

England following the emergence of an industrial urban proletariat.

11 This discussion of indigeneity and indigenization does not engage directly with conflicting claims about whose 'indigenousness' is properly authentic, for example that of southern Africa's original Khoi and San or the more recently arriving Bantu peoples. 'Ironically, in most African cases, the "autochthon" does not actually claim to have come *from* the territory, but rather to have arrived there *first* or perhaps even second' (Dunn 2009: 125).

12 Neither Sobukwe nor Biko was a racial essentialist or single-dimensional nativist as they have sometimes been characterized. Both men had a nuanced understanding of South Africa's syncretic society and political traditions and did not equate 'blackness' simply with being a black African but with the acceptance of the place and worth of African culture and values in South African society (Mangcu 2008).

13 Text of Mbeki's 'I am an African' speech, delivered on 8 May 1996, at www.info.gov.za/aboutgovt/orders/new2002_mbeki.htm.

14 Considering that settler colonialism has been a primary cause of capitalist development in Africa (Good 1976), it is no surprise that South African industrialization generated the continent's most advanced capitalist system, which even during apartheid allowed for the development of a black capitalist class, however subservient and marginal. The means by which an ascendant black capitalist class has been able to effectively project its influence following the end of apartheid relates to four key factors (Randall 1996: 675–84): 1) the political insecurity of white capital, prompting white capitalists to cooperate with the emerging black business class to secure their position in the post-apartheid economy; 2) the explicit promotion of black business by a capable state; 3) the mobilization of opinion against 'fronting' and politician-capitalists, although this is precisely what has transpired according to critics of BEE; and 4) the relatively high degree of sophistication and diversification of the South African economy.

15 The Broad-Based Black Economic Empowerment (BBBEE) Act of 2003 defines 'black people' as a generic term including 'Africans, Coloureds and Indians'. BBBEE refers to the economic empowerment of all 'black' people, generously including women, workers, youth, people with disabilities and people living in rural areas (Republic of South Africa 2004).

16 Three Italian mining companies, however – Marlin Holdings, Marlin Corporation and Red Graniti SA – are suing the South African government for €266 million. The companies claim that holding them, as multinational corporations headquartered outside South Africa, responsible for redress for past injustices in South Africa by making them accountable to South African BEE standards, specifically the South African Mineral and Petroleum Resources Development Act (MPRDA) of 2004, is effectively a form of expropriation of their property. The case is being heard by the World Bank's International Centre for the Settlement of Investment Disputes (ICSID) and will have important implications for the operations of multinational corporations in South Africa (Kruger 2007).

17 For a revisionist analysis of Nongqawuse and her role in the Xhosa cattle-killing movement, an analysis that understands the reasons behind this calamitous sequence of events and the consequences thereof as being 'as much murder as it was suicide', see Peires (1989).

18 Gumede (2008: 264) argues that '[u]ntil he was fired by Mbeki in 2005, Zuma was very much part of the President's inner circle, and appeared to have no qualms over Mbeki's leadership style. In fact, he was an important executioner of his leader's will.'

19 Given the distinction made here between the BCM and the PAC it is worth mentioning PAC leader Robert Sobukwe's nuanced view on white South Africans, a view that has generally been marginalized when the radical and sometimes seemingly anti-white nature of the PAC has been emphasized. Sobukwe states that '[when] I say Africa for the Africans I mean those, of any colour, who accept Africa as their home' (Sobukwe, quoted in Mangcu 2008: 3).

20 Text of Mandela's 'I am prepared to die' speech, delivered on 20 April 1964 at the opening of the defence case at the Rivonia Trial at the Pretoria Supreme Court, at www.anc.org.za/ancdocs/history/rivonia.html.

Conclusion: comparative lessons from southern Africa

1 On modus vivendi, see Gray (2000) and Horton's (2006) critique of Gray.

Bibliography

Aboobaker, G. (2001) Interview with author, Pretoria, 28 September.

Abrahamsen, R. (2000) *Disciplining Democracy: Development Discourse and Good Governance in Africa*, London: Zed Books.

— (2003) 'African studies and the postcolonial challenge', *African Affairs*, 102(407).

Acemoglu, D., S. Johnson and J. Robinson (2003) 'An African success story: Botswana', in D. Rodrik (ed.), *In Search of Prosperity: Analytic Narratives on Economic Growth*, Princeton, NJ: Princeton University Press.

Adam, H., F. Van Zyl Slabbert and K. Moodley (1998) *Comrades in Business: Post-Liberation Politics in South Africa*, Utrecht: International Books.

Africa Research Bulletin (2008) 'Zimbabwe: foreign company takeover', 45(2).

Alexander, J. (2006) *The Unsettled Land: State-making and the Politics of Land in Zimbabwe, 1893–2003*, Oxford: James Currey.

Alexander, N. (2003) *An Ordinary Country: Issues in the Transition from Apartheid to Democracy in South Africa*, New York: Berghahn Books.

Allen, M. H. (2006) *Globalization, Negotiation, and the Failure of Transformation in South Africa*, Basingstoke: Palgrave Macmillan.

Alverson, H. (1978) *Mind in the Heart of Darkness: Value and Self-identity among the Tswana of Southern Africa*, New Haven, CT: Yale University Press.

Amin, S. (1990) *Delinking: Toward a Polycentric World*, London: Zed Books.

Amsden, A. (1989) *Asia's Next Giant: South Korea and Late Industrialization*, Oxford: Oxford University Press.

ANC (1977) 'Colonialism of a special type', Statement of the Lisbon Conference, March, www.anc.org. za/ancdocs/history/special.html, accessed 4 July 2007.

— (1998) 'The state, property relations, and social transformation: a discussion paper towards the Alliance Summit', *Umrabulo*, 5, www.anc.org.za/ancdocs/pubs/ umrabulo/articles/sprst.html, accessed 5 September 2007.

— (2005) 'Consolidated report on the strategic context of the national democratic revolution and the state of organisation', ANC National General Council, 29 June–3 July 2005, www.anc. org.za/ancdocs/ngcouncils/2005/ consolidated_report2.html, accessed 26 March 2009.

Andreasson, S. (2001) 'Divergent paths of development: the modern world-system and democratization in South Africa and Zambia', *Journal of World-Systems Research*, 7(2).

— (2003) 'Economic reforms and "virtual democracy" in South Africa and Zimbabwe: the incompatibility of liberalisation, inclusion and development', *Journal of Contemporary African Studies*, 21(3).

— (2005a) 'Orientalism and African development studies: the "reductive repetition" motif in theories of African underdevelopment', *Third World Quarterly*, 26(6).

— (2005b) 'Accumulation and growth to what end? Reassessing the modern faith in progress in the "age of development"', *Capitalism Nature Socialism*, 16(4).

— (2006a) 'Stand and deliver: private property and the politics of global dispossession', *Political Studies*, 54(1).

— (2006b) 'The African National Congress and its critics: "predatory liberalism", black empowerment and intra-alliance tensions in post-apartheid South Africa', *Democratization*, 13(2).

— (2007a) 'The resilience of comprador capitalism: "new" economic groups in southern Africa', in F. Jilberto, A. E. and B. Hogenboom (eds), *Big Business and Economic Development: Conglomerates and Economic Groups in Developing Countries and Transition Economies under Globalization*, London: Routledge.

— (2007b) 'Can the "developmental state" save southern Africa?', *Global Dialogue: An International Affairs Review*, 12(1).

— (forthcoming) 'Understanding corporate governance reform in South Africa: Anglo-American divergence, the King Reports, and hybridization', *Business and Society*.

Andrews, D. M. (1994) 'Capital mobility and state autonomy: toward a structural theory of international monetary relations', *International Studies Quarterly*, 38(2).

Arrighi, G. (1996) *The Long Twentieth Century: Money, Power, and the Origins of Our Times*, London: Verso.

— (2002) 'The African crisis: world systemic and regional aspects', *New Left Review*, 15, May/June.

Asante, M. K. (1987) *The Afrocentric Idea*, Philadelphia, PA: Temple University Press.

Atkinson, D. (2007) 'Taking to the streets: has developmental local government failed in South Africa?', in S. Buhlungu, J. Daniel, R. Southall and J. Lutchman (eds), *State of the Nation: South Africa 2007*, Cape Town: HSRC Press.

Auty, R. M. (1993) *Sustaining Development in Mineral Economies: The Resource Curse Thesis*, London: Routledge.

Axelrod, R. (1984) *The Evolution of Cooperation*, New York: Basic Books.

Ayittey, G. B. N. (1999) *Africa in Chaos*, New York: St Martin's Press.

Bakshi, R. (2004) 'Gross National Happiness', *post-autistic economics review*, 26(2), www.btinternet.com/˜pae_news/review/issue26.htm, accessed 14 December 2007.

Baran, P. A. (1957) *The Political Economy of Growth*, New York: Monthly Review Press.

Barro, R. J. (1991) 'Economic growth in a cross-section of countries', *Quarterly Journal of Economics*, 106(2).

Basdevant, O. (2008) 'Are diamonds forever? Using the Permanent Income Hypothesis to analyze Botswana's reliance on diamond revenue', IMF Working Paper no. 08/80, www.imf.org/external/pubs/ft/wp/2008/wp0880.pdf, accessed 28 July 2008.

Bassett, C. (2008) 'South Africa: revisiting capital's "formative action"', *Review of African Political Economy*, 116.

Bates, R. H. (1981) *Markets and States in Tropical Africa: The Political Basis of Agricultural Policies*, Berkeley: University of California Press.

— (2008) *When Things Fell Apart: State Failure in Late-Century Africa*, Cambridge: Cambridge University Press.

Bayart, J.-F. (1993) *The State in Africa: The Politics of the Belly*, London: Longman.

Bayart, J.-F., S. Ellis and B. Hibou (1999) *The Criminalization of the State in Africa*, Oxford: James Currey.

Beach, D. (1986) *War and Politics in Zimbabwe: 1840–1900*, Gweru: Mambo Press.

Bearak, D. (2008) 'In destitute Swaziland, leader lives royally', *New York Times*, 5 September, www.nytimes.com/2008/09/06/world/africa/06king.html, accessed 6 September 2008.

Beaulier, S. A. and J. R. Subrick (2006) 'The political foundations of development: the case of Botswana', *Constitutional Political Economy*, 17(2).

Beinart, W. (2001) *Twentieth-Century South Africa*, Oxford: Oxford University Press.

Bekerie, A. (1994) 'The four corners of a circle: Afrocentricity as a model of synthesis', *Journal of Black Studies*, 25(2).

Benson, M. (1966) *South Africa: The Struggle for a Birthright*, London: Penguin.

Berger, S. (ed.) (1981) *Organizing Interests in Western Europe: Pluralism, Corporatism, and the Transformation of Politics*, Cambridge: Cambridge University Press.

Bernal, M. (1987) *Black Athena: The Afroasiatic Roots of Classical Civilization*, New Brunswick: Rutgers University Press.

Bernstein, H. (2005) 'Rural land and land struggles in sub-Saharan Africa', in S. Moyo and P. Yeros (eds), *Reclaiming the Land: The Resurgence of Rural Movements in Africa, Asia and Latin America*, London: Zed Books.

Bessis, S. (2003) *Western Supremacy: The Triumph of an Idea*, London: Zed Books.

Bhagwati, J. N. (1982) 'Directly Unproductive, Profit-seeking (DUP) activities', *Journal of Political Economy*, 90, October.

Bhengu, M. J. (1996) *Ubuntu: The Essence of Democracy*, Cape Town: Novalis Press.

BIDPA (Botswana Institute for Development Policy Analysis) Official (2001) Anonymous interview with author, Gaborone, 1 October.

Biko, S. (1978) *I Write What I Like: A Selection of His Writings Edited with a Personal Memoir by Aelred Stubbs, CR*, London: Bowerdean Press.

Bird, A. and G. Schreiner (1992) 'COSATU at the crossroads: towards tripartite corporatism or democratic socialism?', *South African Labour Bulletin*, 16(6).

Blyth, M. (2002) *Great Transformations: Economic Ideas and Institutional Change in the Twentieth Century*, Baltimore, MD: Johns Hopkins University Press.

Bond, P. (1998) *Uneven Zimbabwe: A Study of Finance, Development, and Underdevelopment*, Trenton, NJ: Africa World Press.

— (1999) 'Political reawakening in Zimbabwe', *Monthly Review*, 50(11).

— (2000) *Elite Transition: From*

Apartheid to Neoliberalism in South Africa, London: Pluto Press.

— (2001a) 'Radical rhetoric and the working class during Zimbabwean nationalism's dying days', *Journal of World-Systems Research*, 7(1).

— (2001b) *Against Global Apartheid: South Africa Meets the World Bank, IMF and International Finance*, Lansdowne: University of Cape Town Press.

— (2001c) Interview with author, Johannesburg, 10 September.

— (2004a) 'The ANC's "left turn" and South African sub-imperialism', *Review of African Political Economy*, 102.

— (2004b) *Talk Left, Walk Right: South Africa's Frustrated Global Reforms*, Scottsville: University of KwaZulu-Natal Press.

— (2006) *Looting Africa: The Economics of Exploitation*, London: Zed Books.

— (2007a) 'Competing explanations of Zimbabwe's long crisis', *Safundi: The Journal of South African and American Studies*, 8(2).

— (2007b) 'Introduction: two economies – or one system of superexploitation', *Africanus*, special issue (November).

— (2007c) 'Primitive accumulation, enclavity, rural marginalisation and articulation', *Review of African Political Economy*, 34(111).

Bond, P. and M. Manyanya (2002) *Zimbabwe's Plunge: Exhausted Nationalism, Neoliberalism and the Search for Social Justice*, Pietermaritzburg: University of Natal Press.

Bond, P. and R. Saunders (2005) 'Labor, the state, and the struggle for a democratic Zimbabwe', *Monthly Review*, 57(7).

Bongma, E. K. (2004) 'Reflections on Thabo Mbeki's African Renais-

sance', *Journal of Southern African Studies*, 30(2).

Booysen, S. (2007) 'With the ballot and the brick: the politics of attaining service delivery', *Progress in Development Studies*, 7(1).

Botswana Vision 2016 Council (2004) 'A long term vision for Botswana: foreword', www.vision2016.co.bw/ PDF%27s/English%20Full%2 oversion.pdf, accessed 11 May 2009.

Bracking, S. (2005) 'Development denied: autocratic militarism in post-election Zimbabwe', *Review of African Political Economy*, 104/105.

Bracking, S. and L. Cliffe (2009) 'Plans for Zimbabwe aid package: blueprint for recovery of shock therapy prescription for liberalisation?', *Review of African Political Economy*, 36(119).

Bracking, S. and G. Harrison (2003) 'Africa, imperialism and new forms of accumulation', *Review of African Political Economy*, 30(95).

Bradley, M. T. (2005) '"The Other": precursory African conceptions of democracy', *International Studies Review*, 7(3).

Bradshaw, Y. and S. N. Ndegwa (eds) (2000) *The Uncertain Promise of Southern Africa*, Bloomington: Indiana University Press.

Bratton, M. and E. Masunungure (2008) 'Zimbabwe's long agony', *Journal of Democracy*, 19(4).

Bratton, M. and N. van de Walle (1994) 'Neopatrimonial regimes and political transitions in Africa', *World Politics*, 46(4).

— (1997) *Democratic Experiments in Africa*, Cambridge: Cambridge University Press.

Brett, E. A. (2005) 'From corporatism to liberalization in Zimbabwe: economic policy regimes and political crisis, 1980–97', *International Political Science Review*, 26(1).

Brockmann, H., J. Delhey, C. Welzel and H. Yuan (2009) 'The China puzzle: falling happiness in a rising economy', *Journal of Happiness Studies*, 10(4).

Budgen, S., S. Kouvelakis and S. Zizek (eds) (2007) *Lenin Reloaded: Toward a Politics of Truth*, London: Duke University Press.

Buhlungu, S. (2004) 'The Anti-Privatisation Forum: a profile of a post-apartheid social movement', Centre for Civil Society and the School of Development Studies, University of Kwa-Zulu Natal, www.nu.ac.za/ccs/files/Buhlungu %20APF%20Research%20 Report. pdf, accessed 5 September 2008.

Bundy, C. (1982) 'The emergence and decline of a South African peasantry', in M. Murray (ed.), *South African Capitalism and Black Political Opposition*, Cambridge: Schenkman Publishing.

Burke, E. (1986 [1790]) *Reflections on the Revolution in France*, London: Penguin.

Bush, R. (2007) *Poverty and Neoliberalism: Persistence and Reproduction of Poverty in the Global South*, London: Pluto Press.

Callaghy, T. M. (1988) 'The state and the development of capitalism in Africa: theoretical, historical and comparative reflections', in D. Rothchild and N. Chazan (eds), *The Precarious Balance: State and Society in Africa*, Boulder, CO: Westview Press.

Carmody, P. (2002) 'Between globalisation and (post) apartheid: the political economy of restructuring in South Africa', *Journal of Southern African Studies*, 28(2).

Carmody, P. and S. Taylor (2003) 'Industry and the urban sector in Zimbabwe's political economy', *African Studies Quarterly*, 7(2/3), web.africa.ufl.edu/asq/v7/v7i2a3. htm, accessed 13 November 2008.

Carroll, B. W. and T. Carroll (1997) 'State and ethnicity in Botswana and Mauritius: a democratic route to development?', *Journal of Development Studies*, 33(4).

Carroll, R. (2006) 'South Africa's "Native Club" stirs unease', *Guardian* (UK), 15 June, www. guardian.co.uk/world/2006/ jun/15/southafrica.rorycarroll, accessed 12 December 2008.

Castells, M. (1992) 'Four Asian Tigers with a dragon head: a comparative analysis of the state, economy, and society in the Asian Pacific Rim', in R. Appelbaum and J. Henderson (eds), *States and Development in the Asian Pacific Rim*, Newbury Park, CA: Sage.

CCJP (Catholic Commission for Justice and Peace) (1999) 'Breaking the silence, building true peace: a report on the disturbances in Matabeleland and the Midlands, 1980–1988 – summary report', Harare: Catholic Commission for Justice and Peace in Zimbabwe.

Chabal, P. and J.-P. Daloz (1999) *Africa Works: Disorder as Political Instrument*, Oxford: James Currey.

Chabane, N., A. Goldstein and S. Roberts (2007) 'The changing face and strategies of big business in South Africa: more than a decade of political democracy', *Industrial and Corporate Change*, 15(3).

Chan, S. (2005) 'The memory of violence: trauma in the writings of Alexander Kanengoni and Yvonne Vera and the idea of unreconciled citizenship in Zimbabwe', *Third World Quarterly*, 26(2).

Chisvo, M. (2007) *Zimbabwe: A Hitch-hiker's Guide to a Failed State*, UpFront Publishing.

Colclough, C. and S. McCarthy (1980) *The Political Economy of Botswana: A Study of Growth and Distribution*, Oxford: Oxford University Press.

Collier, P. (2007) *The Bottom Billion: Why the Poorest Countries are Failing and What Can be Done about It*, Oxford: Oxford University Press.

Corbridge, S. (1998) '"Beneath the pavement, only soil": the poverty of post-development', *Journal of Development Studies*, 34(6).

Dale, R. (1995) *Botswana's Search for Autonomy in Southern Africa*, Westport, CT: Greenwood.

Dallmayr, F. (2002) '"Asian values" and global human rights', *Philosophy East and West*, 52(2).

Dansereau, S. and M. Zamponi (2005) 'Zimbabwe – the political economy of decline', Discussion Paper 27, Nordiska Afrika-institutet, Uppsala, www.nai. uu.se/publications/download. html/91-7106-541-5.pdf?id=25111, accessed 14 January 2009.

Darnolf, S. and L. Laakso (eds) (2003) *Twenty Years of Independence in Zimbabwe: From Liberation to Authoritarianism*, London: Palgrave Macmillan.

Dashwood, H. S. (2000) *Zimbabwe: The Political Economy of Transformation*, Toronto: University of Toronto Press.

Davidson, B. (1990) *African Civilization Revisited*, Trenton, NJ: Africa World Press.

De Angelis, M. (2007) *The Beginning of History: Value Struggles and Global Capital*, London: Pluto Press.

De Kiewiet, C. W. (1941) *A History of South Africa: Social and Economic*, Oxford: Clarendon Press.

Desai, A. (2002) *We are the Poors: Community Struggles in Post-Apartheid South Africa*, New York: Monthly Review Press.

Deutch, J.-G., P. Probst and H. Schmidt (eds) (2002) *African Modernities*, London: Heinemann.

Diamant, A. (1981) 'Bureaucracy and public policy in neocorporatist settings: some European lessons', *Comparative Politics*, 14, October.

Dlamini-Zuma, N. (2009) 'Welcome address by Minister Dr Nkosazana Dlamini-Zuma to the SADC Council of Ministers meeting', Cape Town, 26 February, www. politicsweb.co.za/ politicsweb/ view/ politicsweb/en/ page71656? oid=119180&sn=Detail, accessed 11 March 2009.

Doner, R. F. (1992) 'Limits of state strength: toward an institutionalist view of economic development', *World Politics*, 44(3).

Donnelly, S. (2004) 'How Bhutan can measure and develop GNH', Centre for Bhutan Studies, www. bhutanstudies.org.bt/admin/ pubFiles/Gnh&dev-16.pdf, accessed 14 December 2007.

Dore, R. (2000) *Stock Market Capitalism: Welfare Capitalism: Japan and Germany versus the Anglo-Saxons*, New York: Oxford University Press.

Dorman, S. R. (2003) 'NGOs and the constitutional debate in Zimbabwe: from inclusion to exclusion', *Journal of Southern African Studies*, 29(4).

Du Toit, P. (1995) *State-Building and Democracy in Southern Africa: A Comparative Study of Botswana, South Africa and Zimbabwe*, Pretoria: Human Sciences Research Council Publishers.

Dunn, K. C. (2009) '"Sons of the soil" and contemporary state making: autochthony, uncertainty and political violence in Africa', *Third World Quarterly*, 30(1).

Dunning, T. (2005) 'Resource dependence, economic performance, and political stability', *Journal of Conflict Resolution*, 49(4).

Durkheim, E. (1984 [1893]) *The Division of Labor in Society*, New York: Free Press.

Easterly, W. (2001) *The Elusive Quest for Growth: Economists' Adventures and Misadventures in the Tropics*, Cambridge, MA: MIT University Press.

Easterly, W. and R. Levine (1997) 'Africa's growth tragedy: policies and ethnic divisions', *Quarterly Journal of Economics*, 112(4).

Easterly, W. and S. Rebelo (1993) 'Fiscal policy and growth: an empirical investigation', *Journal of Monetary Economics*, 32(2).

Eisenstadt, S. N. (1973) *Traditional Patrimonialism and Modern Neopatrimonialism*, London: Sage.

Ekeh, P. P. (1975) 'Colonialism and the two publics in Africa: a theoretical statement', *Comparative Studies in Society and History*, 17(1).

Englebert, P. (2000) *State Legitimacy and Development in Africa*, London: Lynne Rienner Publishers.

Erdmann, G. and U. Engel (2006) 'Neopatrimonialism revisited – beyond a catch-all concept', German Institute of Global and Area Studies, Legitimacy and Efficiency of Political Systems Working Paper no. 16, repec.giga-hamburg. de/pdf/giga_06_wp16_erdmann-engel.pdf, accessed 17 May 2009.

Escobar, A. (1995) *Encountering Development: The Making and Unmaking of the Third World*, Princeton, NJ: Princeton University Press.

Esteva, G. (1985) 'Development: metaphor, myth, threat', *Development: Seeds of Change*, 3.

— (1995) 'Beyond development and modernity: regenerating the art of living', in A. Ruprecht and C. Taiana (eds), *The Reordering of Culture: Latin America, the Caribbean and Canada in the Hood*, Ottawa: Carleton University Press.

Esteva, G. and M. S. Prakash (1998) *Grassroots Post-Modernism: Remaking the Soil of Cultures*, London: Zed Books.

Etounga-Manguelle, D. (2000) 'Does Africa need a cultural adjustment programme?', in S. P. Huntington and L. E. Harrison (eds), *Culture Matters: How Values Shape Human Progress*, New York: Basic Books.

Evans, P. B. (1979) *Dependent Development: The Alliance of Multinational, State, and Local Capital in Brazil*, Princeton, NJ: Princeton University Press.

— (1989) 'Predatory, developmental and other apparatuses: a comparative political economy perspective on the Third World state', *Sociological Forum*, 4(4).

Everatt, D. (2008) 'The undeserving poor: poverty and the politics of service delivery in the poorest nodes of South Africa', *Politikon*, 35(3).

Fals-Borda, O. (1985) 'Wisdom as power', *Development: Seeds of Change*, 3.

Fanon, F. (1986 [1952]) *Black Skin, White Masks*, London: Pluto Press.

— (1963) *The Wretched of the Earth*, New York: Grove Press.

Fatton, R. (1990) 'Liberal democracy in Africa', *Political Science Quarterly*, 105(3).

Feinstein, A. (2007) *After the Party: A Personal and Political Journey inside the ANC*, Johannesburg: Jonathan Ball.

Feinstein, C. H. (2005) *An Economic History of South Africa: Conquest, Discrimination and Development*, Cambridge: Cambridge University Press.

Feit, E. (1972) 'Generational conflict and African nationalism in South Africa: the African National Congress, 1949–1959', *International Journal of African Historical Studies*, 5(2).

Ferguson, J. (1994) *The Anti-Politics Machine: 'Development', Depoliticization, and Bureaucratic Power in Lesotho*, Minneapolis: University of Minnesota Press.

— (2006) *Global Shadows: Africa in the Neoliberal World Order*, Durham, NC: Duke University Press.

Fig, D. (2005) 'Manufacturing amnesia: Corporate Social Responsibility in South Africa', *International Affairs*, 81(3).

Fine, B. (2008) 'Can South Africa be a developmental state?', HSRC Developmental State Conference, 4–6 June, Cradle of Humankind, Johannesburg, eprints.soas. ac.uk/5618/1/hsrcdsrev__1_.pdf, accessed 8 April 2009.

Fine, B. and Z. Rustomjee (1996) *The Political Economy of South Africa: From Minerals-Energy Complex to Industrialisation*, Boulder, CO: Westview Press.

Frank, A. G. (1966) 'The development of underdevelopment', *Monthly Review*, 18(7).

Freund, B. (2007) 'South Africa: the end of apartheid and the emergence of the "BEE elite"', *Review of African Political Economy*, 114.

Friedman, S. and I. Chipkin (2001) 'A poor voice? The politics of inequality in South Africa', Research Report no. 87, Centre for Policy Studies, Johannesburg.

Friedman, S. and S. Mottiar (2005) 'A rewarding engagement? The Treatment Action Campaign and the politics of HIV/AIDS', *Politics and Society*, 33(4).

Friedman, T. (2006) *The World is Flat: The Globalized World in the Twenty-first Century*, London: Penguin.

Friedrich Ebert Stiftung (Botswana) (2007) 'Non-state actors', www. fes.org.bw/03NSA.htm, accessed 5 September 2008.

Frimpong-Ansah, J. H. (1992) *The Vampire State in Africa: The Political Economy of Decline in Ghana*, London: Africa World Press.

Fukuyama, F. (1992) *The End of History and the Last Man*, London: Hamish Hamilton.

Gaseitsiwe, D. M. (2000) 'Botswana's planning process', Paper presented at the Macroeconomic and Financial Management Institute of Eastern and Southern Africa (MEFMI), Harare, 10–14 May.

Geertz, C. (1973) *The Interpretation of Cultures*, New York: Basic Books.

Gelb, S. (2001) Interview with author, Johannesburg, 5 September.

— (2006) 'Macroeconomic policy in South Africa. From RDP through GEAR to ASGISA', in G. Gunnarsen, P. MacManus, M. Nielsen and H. E. Stolten (eds), *At the End of the Rainbow? Social Identity and Welfare State in the New South Africa*, Copenhagen: Southern Africa Contact.

Gerhart, G. M. (1972) Interview with Steve Biko, in A. Mngxitama, A. Alexander and C. Gibson (eds), *Biko Lives! Contesting the Legacies* of *Steve Biko*, Basingstoke: Palgrave Macmillan.

— (1978) *Black Power in South Africa: The Evolution of an Ideology*, Berkeley: University of California Press.

Gerschenkron, A. (1962) *Economic Backwardness in Historical Perspective*, Cambridge: Belknap.

Geschiere, P. (1997) *The Modernity of Witchcraft: Politics and the Occult in Postcolonial Africa*, Charlottesville: University of Virginia Press.

Gibson, C. (2006) 'Calling everything into question: broken promises, social movements and emergent intellectual currents in post-apartheid South Africa', in C. Gibson (ed.), *Challenging Hegemony: Social Movements and the Quest for a New Humanism in Post-Apartheid South Africa*, Trenton, NJ: Africa World Press.

Giliomee, H. (1998) 'South Africa's emerging dominant-party regime', *Journal of Democracy*, 9(4).

— (2003) 'The making of the apartheid plan, 1929–1948', *Journal of Southern African Studies*, 29(2).

Glaser, D. (2007) 'Should an egalitarian support black economic empowerment?', *Politikon*, 34(2).

Goedel, A. (2005) 'Is Zimbabwe the future of South Africa? The implications for land reform in southern Africa', *Journal of Contemporary African Studies*, 23(3).

Good, K. (1976) 'Settler colonialism: development and class formation', *Journal of Modern African Studies*, 14(4).

— (1996) 'Towards popular participation in Botswana', *Journal of Modern African Studies*, 34(1).

— (1999) 'Enduring elite democracy in Botswana', *Democratization*, 6(1).

— (2002) *The Liberal Model and Africa: Elites against Democracy*, Basingstoke: Palgrave.

— (2005) 'Resource dependency and its consequences: the costs of Botswana's shining gems', *Journal of Contemporary African Studies*, 23(1).

— (2008) *Diamonds, Dispossession and Democracy in Botswana*, Woodbridge: James Currey.

Good, K. and I. Taylor (2008) 'Botswana: a minimalist democracy', *Democratization*, 15(4).

Goodell, G. E., M. J. Aronoff, D. J. Austin, R. V. Cadeliña, D. K. Emmerson, K. Tranberg Hansen, P. Loizos, B. B. Mandal, J. Pettigrew, M. Riesebrodt, A. C. Sinha, T. Thuen, P. L. van den Berghe and J. A. Wiseman (1985) 'Paternalism, patronage, and potlatch: the dynamics of giving and being given to [and comments and reply]', *Current Anthropology*, 26(2).

Gourevitch, P. (1986) *Politics in Hard Times: Comparative Responses to International Economic Crises*, Ithaca, NY: Cornell University Press.

Grant, W. (ed.) (1985) *The Political Economy of Corporatism*, London: Macmillan.

Gray, J. (2000) *Two Faces of Liberalism*, Cambridge: Polity Press.

— (2002) *False Dawn: The Delusions of Global Capitalism*, London: Granta Books.

Grundy, K. W. (2000) 'South Africa: transition to majority rule, transformation to stable democracy', in Y. Bradshaw and S. N. Ndegwa (eds), *The Uncertain Promise of Southern Africa*, Bloomington: Indiana University Press.

Guelke, A. (1999) *South Africa in Transition: The Misunderstood Miracle*, London: I.B.Tauris.

Gumede, W. M. (2007) *Thabo Mbeki and the Battle for the Soul of the ANC*, London: Zed Books.

— (2008) 'South Africa: Jacob Zuma and the difficulties of consolidating South Africa's democracy', *African Affairs*, 107(427).

Gunner, L. (2009) 'Jacob Zuma, the social body and the unruly power of song', *African Affairs*, 108(430).

Habermas, J. (1996) 'Modernity: an unfinished project', in M. Passerin d'Entrèves and S. Benhabib (eds), *Habermas and the Unfinished Project of Modernity: Critical Essays on the Philosophical Discourse of Modernity*, Cambridge: Polity Press.

Habib, A. (1997) 'From pluralism to corporatism: South Africa's labour relations in transition', *Politikon*, 24(1).

Habib, A. and H. Kotzé (2004) 'Civil society, governance and development in an era of globalisation: the South African case', in G. Mhone and O. Edigheji (eds), *Governance in the New South Africa: The Challenges of Globalisation*, Lansdowne: University of Cape Town Press.

Haggard, S. (2000) *The Political Economy of the Asian Financial Crisis*, Washington, DC: Institute for International Economics.

Haggard, S. and R. R. Kaufman (1995) *The Political Economy of Democratic Transitions*, Princeton, NJ: Princeton University Press.

Halisi, C. R. D. (1997) 'From liberation to citizenship: identity and innovation in black South African political thought', *Comparative Studies in Society and History*, 39(1).

Hall, P. A. and D. Soskice (eds) (2001) *Varieties of Capitalism: The Institutional. Foundations of Comparative Advantage*, New York: Oxford University Press.

Hamann, R., S. Khagram and S. Rohan (2008) 'South Africa's charter approach to post-apartheid economic transformation: collaborative governance or hardball bargaining?', *Journal of Southern African Studies*, 34(1).

Hammar, A. (2008) 'In the name of sovereignty: displacement and state making in post-independence Zimbabwe', *Journal of Contemporary African Studies*, 26(4).

Handley, A. (2005) 'Business, government and economic policy-making in the new South Africa, 1990–2000', *Journal of Modern African Studies*, 43(2).

— (2008) *Business and the State in Africa: Economic Policy-making in the Neo-Liberal Era*, Cambridge: Cambridge University Press.

Hanson, M. and J. J. Hentz (1999) 'Neocolonialism and neoliberalism in South Africa and Zambia', *Political Science Quarterly*, 114(3).

Harvey, C. and S. R. Lewis, Jr (1990) *Policy Choice and Development Performance in Botswana*, London: Macmillan Press.

Harvey, D. (2003) *The New Imperialism*, Oxford: Oxford University Press.

Heilbroner, R. L. (1963) *The Great Ascent: The Struggle for Economic Development in Our Time*, New York: Harper & Row.

Hentz, J. J. (2000) 'The two faces of privatisation: political and economic logics in transitional South Africa', *Journal of Modern African Studies*, 38(2).

— (2005) *South Africa and the Logic of Regional Cooperation*,

Bloomington: Indiana University Press.

Hettne, B. (1995) *Development Theory and the Three Worlds: Towards an International Political Economy of Development*, Harlow: Longman.

Hillbom, E. (2008) 'Diamonds or development? A structural assessment of Botswana's forty years of success', *Journal of Modern African Studies*, 46(2).

Hirsch, D. (2005) *Season of Hope: Economic Reform under Mandela and Mbeki*, Scottsville: University of KwaZulu-Natal Press.

Hirschman, A. O. (1970) *Exit, Voice, and Loyalty: Responses to Decline in Firms, Organizations, and States*, Cambridge, MA: Harvard University Press.

Hitchcock, R. K. (1980) 'Tradition, social justice and land reform in central Botswana', *Journal of African Law*, 24(1).

Holm, J. D. and S. Darnolf (2000) 'Democratizing the administrative state in Botswana', in Y. Bradshaw and S. N. Ndegwa (eds), *The Uncertain Promise of Southern Africa*, Bloomington: Indiana University Press.

Holm, J. and P. Molutsi (eds) (1989) *Democracy in Botswana*, Athens: Ohio University Press.

Holmstrom, N. and R. Smith (2000) 'The necessity of gangster capitalism: primitive accumulation in Russia and China', *Monthly Review*, 51(9).

Hoogvelt, A. (2001) *Globalization and the Postcolonial World: The New Political Economy of Development*, Baltimore, MD: Johns Hopkins University Press.

Horton, J. (2006) 'John Gray and the political theory of modus vivendi', *Critical Review of International Social and Political Philosophy*, 9(2).

Hough, M. (2008) 'Violent protest at local government level in South Africa: revolutionary potential?', *Scientia Militaria: South African Journal of Military Studies*, 36(1).

Houngnikpo, M. (2006) *Africa's Elusive Quest for Development*, New York: Palgrave.

Houston, G., I. Liebenberg and W. Dichaba (2001) 'Interest group participation in the National Economic Development and Labour Council', in G. Houston (ed.), *Public Participation in Democratic Governance in South Africa*, Pretoria: Human Sciences Research Council.

Huntington, S. P. (1968) *Political Order in Changing Societies*, New Haven, CT: Yale University Press.

— (1996) *The Clash of Civilizations and the Remaking of World Order*, New York: Simon and Schuster.

Hyam, R. and P. Henshaw (2003) *The Lion and the Springbok: Britain and South Africa since the Boer War*, Cambridge: Cambridge University Press.

Hyden, G. (2005) *African Politics in Comparative Perspective*, Cambridge: Cambridge University Press.

Iheduru, O. (2008) 'Why "Anglo licks the ANC's boots": globalization and state – capital relations in South Africa', *African Affairs*, 107(428).

Illich, I. (1970) *Celebration of Awareness: A Call for Institutional Revolution*, New York: Doubleday.

— (1976) *Limits to Medicine: Medical Nemesis – the Expropriation of Health*, London: Marion Boyars.

ILO (2002) *Botswana: Economic and Socio-political Situation*,

Subregional Office for Southern Africa, Harare, www.ilo.org/ public/english/region/afpro/ mdtharare/country/botswana. htm, accessed 8 May 2009.

Innes, D. (1984) *Anglo: Anglo American and the Rise of Modern South Africa*, Johannesburg: Ravan Press.

Ishemo, S. L. (2004) 'Culture and historical knowledge in Africa: a Cabralian approach', *Review of African Political Economy*, 31(99).

Jahed, M. (2001) Interview with author, Johannesburg, 13 September.

Jana, P. (2001) 'African Renaissance and the Millennium Action Plan', *Quest: An African Journal of Philosophy*, 15(1/2).

Jenkins, C. (2002) 'The Politics of economic policy-making after independence', in C. Jenkins and J. Knight (eds), *The Economic Decline of Zimbabwe: Neither Growth nor Equity*, Basingstoke: Palgrave.

Jessop, B. (1990) *State Theory: Putting Capitalists in Their Place*, University Park, PA: Pennsylvania State University Press.

Johnson, C. (1982) *MITI and the Japanese Miracle*, Stanford, CA: Stanford University Press.

Jongwe, F. (2008) 'Only God can oust me, says Mugabe', *Mail and Guardian*, 21 June, www.mg.co.za/ article/2008-06-21-only-god-can-oust-me-says-mugabe, accessed 4 February 2009.

Josefsson, H. (2001) Interview with author, Johannesburg, 23 October.

Joseph, R. (1999) 'The reconfiguration of power in late twentieth-century Africa', in R. Joseph (ed.), *State, Conflict, and Democracy in Africa*, Boulder, CO: Lynne Rienner.

Kaarsholm, P. and D. James (2000) 'Popular culture and democracy in some Southern contexts: an introduction', *Journal of Southern African Studies*, 26(2).

Kadalie, R. and J. Bertelsmann (2006) 'Is the Native Club another Broederbond or will it plug intellectual vacuum?', *Cape Argus*, 12 June, www.capeargus.co.za/index. php? fSectionId=137&fArticleId= 3287798, accessed 29 April 2009.

Kaplan, R. D. (1994) 'The coming anarchy: how scarcity, crime, overpopulation, tribalism, and disease are rapidly destroying the social fabric of our planet', *Atlantic Monthly*, 273(2).

Kapoor, I. (2008) *The Postcolonial Politics of Development*, Abingdon: Routledge.

Karsten, L. and H. Illa (2005) '*Ubuntu* as a key African management concept: contextual background and practical insights for knowledge application', *Journal of Managerial Psychology*, 20(7).

Kateb, G. (2006) 'Is John Gray a nihilist?', *Critical Review of International Social and Political Philosophy*, 9(2).

Kaynak, E. and E. E. Marandu (2006) 'Tourism market potential analysis in Botswana: a Delphi study', *Journal of Travel Research*, 45.

Keefer, P. and S. Knack (1995) 'Institutions and economic performance: cross-country tests using alternative institutional measures', *Economics and Politics*, 7(3).

Keohane, R. O. and H. V. Milner (eds) (1996) *Internationalization and Domestic Politics*, Cambridge: Cambridge University Press.

Keohane, R. O. and J. S. Nye (1977) *Power and Interdependence: World*

Politics in Transition, Boston, MA: Little, Brown.

Kevane, M. and P. Englebert (1999) 'A developmental state without growth: explaining the paradox of Burkina Faso in a comparative perspective', in K. Wolmuth, H. H. Bass and F. Messner (eds), *Good Governance and Economic Development*, Hamburg: Lit. Verlag.

Kiedel, A. (2007) 'The limits of a smaller, poorer China', *Financial Times*, 13 November, search. ft.com/ftArticle? queryText= smaller+poorer+china&y=0&aje= true&x=0&id=071113000639&ct= 0&nclick_check=1, accessed 13 December 2007.

Koelble, T. A. and E. LiPuma (2006) 'The effects of circulatory capitalism on democratization: observations from South Africa and Brazil', *Democratization*, 13(4).

Kohli, A. (2004) *State-directed Development: Political Power and Industrialization in the Global Periphery*, Cambridge: Cambridge University Press.

Kothari, R. (1990) *Rethinking Development: In Search of Humane Alternatives*, London: Aspect Publications.

Kothari, U. (ed.) (2005) *A Radical History of Development Studies: Individuals, Institutions and Ideologies*, London: Zed Books.

Kriger, N. (2006) 'From patriotic memories to "patriotic history" in Zimbabwe, 1990–2005', *Third World Quarterly*, 27(6).

Krueger, A. O. (1974) 'The political economy of the rent-seeking society', *American Economic Review*, 64, June.

Kruger, T. (2007) 'Italian lawsuit could have implications for South African mineral rights', *Mineweb*, 21 March, www.mineweb.net/ mineweb/view/mineweb/en/ page54?oid=18473&sn=Detail, accessed 9 December 2008.

Laclau, E. (2005) *On Populist Reason*, New York: Verso.

Land, A. (2002) 'Structured public–private sector dialogue: the experience from Botswana', ECDPM Discussion Paper 37, Maastricht: EPDM.

Landes, D. (1969) *The Unbound Prometheus: Technological Change and Industrial Development in Western Europe from 1750 to the Present*, Cambridge: Cambridge University Press.

— (1999) *The Wealth and Poverty of Nations: Why Some are So Rich and Some So Poor*, New York: Norton.

Larmer, M. (2007) '"More fire" next time?: the southern African social forum as locus of social protest, 2003–2005', *Journal of Asian and African Studies*, 42(1).

Larmer, M., P. Dwyer and L. Zeilig (2009) 'Southern African social movements at the 2007 Nairobi World Social Forum', *Global Networks*, 9(1).

Le Vine, V. T. (1980) 'African patrimonial regimes in comparative perspective', *Journal of Modern African Studies*, 18(4).

Lee, M. C. (2003) *The Political Economy of Regionalism in Southern Africa*, Lansdowne: University of Cape Town Press.

Lefkowitz, M. R. and G. MacLean Rogers (eds) (1996) *Black Athena Revisited*, Chapel Hill: University of North Carolina Press.

Lehmbruch, G. and P. C. Schmitter (eds) (1982) *Patterns of Corporatist Policy-making*, London: Sage.

Levy, B. (2007) 'State capacity,

accountability and economic development in Africa', *Commonwealth and Comparative Politics*, 45(4).

Lewis, D., K. Reed and E. Teljeur (2004) 'South Africa: economic policy-making and implementation in Africa: a study of strategic trade and selective industrial policies', in C. Soludo, O. Ogbu and H.-J. Chang (eds), *The Politics of Trade and Industrial Policy in Africa: Forced Consensus?*, Lawrenceville, NJ: Africa World Press.

Lewis, S. R., Jr (1993) 'Policymaking and economic performance: Botswana in comparative perspective', in S. J. Stedman (ed.), *Botswana: The Political Economy of Democratic Development*, Boulder, CO: Lynne Rienner.

Leysens, A. J. (2006) 'Social forces in Southern Africa: transformation from below?', *Journal of Modern African Studies*, 44(1).

Lindberg, S. (2003) '"It's our time to 'chop'": do elections in Africa feed neo-patrimonialism rather than counter-act it?', *Democratization*, 10(2).

Lindqvist, S. (1996) *'Exterminate all the Brutes': One Man's Odyssey into the Heart of Darkness and the Origins of European Genocide*, New York: New Press.

Lipton, M. (1977) *Why Poor People Stay Poor: A Study of Urban Bias in World Development*, London: Temple Smith.

— (1986) *Capitalism and* Apartheid: *South Africa 1910–1986*, Aldershot: Wildwood House.

— (2007) *Liberals, Marxists, and Nationalists: Competing Interpretations of South African History*, Basingstoke: Palgrave Macmillan.

List, F. (1966 [1885]) *The National*

System of Political Economy, New York: Augustus M. Kelley.

Lodge, T. (1999) 'Policy processes within the African National Congress and the Tripartite Alliance', *Politikon*, 26(1).

— (2004) 'The ANC and the development of party politics in modern South Africa', *Journal of Modern African Studies*, 32(4).

Louw, D. J. (2001) 'Ubuntu and the challenges of multiculturalism in post-apartheid South Africa', *Quest: An African Journal of Philosophy*, 15(1/2).

Love, J. (2005) *Southern Africa in World Politics: Local Aspirations and Global Entanglements*, Cambridge: Westview Press.

Lucas, R. (1988) 'On the mechanics of economic development', *Journal of Monetary Economics*, 22(1).

Lunn, J. (2009) 'The role of religion, spirituality and faith in development: a critical theory approach', *Third World Quarterly*, 30(5).

Luxemburg, R. (1970 [1909]) *Reform or Revolution*, New York: Pathfinder.

— (1951 [1913]) *The Accumulation of Capital*, London: Routledge.

Maclean, S. J. (2002) 'Mugabe at war: the political economy of conflict in Zimbabwe', *Third World Quarterly*, 23(3).

Madisha, W. (2005) 'Address by COSATU President, Willie Madisha', Speech delivered at the Harold Wolpe Memorial Seminar, 8 June, www.cosatu.org.za/speeches/2005/wm20050608.htm, accessed 6 March 2009.

Mafolo, T. (2006) 'The third pillar of our transformation', *Umrabulo*, 26, www.anc.org.za/show.php?doc=ancdocs/pubs/umrabulo/umrabulo26/art6.html, accessed 12 December 2008.

Makgoba, M. (2005) 'Wrath of dethroned white males', *Mail and Guardian*, 25 March, www.mg.co.za/article/2005-03-25-wrath-of-dethroned-white-males, accessed 11 December 2008.

Makinda, S. M. (1996) 'Democracy and multi-party politics in Africa', *Journal of Modern African Studies*, 34(4).

Malthus, T. R. (1970 [1803]) *An Essay on the Principle of Population*, London: Penguin.

Mamdani, M. (1996) *Citizen and Subject: Contemporary Africa and the Legacy of Late Colonialism*, Princeton, NJ: Princeton University Press.

— (2008) 'Lessons of Zimbabwe', *London Review of Books*, 30(23), www.lrb.co.uk/v30/n23/mamd01_.html, accessed 12 December 2008.

Mandela, N. (1978) 'Whither the Black Consciousness Movement?', in M. Maharaj (ed.), *Reflections in Prison*, Cape Town: Zebra Press.

Mangcu, X. (2008) *To the Brink: The State of Democracy in South Africa*, Scottsville: University of KwaZulu-Natal Press.

Marais, H. (2001) *South Africa, Limits to Change: The Political Economy of Transition*, London: Zed Books.

Marks, S. (2007) 'Science, social science and pseudo-science in the HIV/AIDS debate in southern Africa', *Journal of Southern African Studies*, 33(4).

Martin, W. G. (2004) 'Beyond Bush: the future of popular movements and US Africa policy', *Review of African Political Economy*, 31(102).

Martinussen, J. (1997) *Society, State and Market: A Guide to Competing Theories of Development*, London: Zed Books.

Marx, K. (1990 [1867]) *Capital*, vol. 1, trans. B. Fowkes, London: Penguin.

Mashingaidze, T. M. (2006) 'The Zimbabwean entrapment: an analysis of the nexus between domestic and foreign policies in a "collapsing" militant state, 1990s–2006', *Alternatives: Turkish Journal of International Relations*, 5(4).

Matambo, K. (2001) Interview with author, Gaborone, 8 October.

Matthews, S. (2004) 'Post-development theory and the question of alternatives: a view from within', *Third World Quarterly*, 25(2).

Maundeni, Z. (2001) 'State culture and development in Botswana and Zimbabwe', *Journal of Modern African Studies*, 40(1).

— (2004) 'Mutual criticism and state/society interaction in Botswana', *Journal of Modern African Studies*, 42(4).

Maxfield, S. and B. R. Schneider (eds) (1997) *Business and the State in Developing Countries*, Ithaca, NY: Cornell University Press.

Mazrui, A. A. (1963) 'Edmund Burke and reflections on the revolution in the Congo', *Comparative Studies in Society and History*, 5(2).

— (1986) *The Africans: A Triple Heritage*, London: BBC Books.

Mbali, M. (2006) 'TAC in the history of patient-driven AIDS activism: the case for historicizing South Africa's new social movements', in C. Gibson (ed.), *Challenging Hegemony: Social Movements and the Quest for a New Humanism in Post-Apartheid South Africa*, Trenton, NJ: Africa World Press.

Mbeki, T. (1984) 'The Fatton Thesis: a rejoinder', *Canadian Journal of African Studies*, 18(3).

— (1985) 'The historical injustice',

in ANC (ed.), *Selected Writings on the Freedom Charter: 1955–1985*, London: African National Congress.

— (2003) 'Letter from the President: bold steps to end the "two nations" divide', *ANC Today*, 3(33).

— (2007) Steve Biko Memorial Lecture, Cape Town, 12 September, www.polity.org.za/attachment. php?aa_id=7218, accessed 4 December 2007.

Mbembe, A. (2002) 'African modes of self-writing', *Public Culture*, 14(1).

— (2006) 'South Africa's second coming: the Nongqwaqse syndrome', *openDemocracy*, 15 June, www. opendemocracy.net/node/3649/ pdf, accessed 4 April 2009.

— (2007) 'Sacré bleu! Mbeki and Sarkozy?', *Mail and Guardian* (Johannesburg), 27 August, www.mg.co.za/articlePage. aspx?articleid=317571&area=/ insight/insight__comment_and_ analysis/, accessed 19 August 2008.

Mbigi, L. and J. Maree (1995) *Ubuntu: The Spirit of African Transformation Management*, Johannesburg: Knowledge Resources.

McDonald, D. A. and G. Ruiters (eds) (2005) *The Age of Commodity: Water Privatization in Southern Africa*, London: Earthscan.

McGowan, P. J. and F. Ahwireng-Obeng (1998) 'Partner or hegemon? South Africa in Africa (Part Two)', *Journal of Contemporary African Studies*, 16(2).

McGreal, C. (2007) 'Mbeki criticised for praising "racist" Sarkozy', *Guardian* (UK), 27 August, www. guardian.co.uk/world/2007/ aug/27/southafrica.france, accessed 19 August 2008.

McGregor, J. (2007) 'Editorial',

Journal of Southern African Studies, 33(3).

McKinley, D. T. (1997) *The ANC and the Liberation Struggle: A Critical Political Biography*, London: Pluto Press.

Meiksins Wood, E. (2003) *Empire of Capital*, London: Verso.

Memmi, A. (2003 [1974]) *The Colonizer and the Colonized*, London: Earthscan.

Meredith, M. (2002) *Our Votes, Our Guns: Robert Mugabe and the Tragedy of Zimbabwe*, New York: PublicAffairs.

— (2007) *Mugabe: Power, Plunder and the Struggle for Zimbabwe's Future*, New York: PublicAffairs.

Mhone, G. C. Z. (2000) 'Enclavity and constrained labour absorptive capacity in southern African economies', International Labour Office/Southern Africa Multidisciplinary Advisory Team Discussion Paper no. 12.

— (2001) Interview with author, Johannesburg, 13 November.

Mhone, G. and P. Bond (2001) 'Botswana and Zimbabwe: relative success and comparative failure?', Discussion Paper no. 2001/38, United Nations University: World Institute for Development Economics Research.

Migdal, J. (1988) *Strong Societies and Weak States: State and Society Relations and State Capabilities in the Third World*, Princeton, NJ: Princeton University Press.

Milazi, M. (2008) 'Markets wipe out BEE gains', *The Times* (Johannesburg), 12 October, www. thetimes.co.za/PrintEdition/ Article.aspx?id=860816, accessed 11 December 2008.

Mistry, P. S. (2004) 'Reasons for sub-Saharan Africa's development deficit that the commission for Africa did not consider', *African Affairs*, 104(417).

Mlambo-Ngcuka, P. (2006a) 'A catalyst for Accelerated and Shared Growth-South Africa (ASGISA): a summary', Media briefing by Deputy President Phumzile Mlambo-Ngcuka, 6 February, www.info.gov.za/speeches/briefings/asgibackground.pdf, accessed 13 April 2009.

— (2006b) Address at the National Imbizo on Ubuntu and Nation-building in South Africa, Botshabelo-Steve Tshwete Municipality, Mpumalanga, South Africa, 17 November, www.nhc.org.za/ index.php?pid=226&ct=1, accessed 14 December 2007.

Mngxitama, A. (2006) 'National Land Committee, 1994–2004: a critical insider's perspective', in C. Gibson (ed.), *Challenging Hegemony: Social Movements and the Quest for a New Humanism in Post-Apartheid South Africa*, Trenton, NJ: Africa World Press.

Mngxitama, A., A. Alexander and C. Gibson (eds) (2008) 'Biko lives', in A. Mngxitama, A. Alexander and C. Gibson (eds), *Biko Lives! Contesting the Legacies of Steve Biko*, Basingstoke: Palgrave Macmillan.

Moore, D. (2003) 'Zimbabwe's triple crisis: primitive accumulation, nation-state formation and democratization in the age of neo-liberal globalization', *African Studies Quarterly*, 7(2/3).

— (2004) 'Marxism and Marxist intellectuals in schizophrenic Zimbabwe: how many rights for Zimbabwe's left? A comment', *Historical Materialism*, 12(4).

— (2007) '"Intellectuals" interpreting Zimbabwe's primitive accumulation: progress to market civilization?', *Safundi: The Journal of South African and American Studies*, 8(2).

— (2008) 'Contesting civil societies in Zimbabwe's interregna', Centre for Civil Society, University of KwaZulu-Natal, www.ukzn.ac.za/ccs/files/moore-zim100.pdf, accessed 5 March 2009.

Moore, M. P. (2008) 'Biko: Africana existentialist philosopher', in A. Mngxitama, A. Alexander and C. Gibson (eds), *Biko Lives! Contesting the Legacies of Steve Biko*, Basingstoke: Palgrave Macmillan.

Morrison, J. S. (1993) 'Botswana's formative late colonial experiences', in S. J. Stedman (ed.), *Botswana: The Political Economy of Democratic Development*, Boulder, CO: Lynne Rienner.

Mosinyi, W. (2008) 'The second diamond revolution', *Mmegi*, 15 August, www.mmegi.bw/index.php?sid=4&aid=28&dir=2008/August/Friday15, accessed 19 August 2008.

Moss, T. J. (2007) *African Development: Making Sense of the Issues and Actors*, London: Lynne Rienner.

Moyo, B. (2008) 'Zimbabwe violence reminiscent of Gukurahundi massacres', *Mail and Guardian*, 16 June, www.thoughtleader.co.za/bhekinkosimoyo/2008/06/16/zimbabwe-violence-reminiscent-of-gukurahundi-massacres-believe-me-you-don%E2%80%99t-want-to-go-there%E2%80%A6/, accessed 15 January 2009.

Moyo, S. and P. Yeros (2005) *Reclaiming the Land: The Resurgence of Rural Movements in Africa, Asia and Latin America*, London: Zed Books.

Mugabe, R. G. (1989) 'The Unity Accord: its promise for the future', in C. Banana (ed.), *Turmoil and Tenacity: Zimbabwe 1890–1990*, Harare: College Press.

— (2004) 'Address by His Excellency, the President and First Secretary of ZANU PF, Cde Robert Mugabe, on the occasion of the 57th Session of the Central Committee', Harare, 2 April, www.zanupfpub.co.zw/address.htm.

Mumbengegwi, C. and R. Mabugu (2002) 'Macroeconomic and Adjustment Policies in Zimbabwe (1980–2000): an introduction and overview', in C. Mumbengegwi (ed.), *Macroeconomic and Structural Adjustment Policies in Zimbabwe*, Basingstoke: Palgrave.

Munck, R. and D. O'Hearn (eds) (1999) *Critical Development Theory: Contributions to a New Paradigm*, London: Zed Books.

Murapa, R. (1977) 'Geography, race, class, and power in Rhodesia', Working Paper, Council for the Development of Economic and Social Research in Africa, presented at the Conference on the Special Problems of Landlocked and Least Developed Countries in Africa, University of Zambia, Lusaka, 27–31 July.

Murithi, T. (2006) 'Practical peacemaking wisdom from Africa: reflections on Ubuntu', *Journal of Pan African Studies*, 1(4).

Muzondidya, J. (2007) 'Jambanja: ideological ambiguities in the politics of land and resource ownership in Zimbabwe', *Journal of Southern African Studies*, 33(2).

Naidoo, J. (1995) Interview with L. Stack, *TransAct*, 2(7).

Naidoo, P. (2007) 'Struggles around the commodification of daily life

in South Africa', *Review of African Political Economy*, 111.

Nandy, A. (1987) *The Intimate Enemy*, Bombay: Oxford University Press.

Nankani, G. (1979) 'Development problems of mineral exporting countries', World Bank Staff Working Papers.

Nattrass, N. (1999) 'The Truth and Reconciliation Commission on business and apartheid: a critical evaluation', *African Affairs*, 98(392).

Ndlovu-Gatsheni, S. J. (2003) 'The post-colonial state and Matebeleland: regional perceptions of civil–military relations, 1980–2002', in R. Williams, G. Cawthra and D. Abrahams (eds), *Ourselves to Know: Civil–Military Relations and Defence Transformation in Southern Africa*, Pretoria: Institute of Security Studies.

— (2007) 'Tracking the historical roots of post-apartheid citizenship problems: the Native Club, restless natives, panicking settlers and the politics of nativism in South Africa', Working Paper 72, Leiden: African Studies Centre, openaccess.leidenuniv.nl/dspace/bitstream/1887/12905/2/ASC-075287668-236-01.pdf, accessed 4 April 2009.

— (2008) 'Black republican tradition, nativism and populist politics in South Africa', *Transformation: Critical Perspectives on Southern Africa*, 68.

— (2009) 'Making sense of Mugabeism in local and global politics: 'so Blair, keep your England and let me keep my Zimbabwe', *Third World Quarterly*, 30(6).

Ndulu, B. J. and S. A. O'Connell (1999) 'Governance and growth in sub-Saharan Africa', *Journal of Economic Perspectives*, 13(3).

Neocosmos, M. (2006a) 'Rethinking politics in southern Africa today: elements of a critique of political liberalism', in C. Gibson (ed.), *Challenging Hegemony: Social Movements and the Quest for a New Humanism in Post-Apartheid South Africa*, Trenton, NJ: Africa World Press.

— (2006b) 'Reflections on development as human emancipation: a proposal for South–South debate on development politics today', Paper presented at the South-South Collaboration, Pretoria.

— (2008) 'The politics of fear and the fear of politics: reflections on xenophobic violence in South Africa', *Journal of Asian and African Studies*, 43(6).

North, D. C. (1990) *Institutions, Institutional Change and Economic Performance*, Cambridge: Cambridge University Press.

Nyamnjoh, F. B. (2004) 'Reconciling "the rhetoric of rights" with competing notions of personhood and agency in Botswana', in H. Englund and F. B. Nyamnjoh (eds), *Rights and the Politics of Recognition in Africa*, London: Zed Books.

— (2007) '"Ever-diminishing circles": the paradoxes of belonging in Botswana', in M. de la Cadena and O. Starn (eds), *Indigenous Experience Today*, Oxford: Berg.

Nzimande, B. (2005) 'Black economic empowerment: notes towards a lecture', University of Pretoria, 4 May, www.sacp.org.za/main. php?include=docs/sp/2005/ sp0607d.html, accessed 20 August 2007.

Odell, M. J., Jr (1985) 'Traditional and modern roles of the village *Kgotla*', in L. A. Picard (ed.), *The Evolution of Modern Botswana*, London: Rex Collings.

O'Donnell, G. (1998) 'Horizontal accountability in new democracies', *Journal of Democracy*, 9(3).

Ollman, B. (1971) *Alienation: Marx's Concept of Man in Capitalist Society*, London: Cambridge University Press.

Olson, M. (1982) *The Rise and Decline of Nations*, New Haven, CT: Yale University Press.

O'Meara, D. (1996) *Forty Lost Years: The Apartheid State and the Politics of the National Party, 1948–1994*, Randburg: Ravan Press.

Onis, Z. (1991) 'Review: the logic of the developmental state', *Comparative Politics*, 24(1).

Osabu-Kle, D. T. (2000) *Compatible Cultural Democracy: The Key to Development in Africa*, Peterborough: Broadview Press.

Painter-Morland, M. (2006) 'Triple bottom-line reporting as social grammar: integrating corporate social responsibility and corporate codes of conduct', *Business Ethics: A European Review*, 15(4).

Parfitt, T. (2002) *The End of Development: Modernity, Post-Modernity and Development*, London: Pluto Press.

— (2009) 'Countdown to ecstasy: development as eschatology', *Third World Quarterly*, 30(4).

Parfitt, T. W. and S. P. Riley (1989) *The African Debt Crisis*, London: Routledge.

Parson, J. (1985) 'The "labour reserve" in historical perspective: toward a political economy of the Bechuanaland Protectorate', in L. A. Picard (ed.), *The Evolution of Modern Botswana*, London: Rex Collings.

— (1993) 'Liberal democracy, the liberal state, and the 1989 general elections in Botswana', in S. J. Stedman (ed.), *Botswana: The Political Economy of Democratic Development*, Boulder, CO: Lynne Rienner

Parsons, Q. N. (1985) 'The evolution of modern Botswana: historical revisions', in L. A. Picard (ed.), *The Evolution of Modern Botswana*, London: Rex Collings.

— (2006) 'Unravelling history and cultural heritage in Botswana', *Journal of Southern African Studies*, 32(4).

Parsons, Q. N., T. Tlou and W. Henderson (1995) *Seretse Khama, 1921–1980*, Gaborone: Botswana Society.

Patel, R. and P. McMichael (2003) 'Third Worldism and the lineages of global fascism: the regrouping of the global South in the neo-liberal era', *Third World Quarterly*, 25(1).

Peet, R. (2007) *Geography of Power: Making Global Economic Policy*, London: Zed Books.

Peires, J. B. (1989) *The Dead Will Arise: Nongqawuse and the Great Xhosa Cattle-Killing Movement of 1856–7*, Johannesburg: Ravan Press.

Pempel, T. J. (1999) *The Politics of the Asian Economic Crisis*, Ithaca, NY: Cornell University Press.

Perelman, M. (2000) *The Invention of Capitalism: Classical Political Economy and the Secret History of Primitive Accumulation*, Durham, NC: Duke University Press.

Phimister, I. and B. Raftopoulos (2004) 'Mugabe, Mbeki and the politics of anti-imperialism', *Review of African Political Economy*, 31(101).

Picard, L. A. (1985) 'From Bechuana-land to Botswana: an overview', in L. A. Picard (ed.), *The Evolution of Modern Botswana*, London: Rex Collings.

Pieterse, J. N. (1998) 'My paradigm or yours? Alternative development, post-development, reflexive development', *Development and Change*, 29.

— (1999) 'Critical holism and the Tao of development', in R. Munck and D. O'Hearn (eds), *Critical Development Theory: Contributions to a New Paradigm*, London: Zed Books.

— (2000) 'After post-development', *Third World Quarterly*, 21(2).

Pillay, P. (2000) *South Africa in the 21st Century: Key socio-economic challenges*, Johannesburg: Friedrich Ebert Stiftung.

Pillay, S. (2008) 'Crime, community and the governance of violence in post-apartheid South Africa', *Politikon*, 35(2).

Piot, C. (1999) *Remotely Global: Village Modernity in West Africa*, Chicago, IL: University of Chicago Press.

Plaatje, S. T. (1982 [1916]) *Native Life in South Africa*, Randburg: Ravan Writers Series.

Polanyi, K. (1944) *The Great Transformation*, Boston, MA: Beacon Press.

Prempeh, E. O. K. (2006) *Against Global Capitalism: African Social Movements Confront Neoliberal Globalization*, Aldershot: Ashgate.

Pretorius, L. (1994) 'The head of government and organized business', in R. Schrire (ed.), *Leadership in the Apartheid State: From Malan to De Klerk*, Cape Town: Oxford University Press.

— (1996) 'Relations between state,

capital and labour in South Africa: towards corporatism?', *Journal of Theoretical Politics*, 8(2).

Price, R. M. (1991) *The Apartheid State in Crisis: Political Transformation in South Africa, 1975–1990*, New York: Oxford University Press.

Prinsloo, E. D. (1998) '*Ubuntu* culture and participatory management', in P. H. Coetzee and A. P. J. Roux (eds), *The African Philosophy Reader*, London: Routledge.

Prinsloo, M. (1984) 'Political restructuring, capital accumulation and the "coming corporatism" in South Africa: some theoretical considerations', *Politikon*, 11(1).

Przeworski, A. and F. Limongi (1993) 'Political regimes and economic growth', *Journal of Economic Perspectives*, 7.

Raath, J. (2009) 'Robert Mugabe packs 61 people into Cabinet', *The Times* (UK), www.timesonline. co.uk/tol/news/world/africa/ article5769080.ece, accessed 11 March 2009.

Raath, J. and C. Philp (2008) 'Robert Mugabe warns Zimbabawe's voters; "How can a ballpoint pen fight a gun?"', *The Times* (UK), 17 June, www.timesonline. co.uk/tol/news/world/africa/ article4152337.ece, accessed 27 October 2008.

Radice, H. (2008) 'The developmental state under global neoliberalism', *Third World Quarterly*, 29(6).

Raftopoulos, B. (1996) 'Fighting for control: the indigenization debate in Zimbabwe', *Southern Africa Report*, 11(4), www.africafiles.org/ article.asp?ID=3875, accessed 12 December 2008.

— (2004) 'Nation, race, history in Zimbabwean politics', in B. Raftopoulos and T. Savage (eds), *Zimbabwe: Injustice and Political Reconciliation*, Cape Town: Institute for Justice and Reconciliation.

— (2006) 'The Zimbabwean crisis and the challenges for the left', *Journal of Southern African Studies*, 32(2).

Raftopoulos, B. and D. Campagnon (2003) 'Indigenization, state bourgeoisie and neo-authoritarian politics', in S. Darnolf and L. Laakso (eds), *Twenty Years of Independence in Zimbabwe: From Liberation to Authoritarianism*, London: Palgrave Macmillan.

Rahnema, M. (1997a) 'Introduction', in M. Rahnema and V. Bawtree (eds), *The Post-Development Reader*, London: Zed Books.

— (1997b) 'Development and the people's immune system: the story of another variety of AIDS', in M. Rahnema and V. Bawtree (eds), *The Post-Development Reader*, London: Zed Books.

Rahnema, M. and V. Bawtree (eds) (1997) *The Post-Development Reader*, London: Zed Books.

Ramose, M. B. (1999) *African Philosophy through Ubuntu*, Harare: Mond Books.

— (2003a) '"African Renaissance": a northbound gaze', in P. H. Coetzee and A. P. J. Roux (eds), *The African Philosophy Reader*, 2nd edn, London: Routledge.

— (2003b) 'Globalization and *ubuntu*', in P. H. Coetzee and A. P. J. Roux (eds), *The African Philosophy Reader*, 2nd edn, London: Routledge.

Randall, D. J. (1996) 'Prospects for the development of a black business class in South Africa', *Journal of Modern African Studies*, 34(4).

Ranger, T. (2004) 'Nationalist

historiography, patriotic history and the history of the nation: the struggle over the past in Zimbabwe', *Journal of Southern African Studies*, 30(2).

Rapley, J. (2002) *Understanding Development: Theory and Practice in the Third World*, London: Lynne Rienner.

Rapoo, T. (1996) *Making the Means Justify the Ends: The Theory and Practice of the RDP*, Johannesburg: Centre for Policy Studies.

Reno, W. (1998) *Warlord Politics and African States*, Boulder, CO: Lynne Rienner.

Republic of Botswana (1997) *Vision 2016: Towards Prosperity for All*, Gaborone: Government Printer.

— (2007) 'State of the Nation Address by His Excellency Mr Festus G. Mogae, President of the Republic of Botswana, to the opening of the Fourth Session of the Ninth Parliament, "Achievements, challenges and opportunities"', Gaborone, 5 November, www.gov.bw/docs/sotn-2007.pdf, accessed 11 May 2009.

Republic of South Africa (2004) Broad-based Black Economic Empowerment Act, no. 53, 2003, *Government Gazette*, 9 January, llnw.creamermedia.co.za/articles/attachments/00983_brobasblae coempa53.pdf, accessed 10 December 2008.

Revkin, K. (2007) 'Poor countries to bear brunt as world warms', *New York Times*, 1 April, www.nytimes.com/2007/04/01/science/earth/01climate.html, accessed 14 December 2007.

Rist, G. (2002) *The History of Development: From Western Origins to Global Faith*, London: Zed Books.

— (2007) 'Development as a buzz-word', *Development in Practice*, 17(4/5).

Robinson, P. (2002) 'Macroeconomic performance under the economic Structural Adjustment Program: an essay on iatrogenic effects', in C. Mumbengegwi (ed.), *Macroeconomic and Structural Adjustment Policies in Zimbabwe*, Basingstoke: Palgrave.

Rodney, W. (1982) *How Europe Underdeveloped Africa*, Washington, DC: Howard University Press.

Rodrik, D. (1996) 'Understanding economic policy reform', *Journal of Economic Literature*, 34(1).

Romer, P. M. (1986) 'Increasing returns and long-run growth', *Journal of Political Economy*, 94(5).

Ross, M. L. (1999) 'The political economy of the resource curse', *World Politics*, 51(2).

Rossouw, G. J. (2005) 'Business ethics and corporate governance in Africa', *Business and Society*, 44(1).

Rossouw, G. J., A. van der Watt and D. P. Malan (2002) 'Corporate governance in South Africa', *Journal of Business Ethics*, 37(3).

Rostow, W. W. (1960) *The Stages of Economic Growth: A Non-Communist Manifesto*, Cambridge: Cambridge University Press.

Roux, E. (1964) *Time Longer than Rope: A History of the Black Man's Struggle for Freedom in South Africa*, Madison: University of Wisconsin Press.

Rubinstein, R. E. and J. Crocker (1994) 'Challenging Huntington', *Foreign Policy*, 96, Autumn.

Rutherford, B. (2008) 'Conditional belonging: farm workers and the cultural politics of recognition in Zimbabwe', *Development and Change*, 39(1).

Sachikonye, L. M. (2002) 'Whither

Zimbabwe? Crisis and democrati-sation', *Review of African Political Economy*, 29(91).

Sachs, J. D. (2005) *The End of Poverty: How We Can Make It Happen in Our Lifetime*, London: Penguin.

Sachs, J. D. and A. M. Warner (2001) 'The curse of natural resources', *European Economic Review*, 45(4/6).

Sachs, W. (ed.) (1992) *The Development Dictionary: A Guide to Knowledge as Power*, London: Zed Books.

SACP (South African Communist Party) (2007) 'The South Afri-can road to socialism, draft programme of the SACP 2007', *Bua Komanisi*, 6(2), www.sacp. org.za/main.php?include=pubs/buakomanis/2007/vol6-2.html, accessed 12 July 2007.

Samatar, A. I. (1999) *An African Miracle: State and Class Leadership and Colonial Legacy in Botswana Development*, Portsmouth: Heine-mann.

Samuels, R. J. (1987) *The Business of the Japanese State: Energy Markets in Comparative and Historical Perspective*, Ithaca, NY: Cornell University Press.

Sandbrook, R. (1985) *The Politics of Africa's Economic Stagnation*, Cambridge: Cambridge University Press.

— (1993) *The Politics of Africa's Economic Recovery*, Cambridge: Cambridge University Press.

— (2000) *Closing the Circle: Democra-tization and Development in Africa*, London: Zed Books.

Saul, J. (1986) 'South Africa: the question of strategy', *New Left Review*, 160.

— (1997) '"For fear of being con-demned as old fashioned": liberal democracy vs. popular democracy

in sub-Saharan Africa', *Review of African Political Economy*, 24(73).

— (2001) 'Cry for the beloved coun-try: the post-apartheid denoue-ment', *Review of African Political Economy*, 89.

— (2003) 'Africa: the next liberation struggle?', *Review of African Politi-cal Economy*, 30(96).

— (2005) *The Next Liberation Strug-gle: Capitalism, Socialism and Democracy in Southern Africa*, London: Merlin Press.

— (2007) 'The strange death of liberated southern Africa', Seminar paper, Centre for Civil Society, University of Kwa-Zulu Natal, 3 April, www.nu.ac.za/ccs/files/saul%20the%20Strange%20Death%20of%20Liberated%20Southern%20Africa.pdf, accessed 11 January 2009.

Saul, J. and S. Gelb (1986) *The Crisis in South Africa*, revised edn, New York: Monthly Review Press.

Scarnecchia, T. (2006) 'The "fascist cycle" in Zimbabwe, 2000–2005', *Journal of Southern African Studies*, 32(2).

Schapera, I. (1952) *The Ethnic Compo-sition of Tswana Tribes*, London: Macmillan.

— (1953) *The Tswana*, London: Inter-national African Institute.

Schmitter, P. (1974) 'Still the century of corporatism?', *Review of Poli-tics*, 36(1).

Schneider, B. R. (2004) *Business Politics and the State in Twentieth-century Latin America*, Cambridge: Cambridge University Press.

Schoeman, B. M. (1982) *Die Broeder-bond en die Afrikaner-politiek*, Pretoria: Aktuele Publikasies.

Schrire, R. (1991) *Adapt or Die: The End of White Politics in South Africa*, London: Hurst & Co.

Schumpeter, J. A. (1947) *Capitalism, Socialism, and Democracy*, 2nd edn, London: G. Allen & Unwin.

Schwartz, R. (2001) *Coming to Terms: Zimbabwe in the International Arena*, London: I. B. Tauris.

Seabrook, J. (1998) *The Race for Riches: The Human Cost of Wealth*, Basingstoke: Marshall Pickering.

Sebudubudu, D. and B. Z. Osei-Hwedie (2006) 'Pitfalls of parliamentary democracy in Botswana', *Afrika Spectrum*, 41(1).

Seddon, D. and L. Zeilig (2005) 'Class and protest in Africa: new waves', *Review of African Political Economy*, 103.

Seers, D. (1963) 'The limitations of the special case', *Oxford Institute of Economics and Statistics Bulletin*, 25(2).

Sen, A. (1999) *Development as Freedom*, Oxford: Oxford University Press.

Setiloane, G. M. (1976) *The Image of God among the Sotho-Tswana*, Rotterdam: A. A. Balkema.

Shanin, T. (1997) 'The Idea of progress', in M. Rahnema and V. Bawtree (eds), *The Post-Development Reader*, London: Zed Books.

Shaw, T. M. (1989) 'Corporatism in Zimbabwe: revolution restrained', in J. E. Nyang'oro and T. J. Shaw (eds), *Corporatism in Africa: Comparative Analysis and Practice*, Boulder, CO: Westview Press.

— (1994) 'South Africa: the corporatist/regionalist juncture', *Third World Quarterly*, 15(2).

Shaw, W. H. (2003) '"They stole our land": debating the expropriation of white farms in Zimbabwe', *Journal of Modern African Studies*, 41(1).

Shiva, V. (1989) *Staying Alive: Women,* *Ecology and Development*, London: Zed Books.

— (2004) 'The suicide economy of corporate globalization', *ZNet* commentary, 19 February, www.zmag.org/Sustainers/Content/2004-02/19shiva.cfm, accessed 6 September 2007.

Simons, J. and R. Simons (1983 [1969]) *Class and Colour in South Africa 1850–1950*, London: International Defence and Aid Fund for Southern Africa.

Singer, P. (2002) *One World: The Ethics of Globalization*, New Haven, CT: Yale University Press.

Sitas, A. (2008) 'From Marx to Gandhi', *Mail and Guardian* (Johannesburg), 31 March, www.mg.co.za/articlePage. aspx?articleid=335748&area=/insight/insight__national/, accessed 1 May 2008.

Sithole, M. (1997) 'Zimbabwe's eroding authoritarianism', *Journal of Democracy*, 8(1).

— (2000) 'Zimbabwe: the erosion of authoritarianism and prospects for democracy', in Y. Bradshaw and S. N. Ndegwa (eds), *The Uncertain Promise of Southern Africa*, Bloomington: Indiana University Press.

— (2001) 'Fighting authoritarianism in Zimbabwe', *Journal of Democracy*, 12(1).

Smith, A. (1937 [1776]) *An Inquiry into the Nature and Causes of the Wealth of Nations*, New York: Modern Library.

Söderbaum, F. (2008) 'Regionalisation and civil society: the case of southern Africa', *New Political Economy*, 12(3).

Sono, T. (1994) *Dilemmas of African Intellectuals in South Africa*, Pretoria: UNISA.

Southall, R. (1994), 'The South African elections of 1994: the remaking of a dominant-party state', *Journal of Modern African Studies*, 32(4).

— (2003) 'Democracy in southern Africa: moving beyond a difficult legacy', *Review of African Political Economy*, 30(96).

— (2004) 'The ANC and black capitalism in South Africa', *Review of African Political Economy*, 31(100).

— (2006a) 'Ten propositions about Black Economic Empowerment in South Africa', *Review of African Political Economy*, 111.

— (2006b) 'Introduction: can South Africa be a developmental state?', in S. Buhlungu, J. Daniel, R. Southall and J. Lutchman (eds), *State of the Nation: South Africa 2005–06*, Cape Town: HSRC Press.

— (2008) 'The ANC for sale? Money, morality and business in South Africa', *Review of African Political Economy*, 116.

Sparks, A. (1996) *Tomorrow is Another Country: The Inside Story of South Africa's Negotiated Revolution*, London: Mandarin.

Stadler, A. (1987) *The Political Economy of Modern South Africa*, New York: St Martin's Press.

Stedman, S. J. (ed.) (1993) *Botswana: The Political Economy of Democratic Development*, Boulder, CO: Lynne Rienner.

Stiff, P. (2002) *Cry Zimbabwe: Independence – Twenty Years On*, Johannesburg: Galago Publishing.

Storey, A. (2000) 'Post-development theory: romanticism and Pontius Pilate politics', *Development*, 43(4).

Strauss-Kahn, D. (2008) 'Statement by IMF Managing Director Strauss-Kahn on Zimbabwe', IMF External Relations Department, www.

imf.org/external/np/sec/pr/2008/pro8207.htm, accessed 27 February 2009.

Swan, M. (1985) *Gandhi: The South African Experience*, Johannesburg: Ravan Press.

Swenson, P. (1991) 'Bringing capital back in, or social democracy reconsidered: employer power, cross-class alliances, and centralization of industrial relations in Denmark and Sweden', *World Politics*, 43(4).

Sylvester, C. (2006) 'Bare life as a development/postcolonial problematic', *Geographical Journal*, 172(1).

Tawney, R. H. (1921) *The Acquisitive Society*, London: Bell.

Taylor, I. (2003) 'As Good as It Gets? Botswana's "democratic development"', *Journal of Contemporary African Studies*, 21(2).

— (2004) 'The HIV/AIDS pandemic in Botswana: implications for the "African Miracle"', in N. Poku and A. Whiteside (eds), *The Political Economy of AIDS in Africa*, Aldershot: Ashgate.

Taylor, I. and G. Mokhawa (2003) 'Not forever: Botswana, conflict, diamonds, and the Bushmen', *African Affairs*, 102.

Taylor, S. D. (2007) *Business and the State in Southern Africa: The Politics of Economic Reform*, Boulder, CO: Lynne Rienner.

Tendi, B-M. (2008) 'Patriotic history and public intellectuals critical of power', *Journal of Southern African Studies*, 34(2).

Thelen, K. and S. Steinmo (1992) 'Historical institutionalism in comparative politics', in S. Steinmo, K. Thelen and F. Longstreth (eds), *Structuring Politics: Historical Institutionalism in*

Comparative Analysis, Cambridge: Cambridge University Press.

Thompson, L. (2001) *A History of South Africa*, 3rd edn, New Haven, CT: Yale University Press.

Thompson, M. R. (2001) 'Whatever happened to "Asian values"?', *Journal of Democracy*, 12(4).

Thurlow, J. (2007) 'Is HIV/AIDS undermining Botswana's "success story"? Implications for development strategy', IFPRI Discussion Papers 697, International Food Policy Research Institute (IFPRI), www.ifpri.org/pubs/dp/ifpridp00697.pdf, accessed 29 July 2008.

Todd, J. G. (2007) *Through the Darkness: A Life in Zimbabwe*, Cape Town: Zebra Press.

Trapido, S. (1971) 'South Africa in a comparative study of industrialisation', *Journal of Development*, 7.

Tsie, B. (1996) 'The Political context of Botswana's development performance', *Journal of Modern African Studies*, 22(4).

Tucker, V. (1999) 'The myth of development: a critique of a Euro-centric discourse', in R. Munck and D. O'Hearn (eds), *Critical Development Theory: Contributions to a New Paradigm*, London: Zed Books.

Turrell, R. V. (1987) '"Finance ... the governor of the imperial engine": Hobson and the case of Rothschild and Rhodes', *Journal of Southern African Studies*, 13(3).

Underhill, G. R. D. and X. Zhang (2005) 'The changing state–market condominium in East Asia: rethinking the political underpinnings of development', *New Political Economy*, 10(1).

UNDP (United Nations Development Programme) (2008)

Comprehensive Economic Recovery in Zimbabwe: A Discussion Document, United Nations Development Programme, Zimbabwe, www.undp.org.zw/images/stories/Docs/Publications/Comp EconoRec2008.pdf, accessed 27 February 2009.

Vale, P. and S. Maseko (1998) 'South Africa and the African Renaissance', *International Affairs*, 74(2).

Van Binsbergen, W. (2001) '*Ubuntu* and the globalization of southern African thought and society', *Quest: An African Journal of Philosophy*, 15(1/2).

Van der Merwe, W. L. (1996) 'Philosophy and the multi-cultural context of (post)apartheid South Africa', *Ethical Perspectives*, 3(2).

Van der Westhuizen, J. (2002) *Adapting to Globalization: Malaysia, South Africa, and the Challenges of Ethnic Redistribution with Growth*, Westport, CT: Praeger.

Van de Walle, N. (2001) *African Economies and the Politics of Permanent Crisis, 1979–1999*, Cambridge: Cambridge University Press.

— (2003) 'Presidentialism and clientelism in Africa's emerging party systems', *Journal of Modern African Studies*, 41(2).

Van Kessel, I. (2001) 'In search of an African Renaissance: an agenda for modernisation, neo-traditionalism or Africanisation?', *Quest: An African Journal of Philosophy*, 15(1/2).

Venter, E. (2004) 'The notion of Ubuntu and communalism in African educational discourse', *Studies in Philosophy and Education*, 23(2/3).

Vieira, S. and I. Wallerstein (1992) 'Conclusion', in S. Vieira, W. G. Martin and I. Wallerstein (eds), *How Fast the Wind? Southern Africa, 1975–2000*, Trenton, NJ: Africa World Press.

Wade, R. (1990) *Governing the Market: Economic Theory and the Role of Government in East Asian Industrialization*, Princeton, NJ: Princeton University Press.

Wade, R. H. (2003) 'What strategies are viable for developing countries today? The World Trade Organization and the shrinking of "development space"', *Review of International Political Economy*, 10(4).

— (2004) 'Is globalization reducing poverty and inequality?', *World Development*, 32(4).

Waldmeir, P. (1997) *Anatomy of a Miracle: The End of Apartheid and the Birth of the New South Africa*, New York: Norton.

Wallerstein, I. (1974) 'The rise and future demise of the world capitalist system: concepts for comparative analysis', *Comparative Studies in History and Society*, 16.

Walter, A. (2005) 'Understanding financial globalization in international political economy', in N. Phillips (ed.), *Globalizing International Political Economy*, Basingstoke: Palgrave Macmillan.

Waltz, K. (2000) 'Globalization and American power', *The National Interest*, 59.

Ward, A. (1998) 'Changes in the political economy of the new South Africa', in F. H. Toase and E. J. Yorke (eds), *The New South Africa*, London: Macmillan.

WCED (World Commission on Environment and Development) (1987) *Our Common Future*, Report of the World Commission on Environment and Development, with an introduction by Gro Harlem Brundtland, Oxford: Oxford University Press.

Weber, M. (1968 [1922]) *Economy and Society: An Outline of Interpretive Sociology*, New York: Bedminster Press.

Weinrich, A. K. (1971) *Chiefs and Councils in Rhodesia: Transition from Patriarchal to Bureaucratic Power*, London: Heinemann.

Werbner, R. (2004) *Reasonable Radicals and Citizenship in Botswana: The Public Anthropology of Kalanga Elites*, Bloomington: Indiana University Press.

West, A. (2006) 'Theorising South Africa's corporate governance', *Journal of Business Ethics*, 68(4).

Wheeler, D. (1984) 'Sources of stagnation in sub-Saharan Africa', *World Development*, 12(1).

Widner, J. A. (ed.) (1994) *Economic Change and Political Liberalization in Sub-Saharan Africa*, Baltimore, MD: Johns Hopkins University Press.

Williamson, J. (1993) 'Development and the "Washington Consensus"', *World Development*, 21(8).

Wilson, J. (2001) Interview with author, Johannesburg, 13 September.

Woo-Cumings, M. (ed.) (1999) *The Developmental State*, Ithaca, NY: Cornell University Press.

Worby, E. (2001) 'A redivided land? New agrarian conflicts and questions in Zimbabwe', *Journal of Agrarian Change*, 1(4).

— (2003) 'The end of modernity in Zimbabwe? Passages from development to sovereignty', in A. Hammar, B. Raftopoulos and S. Jensen (eds), *Zimbabwe's Unfinished Business: Rethinking Land, State and Nation in the Context of Crisis*, Harare: Weaver Press.

Bibliography

World Bank (1981) *Accelerated Development in Sub-Saharan Africa: An Agenda for Action*, Washington, DC: World Bank.

— (1992) *Governance and Development*, Washington, DC: World Bank.

— (1994) *Adjustment in Africa: Reforms, Results, and the Road Ahead*, Oxford: Oxford University Press.

— (1995a) *Performance Audit Report: Zimbabwe: Structural Adjustment Program*, Washington, DC: Operations Evaluation Department, World Bank.

— (1995b) *Project Completion Report: Zimbabwe: Structural Adjustment Program*, Washington, DC: Country Operations Division, Southern Africa Department, World Bank.

Wright, M. (2001) Interview with author, Gaborone, 4 October.

Yates, P. (1980) 'The prospects for socialist transition in Zimbabwe', *Review of African Political Economy*, 7(18).

Youde, J. R. (2007) 'Why look East? Zimbabwean foreign policy and China', *Africa Today*, 53(3).

Zartman, W. I. (ed.) (1995) *Collapsed States: The Disintegration and Restoration of Legitimate Authority*, Boulder, CO: Lynne Rienner.

Ziai, A. (2004) 'The ambivalence of post-development: between reactionary populism and radical democracy', *Third World Quarterly*, 25(6).

Index